**Dr. Albert H. Dunn,** (D.C.S., Harvard Business School) has been a management consultant for the Pfitzer Company, Syracuse China, Westinghouse, and the Department of Defense. He is a member of the University of Delaware faculty, and has taught at Syracuse University and the Harvard Business School.

**Dr. Eugene M. Johnson,** (D.B.A., Washington University) has presented sales management seminars for Syracuse University, the University of Tennessee, the Goodyear International Corporation, and the Virginia National Bank. He has taught at St. Louis University and the University of Delaware and is a member of the University of Rhode Island faculty.

E 70

# MANAGING YOUR
# SALES
# TEAM

## ALBERT H. DUNN & EUGENE M. JOHNSON

A SPECTRUM BOOK

PRENTICE-HALL, INC., Englewood Cliffs, New Jersey 07632

*Library of Congress Cataloging in Publication Data*

DUNN, ALBERT H
    Managing your sales team.

    (A Spectrum Book)
    Includes bibliographies and index.
    1. Sales management.   I. Johnson, Eugene M.,
joint author.   II. Title.
HF5438.4.D86        658.8'1        80-14554
ISBN   0-13-550905-X
ISBN   0-13-550897-5 (pbk.)

Editorial/production supervision and interior design by Suse L. Cioffi
Cover design by Ira Shapiro
Manufacturing buyer: Barbara Frick

Printed in the United States of America

PRENTICE-HALL INTERNATIONAL, INC., *London*
PRENTICE-HALL OF AUSTRALIA PTY. LIMITED, *Sydney*
PRENTICE-HALL OF CANADA, LTD., *Toronto*
PRENTICE-HALL OF INDIA PRIVATE LIMITED, *New Delhi*
PRENTICE-HALL OF JAPAN, INC., *Tokyo*
PRENTICE-HALL OF SOUTHEAST ASIA PTE. LTD., *Singapore*
WHITEHALL BOOKS LIMITED, *Wellington, New Zealand*

To Jean and Carolyn

# CONTENTS

# YOU AND
# SUCCESSFUL MANAGING

*Managing Your Sales Team* is not a textbook in the traditional meaning of that term, although it is applicable in college sales management courses, continuing education seminars, industry and company management training programs. This is a learning workbook designed for people who expect to become sales managers and for sales managers who wish to improve their skills and insights. Consequently, this is a down-to-earth book, based on the experiences and knowledge of thousands of successful sales managers and their companies.

## What Is Personal Selling?

Personal selling is an occupation with a long, often misunderstood history. It has been correctly said that nothing happens in our economy until a sale is made. Salespeople and their managers "make it happen." Professional salespeople do this through their personal contacts and influence with customers; not by persuading buyers to purchase something they do not want or need, but by satisfying customers' needs and solving their problems.

There are many types of selling and salespeople, ranging from clerks who simply ring up orders to sales reps who sell complex computer installations. This book is concerned with managing those people who are members of a company's own sales force. It is not about managing those people who are primarily order takers (such as retail clerks) or who are independent sales agents, although many of the ideas and concepts presented are also applicable to these types of salespeople.

This book is about managing salespeople on the front lines. It is not about the management of personal selling as seen from the top levels of sales management in a *Fortune* 500 company. It is, instead, concerned with the day-to-day personal supervision of people who sell.

## What Is Sales Management?

The management of people who sell is a difficult, but rewarding profession. Successful sales management is an art assisted by science. *Art* is the application of skill and imagination to achieve a satisfactory result. It is personal and subjective. *Science* is the observation and classification of facts in order to establish general rules and laws. It is impersonal and objective. The successful sales manager is an artist applying personal skills and imagination, assisted by the general laws of science. This means that sales management is highly personal and subjective; to learn it, one must become personally involved. This art cannot be acquired simply by memorizing general laws. You must participate in the learning.

## What Is This Book?

This book is designed to help you become involved in the further development of your own sales management skills and insights. Throughout the book you will be challenged to apply what you are learning to yourself and your company (or one you know well) with the aid of cases, analytical checklists, self-quizzes, brain teasers, and thought provokers. Investigation and observation activities are suggested by which you can broaden your understanding of sales management as an art assisted by science. Each chapter is followed by a list of selected references, which you may read for additional insights about the chapter topics. You will maximize the value of this book if you follow the special instructions as fully as possible.

## What Should You Expect?

As a sales manager, or as someone preparing for this career, you should expect this book to sharpen your personal skills and provide greater insight into the sales management process. In doing so, you will be preparing to produce greater and more profitable sales for your company and to enjoy greater personal reward and satisfaction from your job.

# 1

# MANAGING PEOPLE
# WHO SELL: AN OVERVIEW

*After reading this chapter, you should be able to demonstrate your learning as follows:*
- *Explain the important historical developments in the evolution of sales management.*
- *Understand the elements of the marketing mix.*
- *Identify the major environmental forces affecting selling and sales management.*
- *Describe and explain the management process.*
- *Detail the specific management functions of the sales manager.*
- *Show in specific ways how the sales manager's job is different from the job of other managers in the company.*
- *Explain the role of personal selling in the marketing mix.*

A strong, dynamic sales force, the backbone of a successful company, does not just happen; it has to be developed and nurtured. In this book we are concerned with what the sales manager must do—and do well—to create and maintain a strong sales force.

In Chapter 1 we will analyze the job of the sales manager. This will involve a brief look at the history of sales management, the environmental forces affecting selling and sales management, the role of selling, and the process of management. We will conclude with a description of the sales manager's important functions and responsibilities. Before turning to the evolution of sales management, consider the problem that follows.

## Learning Exercise

Brett Clarke has recently been promoted from salesman to territory manager. He has 12 sales reps. Clarke's supervisor, Susan Malloy, is with him on one of her regular field trips and this conversation takes place:

SUSAN: From what I can see, Brett, you're making a smooth changeover from sales rep to territory manager. Are you having any problems? Any difficulties?

BRETT: I don't think so, Susan. It seems to me it's been smooth—but I do get static from my wife once in a while about working nights and weekends to keep up with the damn paper work. I don't ever seem to have enough time!

SUSAN: Are you doing much selling yourself?

BRETT: Oh, yes. I've kept my nine largest customers as house accounts, and I have to keep giving those guys the same service I did before. Also, by selling to them myself, I keep a feel on market conditions . . . I'd never be able to do all this without my secretary. She's a gem! Handles all the administrative details with the salespeople for me.

*Do you think Clarke is doing a good job in his new position? What are your reasons?* _____

_____

_____

_____

*Should Susan Malloy take any action? Why or why not?* _____

_____

_____

_____

*If you said that Malloy should take some action, what should she do? How should she go about doing this?* _____

_____

_____

_____

## HISTORY OF SALES MANAGEMENT

Brett Clarke and Susan Malloy are sales supervisors. They are deeply engaged in the sales management *process*. Let's begin our overview of selling and sales management by reviewing the historical development of sales management; what that process is now, is importantly the result of its long history.

### Early Developments

Selling has been a productive human activity since the beginning of modern civilization, but formal study of selling and sales management did not begin until the early 1900s when courses in the distributive trades were first offered.[1] It was during this period that businesspeople recognized the importance of demand creation. With the great expansion of production and the introduction of new products, conventional sales practices became inadequate. The twentieth century called for creative, dynamic approaches to selling and sales management.

Early thoughts on managing salespeople developed along contrasting lines. One viewpoint highlighted the independence of salespeople. The sales rep who worked alone, almost as an independent businessperson, had no desire to be regulated by the company. Further, the belief that mastery of selling techniques led to sales success resulted in growing demands for sales training. As this viewpoint was accepted, the practice of sales management emerged. The sales manager served as a link between salespeople and the company.

The next development was the recognition that personal selling is an integral part of the total marketing effort. Sales managers are essential, since they are responsible for coordinating the company's sales efforts.

Since World War II, even more emphasis has been given to sales management, due to the development of the view of salespeople as problem solvers and the marketing management concept.

### Problem Solver

The modern view of selling sees sales reps as more than accomplished persuaders. They are problem solvers able to meet the needs and conditions of individual customers. Because of this, personal selling must

---

[1]For an informative review of the history of sales management, see Robert Bartels, *The Development of Marketing Thought*, (Homewood, Ill.: Richard D. Irwin), 1962.

now be flexible and creative, not simply persuasive. In response to this change, through the 1970s companies have substantially revised their methods of hiring, training, and organizing sales reps to adapt to new market conditions.

In addition there is now general recognition that personal selling is more than just making a sale. Salespeople are often involved in several other important aspects of the total marketing process, distribution, credit, the customer's use or promotion of the product, and delivery.

With each change in the role of personal selling, sales management has become more and more important to a company's success.

## Marketing Management Concept

In the late 1950s, a new philosophy of business management developed. Known as the marketing management concept, it is based on three major propositions: customer orientation, coordination of all customer-related activities, and profit direction.

*Customer orientation* is the key to the marketing management concept. Sales managers must shift from an internal company perspective to the customer's viewpoint. Successful marketing requires a complete understanding of customers—their needs, attitudes, and buying behavior. Thus, a car sales rep who knows that the present customer is the head of a family, with budget constraints, realizes that a sleek sports model will not fit this customer's needs.

Two examples from business history demonstrate the importance of customer orientation. Two early inventors, Obed Hussey and Cyrus McCormick, developed reapers to harvest grain. McCormick's company became International Harvester, still a leading producer of farm equipment. Hussey and his machine, which was just as good, faded into obscurity. Why did McCormick succeed and Hussey fail? The answer is simple— customer orientation. McCormick moved his factory to Chicago, close to grain country; maintained an adequate inventory for rush orders; allowed farmers to pay on an installment plan keyed to harvest conditions; established a fair price and stuck by it; guaranteed his products; and built an excellent reputation as a friend of the farmers. Although these customer-oriented practices are not unusual today, they established McCormick as the leading farm-equipment producer of his time.

The second example also involves a familiar name—Isaac Singer. Although Singer worked on an early sewing machine, Elias Howe is given historical credit for inventing the basic sewing machine. So why don't we have Howe Sewing Centers around the world today? Again, the difference is customer orientation. Singer developed a consumer install-ment plan and franchised agency system. Also, Singer was one of the first Americans to recognize the importance of international marketing, serv-ing customers in many nations. The Singer sewing machine is now known throughout the world.

The second fundamental of the marketing concept is *coordination* between all of the customer-serving functions of the business. For in-stance, when a sales rep writes a large order, production schedules must be adequate to fill it.

Finally, with the marketing management concept, the sales or-ganization is *profit-directed*. Customer satisfaction and loyalty are the only way to profit.

## ENVIRONMENT OF SALES MANAGEMENT

What are the conditions under which all sales managers operate? All business managers work under constantly changing conditions, but most especially sales managers. New products are introduced, a competitor cuts the price, new government rulings that affect a particular business are issued, new territories are opened—change never stops. A sales manager once said, "The only thing I can be sure about when I get to the office in the morning is that something will be changed from yesterday."

### Learning Exercise

*Identify one important change that has taken place in your business over the last year. What optional courses of action might you or your management have taken in response to this change?* _____

_____

_____

_____

You probably identified the three possible responses to change—adapt to it, move against the change, or try to alter it in some way. This is the kind of thinking that successful sales managers display in their responses to the constantly changing environment of sales. What alternatives do I have? What are the risks and possible gains of each?

## Adapt to Change

Usually the easiest and safest course of action is to try to adapt sales operations to changes in the environment. Example: more and more women and minorities are being hired as sales reps. You begin to recruit these people specifically.

## Move Counter to the Change

This course of action involves more risk, but it can have a greater payoff. Example: there is a distinct trend in your industry to produce products with more and more extra features to sell at higher prices. You counsel your management to try for a "low end" market position by continuing to sell the standard product at a lower price.

## Try to Alter the Change

Obviously in some change situations, altering change is not possible because changes stem from uncontrollable forces in economics, the culture, or government. But in other situations, advertising, public relations, publicity, and personal selling can influence the change in your favor. Example: you are a district sales manager for a large petroleum company. Your dealers have become increasingly critical of your company's sales policies, especially those related to tires, batteries, and accessories. You indoctrinate your sales reps on how to explain and justify these policies to their dealer customers.

Not only is the job environment of the sales manager dynamic and ever-changing, but it is made up of a number of special interest groups and other sorts of constraints, which managers must understand and deal with. Let's consider each of these briefly.

## Customers

Customers are clearly critical to success. The successful sales rep and manager know their customers intimately, who and where they are, how, when, and why they buy, their needs and operations, even their personal idiosyncracies.

## Law

The extent and complexity of federal and state laws that govern buying and selling boggle the mind. There are basic laws that govern all selling in interstate commerce. These are aimed at preventing monopoly. There are federal laws for specific industries, such as food, drug, and cosmetics. There are state laws regulating sales transactions. Under these laws, salespeople are considered the agents of their company, and the penalties on the company and the salespeople individually for violation of the laws can be substantial!

The cardinal rule here for sales managers is: you and your reps must know enough about the law to recognize situations in which you need professional legal advice. The laws are so numerous and complex that anytime sales reps or managers make amateur legal decisions on borderline transactions, they court disaster for their companies and themselves.

## Economic Conditions

We all know how general economic conditions affect sales. What is often overlooked is that general economic conditions are an *average* between the best and the worst. But the economic condition of a specific industry, geographical area, population group, or level in the distribution chain can be quite different from the general economic condition at any particular time. Sales managers must recognize and deal with the differences in economic conditions between the various elements of the economy that pertain to them.

## Competition

It is obvious that competitors are a critical force in the sales manager's environment, but it is not always obvious who the competitors are. An example:

> In the 1970s, Cunard operated the *Queen Elizabeth II,* the largest luxury liner afloat. The ship was in constant service around the world, but during the summer months the schedule was largely taken up with five-day trips from New York City to England or return. Shortly after taking office, the new Cunard president asked his senior executives to identify the *QE II's* major competitor on summer trans-Atlantic crossings. They were stunned at the question. Of course, it was the airlines.

How would you have answered the president's question? When you consider it carefully, for speed a five-day Atlantic crossing on the *QE*

*II* could never compete with a seven-hour crossing by air. So what *really* is the competition? It is the alternative uses of vacation time. Would potential customers rather spend five days vacationing while getting across the Atlantic, or get across quickly and have more time to enjoy their vacations there? The *QE II* competes with all of the interesting and pleasurable sites and activities that the vacationer goes abroad to enjoy. In a nutshell: would potential customers rather have an interesting and memorable vacation while getting across the ocean and less time when they are there, or more time to be there when they arrive?

Having accurately identified what the competition is, another condition must be recognized. Sales managers have virtually no control over the actions of competitors who are a major limiting constraint on company sales and profits. Sales managers must therefore see to it that they and their reps know everything they possibly can about competitors' activities. They must be keen "market intelligence" sources for higher management.

### Cost of Sales Operations

On a per-customer-contact basis, personal selling is by far the most expensive promotion technique of all those available to sales program planners. Not infrequently we find that sales managers are responsi-

---

**ENVIRONMENTAL CHECKLIST**

| FORCES IN THE ENVIRONMENT | IMPACT ON YOUR COMPANY | YOUR COMPANY'S REACTION |
|---|---|---|
| A. Customers | | |
|    1. Who they are | _____ | _____ |
|    2. Their buying habits | _____ | _____ |
| B. Law | | |
|    1. Federal | _____ | _____ |
|    2. State/Local | _____ | _____ |
| C. Economic Conditions | | |
|    1. National | _____ | _____ |
|    2. Regional/Local | _____ | _____ |
| D. Competition | | |
|    1. Who or what it is | _____ | _____ |
|    2. Their operations | _____ | _____ |
| E. Cost of Sales Operations | | |
| | _____ | _____ |

---

ble for their controllable costs and, therefore, the profits that are generated by their units. When this is the case, sales managers must fully
understand the nature of the costs for which they are responsible. They
must manage their units as profit-generating centers.

In summary, environmental forces exert great influence on the
decisions that sales managers make and how they operate. These forces
are condensed in the previous checklist. Think about your company.
What are the environmental forces affecting sales? What is the impact of
these forces? How does your sales management react to these forces?

## ROLE OF SELLING IN MARKETING

With an understanding of the evolution of sales management and the
conditions under which the process takes place, we move to the role and
function of personal selling in your company's marketing program. To
start we must understand the *marketing mix,* which is the total package of
the various techniques a company uses to satisfy its customers' needs and
to stimulate sales. The marketing mix also indicates the relative importance of each of the various elements in the mix, for example, 40 percent
of the total promotion budget for advertising, 30 percent for personal
selling, and so on. The marketing mix is not unlike the recipe for cooking
a specific dish—a pinch of salt, cup of flour, and so on, and you have a
particular kind of cake. The elements of the marketing mix are product,
distribution, price, and promotion.

### Product

The features, form of packaging, number of models, degree of
quality, and brand or trademark to be used.

### Distribution

Where and how products are offered for sale, the wholesalers,
distributors, retailers, salespeople, and others who are responsible for
getting goods or services to customers.

### Price

The amount charged for the product that gives a satisfactory
return on the company's investment and still is within the customer's
ability to pay.

## Promotion

Advertising, sales promotion, personal selling, and publicity with one or both of these objectives:

1. *Persuasion*—attempts to influence people to do something, buy a G.E. dishwasher, prevent forest fires, join the U.S. Army.
2. *Information*—informs people of the availability of a product or seller.

### Elements in the Promotion Component of the Marketing Mix

To place personal selling in perspective in the company's promotion mix, we must briefly summarize the other three elements of promotion.

1. Advertising. Nonpersonal, mass persuasion messages to customers through established media that are usually independent of the advertiser (newspapers, magazines, television, and so on).
2. Publicity. Communication to prospective buyers that is not identified as coming from the company itself and in media not considered to be advertising, such as newspaper stories, about a company or its employees.
3. Sales promotion. All activities that are neither advertising, personal selling, or publicity, such as contests, coupons, displays, and samples.

### Personal Selling in the Marketing Mix

Before we consider what personal selling does in the company's total marketing effort, think about the following situation:

*Choose a company with a sales force, yours or some other, that you know well. As specifically as possible, identify the functions that sales reps perform with and for customers.* _____

_____

_____

_____

*Are you aware of some functions that these reps should perform,*
*but do not, or do not perform well?* _____

_____

_____

_____

Each element in the promotion mix performs certain persuasive communication functions well and efficiently, others inefficiently or not at all. For example, mass media advertising reaches mass markets with good coverage and at low cost per person reached, but it is a very expensive and inefficient way to communicate with specific customers in a market area. What, then, does personal selling do well and efficiently? What roles or functions do companies that rely heavily on personal selling expect from the sales force? What is the nature of the activity that you as a sales manager manage?

Personal selling creates at least four conditions that are critically important in the sales of some goods and services.

### There Is Personalized Persuasion

Sales reps and customers deal face-to-face. Often they live together with customer problems for a period of time. Familiarity, if not friendship, develops between them. The *human* element becomes important in the buying decision. The sales rep *is* the company for the customer. Customers do not deal just with an inanimate business organization, but with human beings from that company whom they see personally and know as people. The selling is *personal* selling.

### Customer Confidence in the Supplier Is Increased

Because the customer deals with a supplier through a person, there is great potential for building the customer's confidence in the supplier's products and procedures. Of course the sales rep can muff this opportunity in a number of ways, such as making delivery promises that cannot be met or misrepresenting the product. But personal selling offers the opportunity for the rep to build a basis of trust and confidence with customers.

### Customers Can Act Immediately

Unlike the other means of promoting sales, the rep can work for some desired action by the customer immediately, here and now. Place the order, commit to a purchasing plan for the next quarter, decide on in-store promotion for the product. Personal selling makes it more difficult for the customer to procrastinate or to forget a promised commitment in the future. It provides the opportunity for the rep to get the action or commitment that is wanted on the spot.

### Can Adjust Immediately to Individual
### Customer Conditions, Needs, and Problems

All of the preceding payoffs of personal selling are important, but probably the most valuable is that sales reps' personal contacts with customers make it possible for them to customize their sales presentations and to handle buyers' problems and complaints on an individual basis. Suggestions and problem solutions that make no sense for one customer may be right on target for another. Only personal selling can deliver customer-by-customer accommodation. In a broad sense, this is the *service* aspect of personal selling, to identify each customer's needs and problems and to respond to them individually.

To summarize, personal selling is one of several forces in the marketing mix. It is expensive, but when correctly used and done well, it is a strong force in creating sales. This is because personal selling brings the human element into sales transactions, increases customer confidence in the supplier, makes it possible for the buyer to act immediately, and facilitates the handling of individual customer problems. This is the role and nature of the business function that you, as a sales manager, supervise.

## THE PROCESS OF MANAGEMENT

In this book we are concerned with the job of the sales manager—the skills, responsibilities, problems, and functions that are involved in managing people who sell. However, before taking an overview of the sales manager's job itself, we must first look at *all* management in business and the management process in general.

To get ready to think about this area, try yourself on the problems that follow.

## Learning Exercise

*From what you know about management, basically what is the management process?* _____

_____

_____

_____

*What are the important conditions under which all business management takes place?* _____

_____

_____

_____

## Management Defined

Compare your answers to the learning exercise with what the experts say.

Management is the process that is necessary to bring the most return from a particular commitment of the company's resources (technical, financial, human, mechanical, and so on), when other alternative commitments are possible. The information on which the commitment is made is always incomplete, and the conditions under which the decision will be carried out are uncertain. The most return is, of course, usually thought of as maximum profit.

There are several important aspects of managing that we should recognize from the beginning.

### Management Is Art Assisted by Science

Because of the increasing use of computers, models, sophisticated problem-analysis systems and techniques, we are tempted to conclude that management is totally scientific and that human skills, experience, and insights play no part in it. This is not the case, nor will it ever be, because: first, management importantly involves people—their feelings, emotions, prejudices, reactions, and behavior can never be completely and scientifically forecasted or "programmed" and, second, in a dynamic economic system, such as in the United States, all management takes place under conditions of uncertainty and constant change. The environment of management will never stand still to be completely programmed. These conditions mean that management can be made *more* scientific and exact, but it can never become a pure science such as physics or chemistry. It is, and will remain, an art assisted by scientific observations and techniques.

### Management Is Getting Things Done Through People

Only in the smallest companies is it possible for managers to do everything themselves. In fact, studies show that this is precisely a major cause of failure in small businesses—lack of management depth. To be effective and succeed, managers must magnify themselves through their people by delegating authority and responsibility to the lowest possible level and involving subordinates as much as they can in the decisions and operations of the enterprise.

### Management Can Be Learned

Because management involves making decisions and acting under conditions of uncertainty, alternate choices, and incomplete knowledge, learning is a critical aspect of the manager's job. But can you learn to manage better? The answer is "yes." Based on the extensive research and experience of schools of business and industry's experience with management development programs, learning to manage better is not easy, but it can be done.

Learning to manage has two forms: formal learning, as from this book, and learning from experience. In the formal learning of management, managers are exposed to the condensed experience, knowledge, and research findings of a number of other managers and teachers of management to become better managers. Learning from experience is a continuing process by which managers work to make their experiences teach them more about themselves and their management job.

## JOB OF THE SALES MANAGER

Against the background of observations about the business management process, we turn to an overview of the sales manager's job. What do sales managers do? What are their duties, responsibilities, and functions?

## Case Study

To orient your thinking, study this case and answer the questions that follow it.

### Sheldon Electronics Company

Ed Nieland is sales manager for the Sheldon Electronics Company, a producer of specialty electronic components that are sold by six sales reps to manufacturers for use in their finished products. Sheldon's management organization is shown in Figure 1-1.

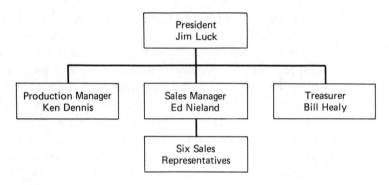

FIGURE 1-1

A researcher is talking to Ed Nieland about what he does as sales manager. The following are extracts from the tape recording of that conversation.

RESEARCHER: Ed, would you explain to me what your job is.

NIELAND: The quick answer is to sell Sheldon products at a profit.

RESEARCHER: I'd already guessed that. (laughter)

RESEARCHER: Put it this way, specifically what do you do day in and day out.

NIELAND: Well, take last week, it wasn't much different from most weeks. (opens his calendar) Now what did I do? (pause) Well, one thing, I had a big hassle with Ken Dennis and his people about the United order. That's a big one! Production said at first they could make the delivery date and now they say they can't.

RESEARCHER:   What else?

NIELAND:   Well, I spent half a day with our new rep and tried to show him a couple of things he's doing wrong. He'll be a good one! Then, there was Al Simms. Good rep, but sometimes he gets off base. He wanted a piece of another territory. He's got good reasons, but his attitude drives me up the wall! We went round and round on that for a couple of days.

RESEARCHER:   Why did that bother you so much?

NIELAND:   Well, never mind about his attitude, but we're cooking up a real big deal with Universal. They're in the piece of territory Al wants. Al doesn't know about it and I can't tell him until its decided. All of us here in management have been working on this deal with Universal for months. If Al sticks his nose into this because of a territory squabble, he could foul up the whole deal. . . . Another thing was Bill Healey and I got together twice during the week to work on his idea about a new discount schedule for one of our best-selling products. Jim Luck sat in on one of our meetings.

RESEARCHER:   What else?

NIELAND:   Well, there were the usual calls from the reps. Can we shave the price? Where's my expense check? What are the credit terms on some oddball deal they've come up with? (pause) Don't remember how many, but there were some letters and calls from customers complaining about something or other. (pause) The usual expense forms to approve. We had a meeting of the Long Range Planning Committee, that's Jim, Ken, Bill, and me, on how fast we should move in introducing our new Trilak system . . . Tuesday my car broke down and it took me two hours to get home from work . . . began planning for the annual yearly sales meeting in a couple of months . . . explained to Bill Healey why Territory Three is so far behind budget. He was very sticky about that one. . . .

*Make a list of the people Ed Nieland dealt with during the week,
identifying them by title or other description.* _____

_____

_____

_____

*What were the different problems or concerns these people had?*

_____

_____

_____

*At what organizational levels did Nieland work last week?* _____

_____

_____

_____

No two sales managers' jobs are exactly alike because of the
differences in company and sales force size, geographical areas covered,
number of customers, and nature of the selling job to be done. For
example, compare Sheldon Electronics with the huge Majestic Company
in a different industry:

| NUMBER OF: | SHELDON COMPANY | MAJESTIC COMPANY |
|---|---|---|
| Sales Reps | 6 | 1,500 |
| Levels of Sales Managers | 1 | 5 |
| Sales Managers, All Levels | 1 | 150 |
| Sales Staff People | 0 | 120 |
| Regular Customers | 150 | 90,000 |
| Company Sales | $5,500,000 | $1,700,000,000 |

Clearly, Ed Nieland's job as sales manager of Sheldon is different
from *any* of the jobs of the sales managers in Majestic. But the differences
are of *structure* and *operations* between companies and industries. They
are not differences in the sales management job itself. All sales managers
do their jobs under similar working conditions and they all have the same

responsibilities. In this section we will consider the basic working conditions and responsibilities of sales managers.

### Sales Management as an Integrated, Interrelated Process

In the chapters that follow we will be studying the individual subelements of the sales manager's job in detail: the recruiting of salespeople, their training, compensation, motivation, evaluation, and supervision. Two important observations about these subelements are: (1) each is interrelated with, and dependent upon, the others and affects their workings, efficiency, and effectiveness, or lack of it, and (2) each must contribute to the attainment of sales success.

Following are two examples of the interrelation between the various activities that the sales manager supervises: (1) a small garden supply chain of retail stores had an excellent recruitment and selection program; however, personal supervision of the clerks was virtually nonexistent, resulting in a poor total selling program, and (2) a small mill supply firm had excellent personal supervision of its outside sales reps, but a very unsatisfactory compensation plan, resulting in an ineffective sales effort.

What the successful sales manager is managing, and what we are studying, is a total, integrated, interactive management system, each part contributing to the common goals of the sales group. This a critically important aspect of the conditions under which sales managers work.

### Uniqueness of Sales Manager's Job

Consider a sales manager you know (perhaps yourself). Is this sales manager's job about the same or different from other managers' jobs in the company?

Similarities:                                    Differences:

_____                    _____

_____                    _____

_____                    _____

In most companies the sales manager's job is greatly different in many important ways from the jobs of other managers in the company. Consider that:

Sales managers spend much of their time in the field (some studies indicate as much as 60 percent of the manager's working time). They must be away from home overnight frequently. They regularly work on an expense account. Only infrequently can they see their subordinates face-to-face, yet they are responsible for their performance. They regularly entertain customers; regularly work evenings and weekends. The sales manager deals with a wide variety of people, each with different interests and problems. Customers hold them responsible for delivery failures and other problems over which they actually have no direct control. Generally they cannot dictate the kind of products their reps sell or at what price and on what delivery schedules and terms of sale. They are the first line of supervision that links the company to its outside environment, competition, economic, and social conditions; the sales manager and the reps are "the company" to customers, competitors, and the general public. They are responsible for coordinating the reps' personal selling efforts with advertising, publicity, sales promotion, and other efforts the company may undertake to promote sales. They must coordinate their reps' activities with other functional specialties in the company, such as warehousing, personnel, delivery, credit, and other departments and functions involved in selling. They coordinate all they and their reps do toward the common company goals.

No other managers in the company work under these conditions and the pressures that are generated on them personally, on their families, and subordinates. These are very important aspects of the sales manager's work conditions. The sales manager's job is unique and difficult.

But let's look at the work conditions of the sales manager from the point of view of pleasures and rewards. The job of the sales manager:

1. *Is varied and ever-changing, not routine and repetitive.* No two customers or sales reps' problems are ever quite alike; the manager gets to know and work with a variety of people. Market conditions, competitors' activities, and the economy are ever-changing.
2. *Is personally rewarding.* Sales managers and their performance are not hidden away somewhere in the organization. They are challenged to produce results, and when they do, it is a source of great personal satisfaction.

3. *Is financially rewarding.* In most companies, sales managers earn substantial incomes and there is good potential for increases.
4. *Often leads to top management.* Various studies over the years have shown that a large number of company chief executives have risen from the ranks of sales managers.

So we see that the work conditions of the sales management job require the manager to be skilled in meshing the various sales management and selling activities into a single strong selling force, as well as coordinating that selling force with related functions in the company. The job is difficult and the working conditions are unlike those prevailing in any other area of management. But sales management offers considerable personal and financial rewards and is a good road to top management. With these work conditions in mind, let us turn to the responsibilities of the sales management job.

## Sales Manager's Job Responsibilities

Sales managers work at all levels. In large companies, such as the Majestic Company, mentioned earlier, there are territory sales managers, district, regional, and national sales managers. In smaller companies, such as Sheldon Electronics, there may be only one or two levels of sales managers. But regardless of the size of the company, all sales managers are responsible to one degree or another for either performing or overseeing four major functions—planning, organizing, supervising, and evaluating sales performance. These are summarized below.

*Planning* for the immediate situation and for the long run:

– establish specific objectives and set up policies, procedures, and plans to attain these objectives.
– transmit objectives, policies, procedures, and plans to subordinate sales supervisers or sales reps.

*Organizing* the sales unit to achieve the objectives:

– break down the selling job for which the manager is responsible into operational parts (jobs).
– create specific job descriptions for these parts.
– recruit and select personnel for these jobs.

*Supervising* the performance of the sales unit to improve its operation:

- issue necessary orders and directions.
- motivate salespeople for high performance.
- train reps for better selling performance.

*Evaluating* sales performance:

- create performance standards and measurements.
- collect and analyze performance information against standards.
- take indicated remedial action.

Because the rest of this book is about supervising people who sell (the sales manager's *operational* responsibilities), we must at this point briefly note some highlights of the sales manager's *planning* responsibilities.

## Planning as a Critical Responsibility

Simply defined, planning is the systematic process by which we decide *what* will be done in the future and *how* it will be done. Planning is not, of course, an effort to control the future. Rather it is directed at being as well prepared as possible for whatever the future may bring. Planning is a future-oriented thought process by which the sales manager tries to have the sales unit perform in the present in a way that will lead to the best possible position in the future. As an example, in the Sheldon Company, the Long Range Planning Committee was concerned last week with the timing of the introduction of a new product in the future.

There is something about human beings that encourages us to neglect planning, to put it aside for another day (that usually never comes). Perhaps this is because planning makes us question our assumptions, look into the future, make firm decisions; all difficult to do, especially when we know from experience that no plan ever works out perfectly in practice. For whatever reason, we tend to neglect planning. But the sales manager cannot!

Sales managers must plan for the maximum allocation of the resources that have been put at their disposal: their time and their reps' time, company money, advertising, and sales promotion aids—all of the resources they have been given to manage. They must plan in order to be as well prepared as possible for future market changes, to respond quickly and effectively to competitive moves, and to coordinate the work of the sales group with other company marketing and promotion activities. At all organizational levels, planning is a prime responsibility of the sales manager.

## Sales Planning Across Functional Areas

In some small companies and at the middle and top levels in large companies, sales planning often requires careful coordination with other company operating areas such as production, finance, warehousing, credit, and advertising. As an example, the Sheldon Company's Long Range Planning Committee is composed of the president, treasurer, production manager, and sales manager.

When this condition exists, special requirements are placed on sales managers. To plan effectively in cooperation with representatives of other company functions, sales managers must know a great deal about these other areas, their objectives, problems, and procedures, and their specialized language. Too often sales managers approach cooperative planning on the assumption that the company exists to serve the sales force. This is, of course, not true. The company exists to generate *profitable* sales, and to do this requires careful consideration of *all* the activities that contribute to profit, only one of which is personal selling.

## WHY THE STUDY OF SALES MANAGEMENT?

Before moving to the detailed consideration of the sales manager's various operating responsibilities, it is highly important that the reader understand how you can *use* what you will study. The principles, observations, research findings, and business experience presented in this book can be universally applied. They are applicable to the selling of products as well as services, to industrial, commercial, and consumer customers, to government buyers, to import and export trade. They are applicable to large and small selling organizations, to selling direct or through distributors, to inexpensive or "big ticket" items.

*The principles themselves are universal, but their adaptation to a particular industry, company, product line, sales force size, price structure, and channel of distribution must rest with each company and sales group.* This requirement is present in every form of learning; the learners must assimilate and adapt what is being taught to their own particular situation and problems. We can, for example, teach the law of gravity, what it is, how it works, and that it applies to all things with weight. But it is up to the learner to understand how the law applies specifically to the production of petroleum products as opposed to the manufacture of air-craft frames. Similarly, the principles of the motivation of sales reps are basic to all salespeople, but how these principles apply to door-to-door cosmetics sales reps are different from how they apply to people selling atomic power generation equipment to public utilities.

In the chapters that follow, we shall consider basic sales management principles in the important areas of recruitment, selection, training, motivation, and evaluation. Readers must adapt these principles to themselves and to their own company's particular selling situation.

## Brain teasers

|  | Agree | Disagree |
|---|---|---|
| 1. The major benefit of personal selling as a promotion technique is the face-to-face relationship the sales rep has with a buyer. | ____ | ____ |
| 2. The highly independent nature of selling precludes any form of sales supervision. | ____ | ____ |
| 3. If a company is truly customer-oriented, it need not worry about profitability. | ____ | ____ |
| 4. In management it is a good generalization that "if you want something done right, do it yourself." | ____ | ____ |
| 5. The sales manager is importantly involved in managing an interrelated, interactive system of activities. | ____ | ____ |
| 6. The sales manager's job is very similar to other management jobs in the company. | ____ | ____ |
| 7. The most effective environmental strategy is to try to change the environment through promotion. | ____ | ____ |
| 8. Most people like to plan and are good at it. | ____ | ____ |
| 9. The marketing mananagement concept essentially emphasizes the manufacture and sale of profitable products. | ____ | ____ |
| 10. The principles of good management are universal, and once they have been learned, they can be applied in any management situation. | ____ | ____ |

## Activities

1. What should be the role of personal selling in the marketing mix of the following companies? Why do you say so? _____

   a) major producer of household cleaning products.
   b) manufacture of expensive machine tools.
   c) local travel agency.
   d) automobile insurance company.

   _____

   _____

   _____

2. Theodore Leavitt of the Harvard Business School has written: "The difference between marketing and selling is more than semantic. Selling focuses on the needs of the seller, marketing on the needs of the buyer." Do you agree with this statement? Do you think Leavitt is a supporter of the marketing management concept? _____

   _____

   _____

   _____

3. Comment on this statement: "Sales planning is very expensive, time-consuming, and anyone with any experience knows that plans seldom, if ever, come near to reflecting future reality. It is therefore a waste of time, effort, money, and expectations to plan."_____

   _____

   _____

   _____

4. Comment on this statement: "The job of sales reps is to sell products or services at a satisfactory profit. So long as they do this, it's nobody's business how or when they get it done."

   _____

   _____

   _____

5. *Interview a sales manager with many years of experience. What major changes in selling and managing does this manager feel have happened during his or her career?* _____

_____

_____

_____

## SELECTED REFERENCES

### History of Sales Management

BARTELS, ROBERT, *The Development of Marketing Thought*. Homewood, Ill.: Richard D. Irwin, 1962.

DAWSON, LESLIE M., "Toward a New Concept of Sales Management," *Journal of Marketing* (April 1970), pp. 33–38.

KEITH, ROBERT J., "The Marketing Revolution," *Journal of Marketing* (January 1960), pp. 35–38.

LEVITT, THEODORE, "Marketing Myopia," *Harvard Business Review* (July–August 1960), pp. 45–56.

"The New Supersalesman: Wired for Success," *Business Week* (January 6, 1973), pp. 44–49.

RIESER, CARL, "The Salesman Isn't Dead—He's Different," *Fortune* (November 1962), pp. 124–27 ff.

### Environment of Sales Management

BOONE, LOUIS E., and DAVID L. KURTZ, "The Environment for Marketing Decisions," in *Contemporary Marketing* (2nd ed.), Hinsdale, Ill.: The Dryden Press, 1977.

DUNN, ALBERT H., EUGENE M. JOHNSON, and DAVID L. KURTZ, "The Environment of Selling," in *Sales Management: Concepts, Practices and Cases*. Morristown, N.J.: General Learning Press, 1974.

MCCARTHY, E. JEROME, "Strategy Planning in an Uncontrollable Environment," in *Essentials of Marketing*. Homewood, Ill.: Richard D. Irwin, 1979.

### Role of Selling in Marketing

JOLSON, MARVIN A., "Personal Selling—a Subset of Marketing," in *Sales Management: A Tactical Approach*. New York: Petrocelli/Charter, 1977.

MAZZE, EDWARD M., *Personal Selling: Choice Against Chance*. St. Paul: West Publishing, 1976.

STANTON, WILLIAM J., and Richard H. Buskirk, "The Field of Sales Management," in *Management for the Sales Force* (5th ed.). Homewood, Ill.: Richard D. Irwin, 1978.

### Process of Management

DONNELLEY, JAMES H., JR., JAMES L. GIBSON, and JOHN M. IVANCEVICH, *Fundamentals of Management*, 3rd ed., Dallas: Business Publications, 1978.

KOONTZ, HAROLD, and CYRIL O'DONNELL, *Management*, 6th ed., New York: McGraw-Hill, 1976.

MINTZBERG, HENRY, "The Manager's Job: Folklore and Fact," *Harvard Business Review*, (July-August 1975), pp. 49–61.

NEWMAN, WILLIAM H., and E. KIRBY WARREN, *The Process of Management*, 4th ed., Englewood Cliffs, N.J.: Prentice-Hall, 1977.

### Job of the Sales Manager

BROWN, RONALD, *From Selling to Managing*. New York: Amacon, 1968.

HANAN, MACK, and others, *Take-Charge Sales Management*. New York: Amacon, 1976.

HORWITZ, VICTOR, "Salesman to Manager: Easy Doesn't Do It," *Sales Management*, April 30, 1973, pp. 30 ff.

"Making Field Managers Managers, Special Report," *Sales and Marketing Management* (December 1978).

SEGAL, MENDEL, *Sales Management for Small and Medium-sized Businesses*. West Nyack, N.Y.: Parker Publishing, 1969.

# 2

# SALES PERSONNEL
# PLANNING AND RECRUITING

*After reading this chapter, you should be able to demonstrate your learning as follows:*
- *List the major steps involved in the sales staffing process.*
- *Given information on the number of salespeople and selling costs, calculate the turnover rate and estimate the cost of turnover for your company.*
- *Given a company's sales goals, determine the number and type of salespeople required.*
- *Plan and coordinate an effective sales recruiting program.*
- *List the major sources of sales recruits, including those for women and minorities, and select the sources that would be most fruitful for the type of sales recruit desired.*
- *Avoid mistakes in complying with affirmative action laws and guidelines.*

Staffing the sales organization is crucial to successful sales management. Any manager, whether a general, university president, football coach, or sales manager, must choose subordinates carefully. A sales manager is only as good as the people in the sales organization. General Dwight D. Eisenhower, Supreme Allied Commander in Europe during World War II, was successful largely because of his ability to choose and coordinate the diverse talents of such military men as General Omar Bradley, Field Marshal Bernard Montgomery, and General George Patton.

In this and the next chapter, we shall explore techniques for analyzing and planning for sales personnel needs, recruiting, screening and selecting salespeople, and orienting new salespeople. These are the first major steps in the sales management process, and the future success of any sales force depends on the sales manager's ability to staff the sales organization. To do this well, a sales manager must be both a sales representative for the company and a judge of the ability of sales applicants to succeed in selling.

## STEPS IN THE STAFFING PROCESS

A systematic approach for staffing the sales organization includes three major steps.

1. *Sales personnel planning.* This has become an essential part of managing the sales force. Two important activities are involved: determining the number of sales reps needed and determining the type of people needed. Realistic estimates of the size and characteristics of the company's future sales force enable management to develop recruitment, selection, and training programs that will make optimum use of the company's existing sales force and meet the sales organization's personnel needs of the future.
2. *Recruiting sales candidates.* Recruiting involves identifying sources of candidates and attracting these people to the company. In the search for sales candidates, the manager must be aware of the best sources for sales recruits and cultivate these sources through personal and indirect recruiting techniques.
3. *Screening and selecting applicants.* Screening is the negative process of elimination. Unqualified and undesirable applicants arc weeded out until only qualified candidates remain. Selection is the positive process of choosing the number of people needed from this group of qualified candidates.

One way of viewing this process is to visualize a funnel. The first step is to determine what to put into the funnel; how many and what type of salespeople are required. Then the funnel is filled with a "pool" of applicants through recruiting efforts. The last two steps are screening the applicants and making final selection decisions. If the entire process has been done properly, the manager will end up with an adequate number of qualified applicants at the base of the funnel.

## SALES PERSONNEL PLANNING

Sales personnel planning has increased in importance because of the shortage of sales applicants. One reason is that many young people are reluctant to consider selling as a career, although the demand for qualified sales reps is increasing.

A second pressure behind increased personnel planning is the expense of sales recruiting and selection. A company cannot afford to make many mistakes. Hiring more sales reps than are needed and hiring the wrong kind of person are costly errors. Careful planning helps avoid these errors. Further, as we shall see in the next section, the costs of sales turnover are high.

Finally, timing is important in the selection process. It is wise to forecast needs for salespeople well in advance of the time they will be employed. This allows for a carefully designed recruitment and selection program. It is also important to hire sales applicants before they are needed so that there is adequate time for proper training.

### Evaluating the Staffing Program

The first step in the planning process is to evaluate the existing staffing program. If you answer "yes" to any of the following questions, your company's program may need revision.

### Is Turnover Excessive?

Turnover is a problem for almost every company and cannot be eliminated entirely. There will always be salespeople who retire, die, quit the company for other positions, or who are considered unfit for selling and are discharged.

What is excessive turnover? Turnover varies according to company, industry, and type of selling, but it is possible to offer some guidelines. Derek A. Newton, whose study, *Sales Force Performance and Turnover,* included responses from over 1,000 sales executives, considers a turnover rate of 10 percent or more excessive.[1] Another study by the

---

[1]Turnover rate equals the number of salespeople who quit or are discharged divided by the average size of a company's sales force during a given period of time (usually a year).

National Industrial Conference Board reported that, on the average, three percent of a company's sales force quit and one percent are discharged during a given year. Thus, a turnover rate greater than four percent is cause for concern and a rate above 10 percent may require immediate action.

### Is the Dollar Investment Lost on People Who Have Left the Company Excessive?

The out-of-pocket costs of turnover are startling. Included are the costs in time, energy, and money of recruiting, selecting, training, and supervising people who ultimately fail to sell. The compensation paid to these salespeople must also be counted. To illustrate this, assume a firm's costs of hiring and training a sales rep are $20,000. If a firm has 200 sales reps and turnover is 10 percent per year, it will incur a cost of $400,000 per year. By cutting the turnover rate in half, this firm could save $200,000 per year.

Let's look at turnover costs in another way. Again, assume expenses of $20,000 to recruit, select, and train a sales rep. If a company has a turnover rate of 10 percent, the cost of each retained sales rep would be $22,222 ($20,000 ÷ .9). If turnover can be reduced to five percent, the cost per retained sales rep would be reduced by over $1000 per person ($20,000 ÷ .95 = $21,053).

### Are Sales Lost Because Salespeople Leave the Company?

When a sales rep leaves, the impact on sales volume is immediate. If the departed rep has switched to a competitor, customers may also switch. A customer's loyalty may be to the sales representative rather than to a product or company.

Even if customers remain loyal to the company, excessive turnover may result in lost sales. It is hard to convince a customer that he or she is dealing with a reputable firm with quality products if a different salesperson appears every few months. Further, the buyer's ordering routine may be interrupted while replacements are recruited, selected, and trained. Sales lost because of turnover may be more costly to the firm in the long run than out-of-pocket selection and training expenses.

Obtain information on your company's sales force. How many salespeople have left the company over the last year? How much have they cost the company in out-of-pocket expenses and disruption of selling routine? Complete the checklist that follows.

---

### CHECKLIST FOR EVALUATING YOUR SELECTION PROGRAM

TURNOVER

| Number of salespeople at beginning of year | | Number of salespeople at end of year | | Average sales force |
|---|---|---|---|---|
| (_____) | + | (_____) | ÷ 2 = | _____ |

| Number of salespeople who left company during the year | | Average sales force | | Turnover rate |
|---|---|---|---|---|
| (_____) | − | (_____) | = | _____% |

COSTS

1. Dollar investment per sales representative

- Recruitment and selection     $ _____
- Training     $ _____
- Supervision     $ _____
- Compensation     $ _____
- Other     $ _____

|  |  | Number of salespeople who left | Total Cost |
|---|---|---|---|
| Total | $ _____ × (_____) | = $ _____ |  |

2. Lost sales (estimate)           +    _____
    Total Costs                  $ _____

---

## Case Study

We have discussed the costs of turnover and presented a method for computing the turnover rate and estimating total costs. Before turning to sales personnel planning techniques, let us apply what we have learned to an actual business problem. Study this problem and answer the questions that follow.

### Sew-More Company

Ron Wilson has recently been appointed assistant to the national sales manager of Sew-More, a national producer and distributor of home sewing notions. Wilson joined Sew-More as a salesman three years ago after graduating from Bedford College, a small New England business school. His sales record was excellent and his new promotion is expected to be the first of many.

One of Ron Wilson's first assignments is to analyze the company's turnover of sales personnel. At the beginning of last year, Sew-More had 240 sales reps and ended the year with 260, a net gain of 20. During the year, 60 new sales reps were hired and trained and 40 left the company.

*What was Sew-More's turnover rate for last year?* _____

_____

*Using the checklist on page 31 as a guide and the following cost data, calculate the total cost of turnover.* _____

| | |
|---|---|
| Recruitment and selection | = $ 800/sales rep |
| Training | = $2400/sales rep |
| Supervision | = $1200/sales rep |
| Compensation (average for 6 months) | = $3600/sales rep |
| Other costs | = $ 400/sales rep |
| Estimated lost sales | = $ 300/sales rep |

*Based on this analysis, do you think Sew-More has a turnover problem?* _____

_____

_____

_____

## Predicting Quantitative Requirements

The general approach to determine the number of salespeople needed is explained by a simple equation:

$$
\begin{array}{ccc}
\text{Sales personnel} & - & \text{Sales personnel} & = & \text{Additional sales personnel} \\
\text{needed} & & \text{available} & & \text{required}
\end{array}
$$

## Sales Personnel Needed

Any forecast of sales personnel needs must be tied to some base point. The most useful base is a reasonably accurate projection of the firm's long-range sales. Usually, a 5-or-10-year forecast is an appropriate planning base.

Trend analysis is used to predict sales personnel needs. Historical data relevant to sales personnel requirements are obtained from company records. Then significant trends are identified and projected into the future. The sales personnel forecast is derived from the projected trend.

To illustrate this technique, Dillon Company has collected data on sales and number of salespeople over the last 20 years. The relationship between these two sets of data can be determined mathematically or graphically. Figure 2-1 shows the graphical relationship. By projecting the trend line, management can derive the sales personnel requirements for future sales levels. For example, if sales are expected to be $75 million, 600 salespeople will be required.

FIGURE 2-1. TREND ANALYSIS

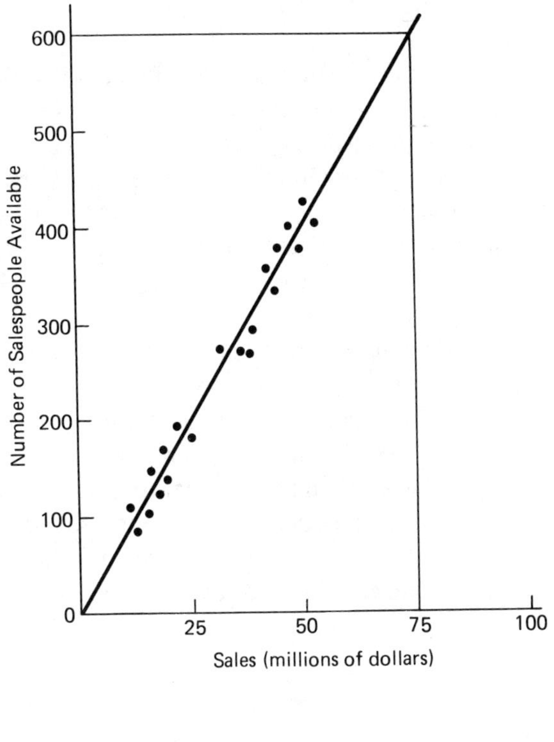

A similar approach is to compute the sales per sales rep ratio and project this trend. For instance, Dillon Company now employs 400 salespeople and has sales of $50 million. The current sales/sales rep figure is $125,000 ($50 million ÷ 400 salespeople. The company predicts sales of $75 million at the end of a five-year planning period. A rough estimate of the number of salespeople the firm will require at the end of five years is 600 salespeople ($75 million ÷ $125,000).

The major weakness of trend analysis is that it assumes future operating conditions will remain the same as in the past. This assumption may be unrealistic in today's fast-changing business world. Sales personnel requirements are affected by productivity changes, economic conditions, new product introductions, promotional strategy revisions, and other marketing policy changes.

To illustrate: Dillon's management decides to increase the advertising support given sales reps. This is expected to improve the sales/sales rep ratio by 2 percent each year. If this happens, in five years sales per sales rep will be almost $138,000. When this is divided into $75 million, the revised estimate of salespeople needed is 544.

## Sales Personnel Available

The starting point for predicting the number of salespeople available within the firm is a comprehensive inventory of sales personnel. A "person-by-person" approach is recommended. The abilities, promotability, and retirement status of salespeople are considered on an individual basis; vacancies are highlighted, and additional personnel requirements are anticipated. This task has been simplified in recent years by the introduction of computerized payroll and personnel coding systems.

Trend analysis is used also to predict the number of salespeople remaining within the firm at some future date. First, historical data on the retirement, turnover, and promotion rates of salespeople are assembled. Then a "total loss rate" is calculated and projected into the future.

For example: Dillon Company's total loss rate is computed as 5 percent a year. Assuming no interim hiring, the company will have slightly more than three-fourths (310 salespeople) of its original sales force available in five years. This year-by-year loss is shown in Figure 2-2.

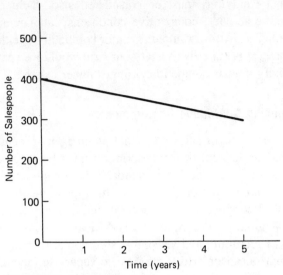

FIGURE 2-2. TOTAL LOSS RATE

### Additional Sales Personnel Required

The final step is to compare the available sales personnel with the forecasted need for salespeople. To achieve its sales goal of $75 million in five years, Dillon Company will need an additional 234 salespeople. This estimate assumes the new advertising support policy will be implemented.

| Sales personnel needed | − | Sales personnel available | = | Additional sales personnel required |
|---|---|---|---|---|
| 544 | − | 310 | = | 234 |

### Other Factors

Before leaving quantitative sales personnel planning, it is wise to point out other factors that will modify the number of salespeople needed by a company. Changes in company policies, promotion policies, retirement plans, and transfer procedures will affect sales personnel planning. For example, if a company stresses maximum promotion from within, the planner must make sure there are qualified salespeople who can be upgraded to management positions. The planner must also compensate for this policy when estimating the potential sales personnel available.

External conditions must be considered also. Included are the level of economic activity, competitive conditions, labor relations, and government policies. If, for example, a major competitor decides to double its sales force, it is quite likely that your firm would lose experienced people, especially if your competitor offered higher salaries.

## Determining Qualitative Requirements

The second part of sales personnel planning is to determine the *type* of salespeople desired. A job description must be prepared before recruiting and selection begin. This includes a list of job specifications, which indicates what the job demands and what type of person is needed.

The job description is an important tool in many areas of sales management. Without job descriptions it is difficult, if not impossible, to do a good job of recruiting and selecting salespeople, to train sales personnel, to assign salespeople to territories, to supervise them or to plan market strategy. Job descriptions are also the key to a good sales evaluation program. Therefore, a key proposition that will be used throughout this book is: *an important, basic tool that allows the sales manager to perform most management functions well is the job description.*

Now let us turn to the steps in creating a good job description and discuss the characteristics that must be present for the job description to be a useful sales management tool in the many management areas where it is required.

## Job Analysis

The first step in creating a good job description is job analysis; the careful and objective study and written summary of the selling job in question. Through the use of company records, direct field observation and whatever other supporting information may be available (such as government statistics and trade association studies), the sales job is analyzed and summarized in light of these critical questions.

### Environmental Factors

What is the nature and extent of the competition that salespeople encounter? What general business conditions must they operate within (for example, purchasing power, level of unemployment)? What industry structure and practices must they work with, such as traditional channels of distribution and industry credit policies? In short, what is the business and social framework within which they will have to sell and in which their work will be supervised and evaluated?

> *Specifically, what is the nature of the social, competitive, and economic environment within which your own company's salespeople must work?* _____
>
> _____
>
> _____
>
> _____

## Performance Factors

How do salespeople presently spend their time: traveling, selling, filling out reports, securing sales promotion support from customers, waiting, entertaining? What specific selling functions do they perform? How much time do they spend on each function and activity? Regardless of how this is finally summarized, it amounts to a time-and-motion study similar to those used in the plant to study the performance of production workers. When it is completed, it will show in detail how the sales reps are spending that valuable asset the company has bought for its use: time.

A large western liquor wholesaler does this job analysis process particularly well. In the annual review of sales performance, the wholesaler has several specially trained supervisors travel for two days each with a sample of sales reps. They note, on a special form, everything the reps do and the approximate time required for each activity. These reports are summarized at headquarters and the results are compared with the job description. This process rechecks and keeps job descriptions up-to-date with environmental and market changes.

## Critical Analysis

With knowledge of the factors in their environment that salespeople must deal with and with information about how they actually spend their time, the last stage in job study is to analyze *how they should* be spending their time and to describe this in a meaningful summary. Should they be performing the functions that they are? Should they be placing the relative emphasis on their various functions that they are? Should they be dealing with competition and other environmental factors in the way they are? Should they be doing more, less, or the same amount of entertaining?

By combining performance and environmental studies of the sales job in an objective, careful, critical analysis of the job, we develop a meaningful summary of what the selling job we are going to describe *should be*.

Does your company make it a practice regularly to study and observe your salespeople at work? If not, should your company be doing this? If so, what is the purpose of this activity? How effective is it and why? Does it assist in making the sales job description more accurate and useful?

_____

_____

### Sales Job Description

We are now ready to move to the systematic development of a good formal sales job description. Working from the systematic, detailed job analysis, outlined above, we produce a detailed, written job description whose purpose is to show:

1.  In detail the components of the sales job, the functions or specific activities salespeople must perform, such as prospecting for new customers, traveling, selling, setting up displays, providing service assistance, and filling out reports.
2.  The ideal or desired division of the sales rep's time between each function: how to divide efforts among many activities, *stated in measurable, relative terms*.

### Characteristics of a Good Job Description

Take a few minutes and write a rough draft job description for your company's salespeople. It is important that you do this before reading further, so you can later compare your draft job description with the characteristics of a good job description, which follow.

A good job description has five characteristics.

## Written

The job description must be committed to paper. Informal, verbal job descriptions are virtually useless in managing the sales force and lead to misunderstanding and friction. Job descriptions that are not written are often worse than no job descriptions at all.

## Accepted

To be useful in their many applications to sales management, job descriptions must be known to, and accepted by, salespeople, their immediate managers, and all other sales executives. Unless the job description is written down and agreed upon by all, misunderstanding and friction will result when it comes to using the job description for selecting, training, and evaluating salespeople. This is because each sales rep and each manager is proceeding on his or her own private understanding of the job content and the relative priorities of various job functions.

One example of this problem is offered by the sales manager of a sulphur company, who reports: "My field managers could never agree on whether or not a particular sales rep was doing a good job, or for that matter, for any given period, if the whole sales force was doing a good or a poor job. We finally realized why—we didn't have any common standards in our job description. We've fixed that now."

## Specific

A job description must be specific, not vague or general in its delineation of the selling functions and the relative emphasis that should be placed on each. As far as possible, the required performance of each function must be *stated in measurable terms,* such as the *number* of calls per day, *dollars* or *units* sold, *number* of displays set up, and the *number* of new accounts opened.

An example of the description of one job element that is vaguely and generally stated comes from a plywood manufacturer: "An important part of the sales rep's job is to make regular calls on the trade." This description is useless in management. What is "important" or "regular" or a "call"? How can you know what the rep is doing against this criterion? You can't.

A useful description of the same function comes from a drug manufacturer:

Our sales reps must call on Class A customers 50 times a year; on Class B customers, 25 times a year, and on Class C customers as frequently as their other duties allow. Our sales reps do not call at all on Class D customers, who are serviced entirely through wholesalers. The classes of customers are established by dollar volume with Class A being . . .

As these examples illustrate, a job description must be specific in order to be useful.

## Inclusive

To be useful in the management of salespeople, the job description must identify all functions they are to perform, and furnish priorities. None can be overlooked or assumed to be evident. If opening new accounts, controlling expenses, or maintaining a certain average order size are important functions of a particular sales job, the job description must specifically identify them as such. In addition, it must provide effective measures or standards of performance for the functions; for example, a bogey average of new accounts opened per week or month, a ratio of dollar expense to dollar sales, a dollar range of average order size.

## Detailed, but Terse

For purposes of sales management, the job description must avoid each of two extremes. One problem is overterseness. Such a job description is very short, quick, and easy to read, but in its brevity, is so generalized as to be useless for management purposes. An illustration of this is the example of the plywood manufacturer cited above. It describes the function in a very few words, but tells nothing that can be used in managing the sales representative's work.

The other extreme that must be avoided is overdetail. In the overdetailed job description, the functions are described in such minute detail that it is difficult or impossible for the sales rep or the manager to use it. A job description must be *only as detailed* as necessary to provide an effective management tool and to show the sales rep what is expected.

In summary, a job description is an ideal, realistic, and detailed statement of the sales rep's job in terms of specific functions, activities, and their relative priority. In total, a job description is a *profile* of the sales job, showing the functions that must be performed and how much time, effort, attention, and emphasis (however measured) should be placed on each activity. Finally, good job descriptions are indispensable in many of the functions of sales management, most especially in recruitment and selection, training, motivation, and supervision.

|  | *Yes* | *No* |
|---|---|---|
| Does your company have written sales job descriptions? | _____ | _____ |
| Are they generally accepted by all members of management as accurate and useful? | _____ | _____ |
| Are they generally accepted by the salespeople as accurate and useful? | _____ | _____ |
| Review the draft job description you wrote earlier in this section. Is it: | | |
| Specific? | _____ | _____ |
| Detailed, but terse? | _____ | _____ |
| Inclusive? | _____ | _____ |

Now that you have studied the material on job description, how could you improve your draft job description made earlier?

As we see, a company's sales job description provides the framework for recruiting and selection. It is the basis for preparing job announcements, advertisements, application blanks, interview forms, the selection of psychological tests, and other selection tools. When these tools are not used, sales managers tend to hire people who are a reflection of their own abilities and qualifications. Selection is often made on the basis of a single outstanding physical, mental, or personality trait. This practice has been called the "halo effect" and has resulted in some costly hiring mistakes. For example, research studies concerning the hiring practices of sales managers reveal that many managers believe tall people make the best salespeople; that anyone who smokes a pipe cannot be a good salesman because he is too contented; that a person who wears blue clothing will be more effective than someone wearing another color; that not owning life insurance is an indication of financial irresponsibility! How many excellent salespeople do you know who do not conform to these standards?

Although the job description will be different for each sales job and selection criteria vary accordingly, there are some general qualities that are preferred in all salespeople.

Before reading further, list those qualities that you would look for in a successful sales representative.

_____        _____

_____        _____

_____        _____

Books and articles on selling and sales management contain many descriptions of successful salespeople. Frequently mentioned characteristics are summarized in the table below. How do they compare with your list?

### CHARACTERISTICS OF SUCCESSFUL SALESPEOPLE

1. Initiative: a "self-starter," interested in selling, strong personal desire for success, able to motivate self, enthusiastic, ego drive.
2. Intelligence: problem-solving ability, technical competence (when necessary), willingness and ability to learn, well organized.
3. Balance: versatile, flexible, variety of interests, well rounded, experienced.
4. Poise: confidence in self, ability to handle pressure situations, sociability.
5. Communications skills: articulate, persuasive, able to establish rapport with others, empathy, high verbal skills.

### Case Study

Let's return to Ron Wilson's review of turnover for the Sew-More Company (pages 31–32). Wilson's next step is to determine what qualities Sew-More's sales reps need. Consider this problem and answer the questions that follow.

The second part of Wilson's analysis of turnover involves a comparison of the 40 sales reps who left the company with a sample of 40 successful sales reps still active with Sew-More. Wilson explained that "The intent is to better understand why we terminate people or why they resign within a short period of time. Knowing these factors, we could design a profile that would help a district sales manager in selecting new sales reps."

The following is a summary of Wilson's major findings.

*Age when hired*

| | |
|---|---|
| Terminated | 34 years |
| Resigned | 29 years |
| Active | 30 years |

*Previous selling experience*

| | |
|---|---|
| Terminated | 21% |
| Resigned | 32% |
| Active | 12% |

*Married with children*

| | |
|---|---|
| Terminated | 71.5% |
| Resigned | 54.5% |
| Active | 100.0% |

*Educational Level*

| | |
|---|---|
| Terminated | 2 years of college |
| Resigned | 3 years of college |
| Active | 1 year of college |

Based on this statistical analysis, Wilson developed this profile as a guide for district sales managers when hiring sales applicants:

Age 26 to 30, married, with two children. At least a high school education with possibly one year of college. Former experience may include factory work, the construction trades, retail store work, or sales in a small company such as a distributor of office equipment, building supply house, and the like. Past experience should show someone who has served long hours with little reward. Previous income should be less than our weekly starting rate, not including bonuses. Before making the job offer, district sales manager should meet with the applicant and applicant's spouse to insure that the spouse fully understands the job and travel required.

*What is your appraisal of the statistical summary Ron Wilson compiled?* _____

_____

_____

_____

_____

*What additional information would you like to have? Why?* _____

_____

_____

_____

*How helpful do you think Wilson's profile will be to Sew-More's district sales managers?* _____

_____

_____

## RECRUITING GUIDELINES

Once sales personnel needs are identified and projected, plans must be made for recruiting applicants. Certain guidelines have been useful for many companies.

### Plan and Organize Recruiting Efforts

Recruiting is essentially a selling activity, and in the same way a sales representative plans and organizes sales efforts, a sales manager must plan and organize the recruiting activities. Also, one must view recruiting as a continuous process, which must be thoughtfully organized. Too often sales managers think about recruiting only when a vacancy occurs. In the rush to fill the vacancy, the manager is likely to overlook an applicant's shortcomings. The effective recruiter always has a few promising candidates in mind to avoid crash recruiting efforts.

One way to avoid a hurried search is to maintain a file of potential sales candidates. In their work, sales managers encounter many potential salespeople. The prudent manager finds out something about these people, records this information, and files it for future reference. When a vacancy occurs, the manager has a list of potential recruits who have already been identified.

### Recruit from All Sources

Every sales manager has a favorite source of sales recruits. A skillful manager will continue to use sources that have proven fruitful.

However, it is desirable to maintain contacts with anyone who might suggest potential sales recruits, since word-of-mouth is an important source of information when recruiting. Referrals can come from those outside the company, clergymen, civic leaders, customers, and suppliers, for instance, as well as from internal company sources.

### Develop Qualified Recruiters

Poorly trained recruiters may discourage qualified applicants or give false encouragement to unacceptable applicants. Also, poor recruiters may make costly mistakes when interviewing women and minority applicants. Recruiting errors have resulted in legal action against the recruiter's company.

Recruiters should be trained to do two important things: to sell the company to applicants and to decide whether the candidate should continue in the recruitment and selection process. Even if the recruiter decides early in the interview that the applicant will not fit the job, the recruiter must be amicable. The applicant may have friends who are attractive potential sales recruits, or the applicant may someday be a customer. Recruiting is a two-way street and a very important public relations activity for the company.

Mobil Corporation has an excellent training program for college recruiters. They are brought to selected college campuses for an intensive seminar. In addition to lectures and discussions, each trainee-recruiter interviews an applicant. These interviews are videotaped and critiqued by the instructor and others in the group. This program has done much to improve Mobil's college recruiting program.

### Review Recruiting Results

To monitor the recruiting program, the sales manager must get feedback on recruiting activities. Improving the process is not possible without such information. Records are kept on the number and quality of sales applicants that come from various recruiting sources. For example, how many qualified applicants responded to an advertisement in a trade journal? These records help the manager judge the effectiveness of recruiting sources.

Another procedure is to follow the progress of successful applicants. How many become successful salespeople? How many leave the company? Are there any significant characteristics of successful and unsuccessful recruits? A pharmaceutical manufacturer found that when forced by market conditions to recruit business students, these recruits were actually more successful sales representatives than the biology, chemistry, and pharmacy students previously hired.

A third technique is to question those applicants who refuse job offers. Why are they refusing? Perhaps they feel that the compensation is too low, that the job does not provide a challenge, or that they need more job security. These and many other possible responses suggest changes to be made in a firm's sales recruiting program.

## SOURCES OF SALES RECRUITS

As already suggested, a sales manager should use several sources of sales recruits. The most frequently used sources are discussed below. But before reading further, list what you consider to be the best sources of sales recruits for your company.

_____

_____

_____

### Company Sources

Don't overlook other employees when searching for sales recruits. People in manufacturing, maintenance, clerical, or warehouse jobs may have latent sales talent. Make sure the company's personnel department is aware of sales personnel needs. Since the personnel manager continuously evaluates qualifications of employees, his or her review may reveal employees with qualifications for sales positions.

The search for sales talent from within can be advantageous. A review of one West Coast company's industrial sales force revealed that five of nine top sales reps and field sales managers had held production positions. Other advantages of recruiting salespeople from nonsales functions are:

1. The sales recruit is more of a known quantity than an outsider.
2. The recruit requires less training and indoctrination because he or she is familiar with the company's products, operations, and policies.

3. Overall company morale is bolstered since employees become aware that opportunities are not restricted to individual departments or divisions.

## Company Salespeople

Like a field sales manager, salespeople become acquainted with many potential sales recruits. They should be encouraged to refer qualified applicants to the company. Some firms, IBM is one, offer a bonus as an incentive to salespeople to recruit others. However, referrals from salespeople must be handled tactfully so as not to cause hard feelings if a referral is rejected.

## Suppliers and Customers

Don't overlook sales reps calling on your company. It is possible they may be dissatisfied and looking for a change. Also, distributors, dealers, and other customers may have suggestions about salespeople who call on them.

## Local Business and Civic Organizations

Participation in community organizations will often provide recruiting leads. Civic organizations (PTA, Chamber of Commerce, Junior Chamber of Commerce), local business associations (Society for the Advancement of Management, American Marketing Association, Sales and Marketing Executives-International), and service organizations (Lions, Kiwanis, Rotary) are all possible sources of sales recruits.

## Professional Associations

Technical, trade, and sales organizations usually maintain informal employment listings for members. They may also publish and distribute lists of job opportunities. For information, contact the executive director of the trade association.

## Educational Institutions

All types of institutions for higher learning—colleges, universities, junior colleges, business schools, adult evening courses, and correspondence schools—are fertile sources of sales recruits. Of course, the institutions contacted will depend on the job qualifications desired.

If sales reps need a technical background, colleges and universities are a main source of recruits. Contacts with professors, placement officers, and administrators will pay off. However, even with many contacts, colleges and universities are limited as sources of sales recruits. Many companies are competing for only a small percentage of college students who will even consider a career in selling.

An effective strategy for recruiting and screening college students is to offer students internships or part-time jobs in selling. Students are always interested in an opportunity to find out what the "real world" of business is like. Providing work/study opportunities gives the company a chance to attract qualified sales recruits and observe them on a job. Students in cooperative programs are often effective in missionary and similar promotion tasks, and many become interested in full-time sales employment as a result of their experiences.

Some companies make a mistake by going after only the top students. When recruiting college students for sales careers, don't concentrate on only those students with outstanding records. Men and women with average or undistinguished records are often more effective salespeople. College dropouts may also be good sales recruits. And don't forget alumni. Most college placement offices maintain an active alumni file. Experienced salespeople frequently contact the placement directors of their alma maters when they decide to change jobs.

Also frequently overlooked are community and junior colleges. These two-year colleges, which have multiplied rapidly, offer a rich source of potential sales recruits. The students are often men and women who recognize the need for higher education, but lack the financial resources or academic motivation for a four-year degree. Many older men and women are enrolled in two-year programs. These students are often married and eager to begin work as soon as possible.

Other rich sources are evening programs of high schools and colleges. People enrolled in these programs are usually employed, but are searching for ways to improve themselves. Courses in public speaking, salesmanship, and marketing are logical places to locate people who are interested in selling. One way to meet and interest these people is to speak to their classes about a career in selling.

## Armed Forces

Placement officers at mustering-out centers may know of armed forces personnel who are interested in selling careers. Some may have prior selling experience. Others will have leadership experience and may possess selling potential.

### Government Agencies

For certain types of sales positions, the United States Employment Service and similar state agencies provide listings of qualified applicants. These agencies may be particularly helpful to the company seeking technical persons who may have been displaced by technological advances or economic changes.

### Job Fairs

Chambers of commerce, professional organizations, civic groups, and government agencies sponsor job fairs, which bring applicants and employers together. These job fairs have the major advantage of providing a large number of initial contacts for very little cost. However, they may not be appropriate for certain types of sales jobs.

Some companies have been successful in running their own job fairs. The American Bankers Life Assurance Company uses a series of "opportunity seminars" to attract and evaluate job applicants. During three evening sessions, interested persons are provided with general and specific job information and are screened for further consideration.

### Unsolicited Applicants

Frequently, sales candidates will contact a company directly. This action shows that the applicant has initiative, but, like everyone else, unsolicited applicants must be checked out carefully. There may be some unusual reason why the applicant is unwilling to go through the normal recruiting channels.

### Employment Agencies

Sales managers who do not have enough time for recruiting might consider using a professional employment agency. However, it is absolutely essential that each manager select an agency that is right for the sales job involved. Some employment agencies do not enjoy a good reputation as sources for salespeople. Also, some agencies just refer applicants to clients with no real concern for the client's or the applicant's needs.

Fortunately, not all agencies are this way. Some specialize in sales jobs and render a valuable recruiting service. The following guide-lines are suggested for using an agency to the best advantage.

1.  Select an agency with a good professional reputation and experi-ence in recruiting salespeople. One indication of an agency's professionalism is whether the agency is a member of the Na-tional Employment Association. Membership means that the agency subscribes to the NEA's Code of Ethics.
2.  Visit the agency personally. Examine its facilities and personnel to be sure the agency is able to screen applicants effectively.
3.  Make sure the agency knows your requirements. Provide the agency's recruiters with a comprehensive description of the job and the required qualifications. Supportive literature about the company will also be helpful.
4.  Develop continuing relationships with agencies that provide good results and eliminate those that are unsuccessful.

### Advertisements

Advertisements placed in newspapers, professional newsletters, and trade journals may result in responses from many sales applicants. If a technically qualified or experienced person is needed, advertising in trade journals or professional newsletters is appropriate. For more general sales jobs, newspaper advertisements are adequate. Advertisements in trade and professional publications are usually placed in a personnel or marketplace section. A newspaper ad will reach more potential sales recruits if it appears in the personnel section of a Sunday newspaper. In most major cities with more than one newspaper, one particular paper is usually the marketplace for personnel.

Recruitment ads must be appealing and informative. To attract readers, the ad needs a strong sales-oriented headline. Include informa-tion about the company, nature of the job, specific qualifications re-quired, compensation, fringe benefits, and opportunities for advance-ment. However, the ad must not promise too much. It should be written in a manner to discourage those who are not qualified from applying. To make it easy for an applicant to reply immediately, a telephone number or place to write is included.

Some companies have begun to recruit sales applicants through radio and television spots. Brief radio announcements of sales openings during early morning and late afternoon commuting hours have drawn well. Although television ads are expensive, they reach large numbers of people and have great impact. The sales manager who wishes to use radio or television advertising is advised to consult an experienced advertising executive before preparing and placing ads.

## EQUAL EMPLOYMENT OPPORTUNITY

Sales managers have a moral and legal obligation to provide equal employment opportunities for all qualified applicants. Further, most companies are expected to develop affirmative action plans that go beyond equal employment opportunity and make a special effort to hire and promote women and minorities. This section will review the legal requirements for recruitment and selection, identify major problem areas, and suggest procedures for recruiting women and minorities.

### Legal Requirements

The United States government, most states, and many counties and cities have laws that are directed toward preventing discriminatory employment practices. The federal government's legal cornerstone for equal employment opportunity is Title VII of the 1964 Civil Rights Act. This law prohibits discrimination because of race, color, religion, sex, or national origin in all employment practices. The Equal Employment Opportunity Commission (EEOC) was created to administer Title VII. In 1972 the EEOC's powers of enforcement were broadened and the agency was given direct access to the courts. Additional legislation in 1967 (Age Discrimination in Employment Act) and 1974 (Rehabilitation Act) included age and physical handicaps under the federal regulations.

Penalties for noncompliance are severe. The EEOC and similar state agencies may take legal action against employers. Substantial financial penalties, such as back pay and salary adjustments, are often levied by the courts. However, in many cases an employer and the EEOC will agree to a negotiated settlement. Such was the case when AT&T agreed in 1973 to make payments of $15 million to 15,000 employees, mostly women.

For those companies that have federal contracts, the Office of Federal Contract Compliance (OFCC) of the Department of Labor has equal employment guidelines that must be adhered to. Any company with 50 or more employees must submit a written affirmative action program to the OFCC. In addition, this agency and the EEOC have the authority to conduct an audit to determine if a company is complying with equal employment opportunity guidelines.

## Major Problems

As noted, the penalties for violating equal employment opportunity regulations are severe. Unfortunately, costly mistakes are made because recruiters and sales managers do not understand the law or are careless in using selection procedures.

The key point to remember is this: If you have any doubt about a recruiting or selection technique or standard, seek qualified legal advice. The penalties are too severe to risk a mistake. Areas of specific concern under the law are application forms, interviews, and employment tests.

*Application forms* must ask only for information that is related to the sales job. By the law, personal information, such as marital status, number of children, and age, should not be requested since this information could be used to prevent or restrict employment. Questions about military discharges and arrest records are also considered discriminatory. Likewise, questions about the applicant's financial status, such as credit accounts, home rental or ownership and bankruptcy are not allowed since the information may result in different treatment for different groups of people. The basic guideline is to seek only that information that is related to what the EEOC calls ''bona fide occupational qualifications,'' that is, information directly related to potential job performance.

*Interviews* are to be based only on job-related questions. The same restrictions on information requested from application forms applies to personal interviews. Further, the sales manager must not express personal opinions or value judgments about women or minorities to the interviewee.

*Psychological tests* have come under fire because some observers feel that tests discriminate against minorities. In fact, court cases and guidelines issued by the EEOC have caused some companies to discontinue testing as a selection technique. This may not be necessary, but a company must be prepared to prove that tests are job related and do not illegally discriminate. If a test is used, it must be validated by a qualified professional.

## Recruiting Female and Minority Applicants

Most sales organizations that have hired older men, women, and minority sales representatives have been pleased with the results. In certain segments of the market and with some types of buyers, minority and female salespeople have been more successful than white, Anglo-Saxon men. Sales selection researchers Herbert Greenberg and Ronald Bern comment:

> Our experience shows that a man of 50 may have more open-mindedness and youthful vigor than a man half his age; that women have the same ranges of business talents as men; that race has nothing to do with ability to sell. . . .[2]

A sales manager would be unwise not to make strong efforts to recruit all types of people for the sales force.

With some modifications, the recruiting sources discussed earlier can be used in recruiting women and minority persons. However, a good affirmative action program cannot just depend on traditional sources of sales recruits. It is wise to develop recruiting messages and media for specific populations and subgroups. Specific suggestions for recruiting female and minority sales applicants follow.

## Consider Present Female and Minority Employees

It is quite possible that a company's present minority or female employees have the potential for sales success. Persons in secretarial, clerical, manufacturing, and similar positions should be considered when sales openings occur. The personnel manager is a good source of information on present employees. Also, a sales manager can ask minority and female employees for referrals.

## Contact Specialized Employment Agencies and Organizations

There are many employment agencies that specialize in placing women and minorities. Information about these agencies and other services can be obtained from local chapters of the National Organization for Women (NOW), National Association for the Advancement of Colored People (NAACP), Urban League, and similar groups. In larger cities these organizations may have their own employment referral services.

---

[2]Herbert M. Greenberg and Ronald L. Bern, *The Successful Salesman: Man and His Manager* (Philadelphia: Auerbach Publishers, 1972), p. 80.

## Contact Women's and Minority
## Educational Institutions

Although times are changing, there are still a number of educational institutions that have predominantly minority or female student enrollments. Also, most large colleges and universities have minority administrators and student advisors who are useful sources for referrals.

## Use Targeted Advertising Messages
## and Media

Certain newspapers, radio and television programs, magazines, and other media appeal to minority and female populations. Recruiting ads placed in these media should be designed to appeal to the special groups. For instance, if photographs are used, females and minorities should be featured in them and copy should be in the appropriate language if the medium is not in English.

## Develop Personal Contacts

Contact respected female and minority members of the community for suggestions. Personal contacts are an effective affirmative action recruiting technique. For example, a leading bank in a major New England city has a woman marketing vice president. This respected executive is an excellent source of information about women who are interested in sales and marketing careers.

### Case Study

After the discussion of equal employment opportunity guidelines, consider this case problem. Answer the questions that follow.

Professional Books, Inc.

Sam Edwards, district sales manager for Professional Books, a large publisher, was interviewing Ellen Rogers, an applicant for a sales position. Here are selected excerpts from the interview:

EDWARDS: Is it Miss or Mrs. Rogers?

ROGERS: It's Mrs. Rogers, but please call me Ellen.

EDWARDS:  What does your husband do, Ellen?

ROGERS:  He's an accountant for Draper Manufacturing Company.

EDWARDS:  What would you do if your husband was transferred to another part of the country?

. . . . . . . . . . . . . . . . . . . . . . . . . . . . . . . . . . . . . . . . . . . . . . . . . . . . . . . . . .

EDWARDS:  Your first territory assignment would require that you be away from home at least one night a week. Do you think your husband would mind?

ROGERS:  No, we've discussed my career plans and he is totally committed to my decision.

EDWARDS:  But does he mind if you have dinner with male customers?

. . . . . . . . . . . . . . . . . . . . . . . . . . . . . . . . . . . . . . . . . . . . . . . . . . . . . . . . . .

EDWARDS:  As you know, we publish many business and engineering textbooks. Since you're a woman, do you think you'll have problems selling to male professors?

ROGERS:  I don't really think so. My major in college was business. Also, there are more women teaching in business and engineering schools.

EDWARDS:  Yes, but what would you do if a man comes on too strong? You're an attractive woman.

*Did Sam Edwards say anything that might be a violation of equal employment opportunity guidelines?* _____

_____

_____

*If you were Ellen Rogers, how would you feel about the questions Edwards asked?* _____

_____

_____

*How could Sam Edwards obtain the information he wants in a different way?* _____

_____

_____

## Brain teasers

|  | *Agree* | *Disagree* |
|---|---|---|
| 1. Recruiting and selection activities require a sales executive to change from seller to buyer. | ____ | ____ |
| 2. Turnover of salespeople can never be eliminated, but improved selection procedures may reduce turnover. | ____ | ____ |
| 3. In today's fast-changing business environment, trend analysis is a foolproof method for forecasting sales personnel needs. | ____ | ____ |
| 4. Job descriptions are very useful in hiring the right kind of people, but they are not used elsewhere in managing salespeople. | ____ | ____ |
| 5. There is agreement among sales managers that selling experience is the most important factor in hiring salespeople. | ____ | ____ |
| 6. Most successful recruiters use only one or two favorite sources of sales recruits. | ____ | ____ |
| 7. Grades are the most important consideration when recruiting sales candidates from colleges and universities. | ____ | ____ |
| 8. Since recruiting is so similar to selling, sales managers do not need any training to recruit. | ____ | ____ |
| 9. Although many employment agencies specialize in sales jobs, the manager still needs to provide the agency with specific job requirements. | ____ | ____ |
| 10. Only information that is related to the sales job should be requested from applicants during interviews. | ____ | ____ |

### Activities

*1. A study of sales turnover reported that younger salespeople are most likely to quit and are most subject to discharge. Also, consumer product salespeople are more likely to quit or be discharged than industrial product salespeople. What do you think are the reasons for greater turnover of younger sales-*

*people and consumer product salespeople? Can you suggest selection safeguards that might cut down on turnover?* _____

_____

_____

_____

2. *Think about your company's needs for salespeople during the next several years. What factors are likely to alter the number of salespeople needed and qualifications that these people must have?* _____

_____

_____

_____

3. *Acquire a copy of a sales rep's job description from your company or another. Analyze its strengths and weaknesses against the criteria set up in this chapter. How could it be improved?*

_____

_____

_____

4. *Briefly list the job features you would want in a sales job and the qualifications you have to offer. How would you go about looking for a job that meets your demands and qualifications? What does this analysis tell you about sales recruiting?* _____

_____

_____

_____

5. *A small regional manufacturer of business forms recruits only experienced sales reps from large national competitors. Is this a wise recruiting policy? Can you suggest other sources and methods of recruiting sales reps?* _____

_____

_____

_____

6. *Interview a female or minority sales representative in your company or another company. How does this person view the sales job? Does he or she have different views of selling than you do? Why or why not?* _____

_____

_____

_____

## SELECTED REFERENCES

### Sales Personnel Planning

DOBBS, JOHN H., "Sales Force Turnover Can Make You—Or Break You," *Sales and Marketing Management,* May 14, 1979, pp. 53–58.

HANAN, MACK, "It's Time to Do Something about Sales Force Turnover," *Sales Management,* February 4, 1974, pp. 47–51.

MAYER, DAVID, and HERBERT M. GREENBERG, "What Makes a Good Salesman?" in *Harvard Business Review* (July-August 1964), pp. 119–25.

MOSS, STAN, "What Sales Executives Look for in New Sales People," *Sales and Marketing Management* (March 1978), pp. 46–48.

SEMLOW, WALTER J., "How Many Salesmen Do You Need?" in *Harvard Business Review* (May–June 1959), pp. 126–32.

### Recruiting

HARTMAN, T. H., "Start Right by Hiring Right," *Sales Management,* April 30, 1973, pp. 70 ff.

LAPP, CHARLES L., and KENNETH J. LACHO, "Finding and Attracting Salespeople," *Louisiana Business Survey* (July 1977), pp. 12–14.

MCMURRAY, ROBERT N., and JAMES S. ARNOLD, *How to Build a Dynamic Sales Organization.* New York: McGraw-Hill, 1968.

STANTON, WILLIAM J., and RICHARD H. BUSKIRK, "Selecting the Sales Force—Recruiting Applicants," in *Management of the Sales Force* (5th ed.). Homewood, Ill.: Richard D. Irwin, 1978.

WALDO, CHARLES N., "Toward More and Better Salesmen," *Sales Management,* April 2, 1973, pp. 34–35.


## Equal Employment Opportunity

"Help Wanted in Avoiding Discrimination," *Today's Manager* (July–August 1976), pp. 3–6.

HILAAEL, T.M., "Three Step Plan for Implementing an Affirmative Action Program," *Personnel Administration,* (July 1976), pp. 35–39.

HURWOOD, DAVID L. "More Blacks and Women in Sales and Marketing," *Conference Board Record* (February 1973), pp. 38–44.

MITNICK, MARGERY M., "Equal Employment Opportunity and Affirmative Action: A Managerial Training Guide," *Personnel Journal* (October 1977), pp. 492–97 ff.

POPISIL, VIVIAN C., "What Can You Ask a Job Applicant?" *Industry Week,* March 1, 1976, pp. 24–28.

# 3

# SCREENING AND SELECTION OF SALES RECRUITS

*After reading this chapter, you should be able to demonstrate your learning as follows:*

- *Given the need for sound selection procedures, identify the difficulties of selection.*
- *List the major screening and selection tools and explain how they are used to select people who sell.*
- *Use each selection tool correctly without violating equal employment opportunity guidelines and privacy laws.*
- *Plan and conduct an effective employment interview.*
- *Design and implement a sound orientation program for new salespeople.*

The final staffing tasks are to screen and select candidates from the list of recruits generated. The tools available for screening and selection are:

1. Application form.
2. References.
3. Interviews—screening and selection.
4. Psychological tests.
5. Medical examination.
6. Trial period.

The sequence of these selection tools will vary. At each step unqualified applicants will be eliminated. After preliminary screening, only the best qualified applicants will remain, and a choice must be made.

Each of these selection tools will be considered in this chapter. First, however, we must consider some of the difficulties of selection.

# PROBLEMS IN SALES SELECTION

When selecting sales reps, the sales manager is challenged by the difficulties of predicting sales success.

## Sales Manager as a Buyer

Recruitment and selection present a transposition problem to the sales manager, especially the manager who has advanced from the ranks of selling. Now he or she must reverse roles. Rather than selling, the sales manager is now a buyer, purchasing the services of people for the company. Industrial consultant Keith Jewell comments: "(The sales manager) must put aside his usual selling attitudes and become, instead, an astute and careful buyer."[1]

## Risk in Predicting

Like most purchases, risk is involved when selecting salespeople. Prediction is hazardous. When you choose a sales applicant, you are predicting that this individual will become an effective sales rep for your company.

Both your company and the applicant have much to gain or lose from this prediction. Your company will incur costs for recruiting, hiring, and training the recruit. Sales losses can be expected if the wrong applicant is chosen. The applicant is gambling a part of a working life. If the applicant selects the wrong job, a portion of a business career is lost and cannot be recovered.

## Complexity of Selling

Further hampering the selection process is the complexity of selling. Unlike many jobs, success in selling does not depend solely upon intellectual qualifications. Sales jobs also impose emotional and temperamental demands on an individual. Consequently, there is difficulty in applying simple concepts of management psychology to the selection of salespeople. Selection techniques must emphasize the personality and emotional demands of selling as well as the ability, experience, and aptitude required.

[1]Keith R. Jewell, "Let's Take the Hocus Pocus out of Hiring," *Sales Management,* February 7, 1964, p. 28.

## Art or Science?

Selection is both an art and a science. Predicting an applicant's future performance involves experience and more than a little luck; this is the art of selection. Experienced managers do not ignore their instincts when selecting salespeople. Chances are good that experienced sales managers are right more often than they are wrong.

Too many sales managers, however, rely solely on their experience and luck. Critics of sales selection argue that these managers fail to follow a tested, systematic procedure when hiring. No company can expect to do a perfect job of selection because people are too complex, and not everyone can meet the rigorous qualifications of selling. However, by following a logical procedure, such as the one described in this chapter, you can expect to improve your selection batting average. This is the science of selection.

## Responsibilities for Selection

In the past many companies have placed the responsibility for recruiting, screening, and selecting salespeople with field sales managers. On the surface this seems appropriate since a field sales manager will ultimately succeed or fail with the people selected. However, it turns out that many field sales managers are poor recruiters and selectors.

Busy field sales managers often fail to use proven hiring practices. Because they are diverted by pressing day-to-day operations, they fail to devote sufficient attention to the vital activity of personnel selection. To save time busy managers may settle for the first available applicant to fill a territory opening, or they may hire in their own image and reject those applicants who don't fit their view of a "good sales rep."

Many field sales managers also lack the training and experience required for effective selection. The specialized techniques of selection, such as interviewing and testing, require extensive preparation. Unless field sales managers have received training in these techniques, it is unlikely that they will be good predictors of sales success. Further, unprepared managers can make embarrassing and costly mistakes that violate equal employment opportunity regulations.

Because field sales managers often fail to recruit and select qualified sales reps, many companies have centralized the sales selection activities. Professional recruiters are used to relieve field sales managers of preliminary hiring chores. Applicants are recruited, tested, and screened by trained personnel specialists, but most companies still leave the final selection to members of sales management.

This shared arrangement is preferable. In a large company with a personnel department, experts handle recruiting, compliance with equal employment opportunity regulations, and preliminary screening. Of course, they receive guidance from the sales department, and final selection decisions remain with sales management. Consequently, it is necessary for field sales managers to understand the selection process since they will be responsible for their part of the recruitment and selection process.

## Case Study

The trend is toward working to make sales selection more scientific, more exact. This case describes the efforts of an insurance company to do this. Study the agent's selection plan and answer the questions that follow.

### Chesapeake Life Insurance Company

Walter Blake, general sales manager for the Chesapeake Life Insurance Company, has developed a numerical rating system for selecting life insurance sales agents. Blake believes that this system will result in higher quality agents and reduce agent turnover.

The selection rating system emphasizes those factors that Blake feels are essential to an agent's success. Five factors are assessed and quantified for each applicant: age, marital status, education, experience, and sales aptitude. The points assigned to these factors are shown below.

| FACTOR | ASSUMPTION | POINT ALLOCATION |
|---|---|---|
| Age | Age is an advantage up to 50. | 21–30: 3 points<br>31–40: 5 points<br>41–50: 3 points<br>51 or older: 0 points |
| Marital status | Marriage increases motivation and stability. | Single or divorced: 0 points<br>Married without children: 3 points<br>Married with children: 5 points |

| FACTOR | ASSUMPTION | POINT ALLOCATION |
|---|---|---|
| Education | College training contributes to success. | 1 point for each year of college; 1 extra point for a graduate degree. |
| Experience | Experience, especially selling experience, is helpful. | 1 point for each year of nonselling business experience up to a maximum of 3; 1 point for each year of field selling experience up to a maximum of 5. |
| Sales aptitude | Aptitude can be measured. | 0 to 7 points based on results of an industry sales aptitude test. |

The points are totaled for an overall rating. Those applicants with 20 or more points (30 is maximum) are considered definite hires; those with between 10 and 20 points are possible hires; and those with fewer than 10 points are eliminated from consideration. Final hiring decisions are based on the numerical rating and a series of personal interviews.

*What is your appraisal of Chesapeake's numerical rating system?*

_____

_____

*In your opinion, what is the role of quantitative rating systems in the selection of people who sell?* _____

_____

_____

_____

## APPLICATION FORMS

Properly constructed, a written application form is an important source of information about a candidate's background and qualifications. Most companies use application forms for two purposes: to collect pertinent information and to aid personal interviewing.

The application form is a means by which the sales manager can review the applicant's background without being influenced by appearance or personality. A typical form records facts about an applicant's educational background, business experience, military service, and outside activities. Other facts pertinent to job success are also included. This information is then used to eliminate candidates who are not qualified.

Specific questions for use in a personal interview are prepared by carefully reviewing an applicant's written responses. For instance, if the applicant indicates activity in several civic organizations, ask: Why did you join _____? What is your personal role? What role do you expect to play in the future?

The application form will also point out possible difficulties that should be pursued in the personal interview. Are there gaps of several months between jobs? Has the applicant changed jobs several times? Perhaps this applicant is a job hopper. These and similar questions will suggest issues for future inquiry.

Each company must prepare its own application form. Only information that will be used in the selection process should be requested. Some companies have found a short application form useful for initial screening, with a comprehensive form completed later by the remaining applicants. Another variation is a weighted application form. These employ specific weights assigned to the information requested. The sales manager mathematically determines how an applicant compares to the minimum qualifying score, and unsatisfactory candidates are quickly eliminated.

## REFERENCES

Character and credit references have several important benefits. First, and most important to the selection process, they provide evaluative information. No matter how promising a candidate may appear, there may be flaws that will go unnoticed. Information from other sources can be verified by checking an applicant's references.

### Character References

Reference checks have public relations value. They indicate that a company has a sincere interest in picking the right people for job openings. Further, a company's name becomes familiar to key persons in the community. Reference checks also reveal to applicants that the company is sincerely interested in them.

New laws designed to protect individual privacy place limitations on references as a selection tool. Damage suits for negative references won by former employees have resulted in many companies limiting what information they will reveal.

Frequently, a line manager will refer a request for a reference to the personnel department. In that case it is likely that only the dates and nature of employment will be disclosed unless the applicant has given written permission to release employment information. Even then, there is disagreement among lawyers whether personnel information can be released to outside parties. Educators are also limited in what they can reveal unless the applicant has provided written authorization. However, many managers and educators will be willing to provide information "off the record."

Before checking references, it is advisable to obtain the applicant's written permission to contact former employers, college professors, and others. However, when checking references, do not just contact an applicant's handpicked references. These persons may not be objective sources of information. If possible, seek out other people who may have unique insights into a person's character and potential for sales success.

The best source of information about an applicant is a previous superior. More than anyone else, a boss knows what a person is really like on the job. The boss knows about the applicant's performance characteristics from personal day-to-day experience. How well does the applicant get along with others? What are the applicant's strengths and weaknesses? What is the person especially good at doing? Perhaps the key question is: Would you rehire this applicant?

For younger applicants who have little or no job experience, educational background is particularly important. Factual information (dates of attendance, courses, grades, degrees received) can be verified by asking the applicant to have an official transcript sent from the registrar's office. Other information about the applicant's character and performance can be obtained by contacting teachers, guidance counselors, faculty advisors, or major professors.

In general, it is most effective to interview references in person. However, personal visits may be difficult to arrange. If so, a telephone call is more effective than a letter. People are reluctant to say anything bad about someone in writing and a telephone call is a prompt, efficient way to get an accurate assessment of the applicant. To be sure all items are covered, prepare a checklist to follow during the call. Written records may also be required in the event legal action is taken by a rejected applicant.

## Credit References

In the past, credit references were used to provide an indication of an applicant's financial responsibility. However, equal employment opportunity guidelines and privacy laws have limited the access of a third party to credit information. If credit references are to be checked, the sales manager must inform the applicant. It is important to remember that the applicant has the right to review any credit information presented to prospective employers. Finally, credit checks are safe to use under the law only if credit worthiness is directly related to job requirements, such as the need for a sales representative to be bonded.

When credit checks are used, they may indicate danger signs such as unusual debts, slow or nonpayment of debts, or refusal of credit. Financial irresponsibility may be symptomatic of other difficulties. Further, someone who is overly concerned with financial problems may be distracted from a total selling effort.

## INTERVIEWS

Interviews are the major source of evaluative information about an applicant. Legal problems with selection tests and references have meant that companies have to rely more heavily on personal interviews. Screening interviews are useful as a preliminary step, and more extensive interviews are very important as part of the final selection process.

An interview is a conversation with a purpose, normally involving two people. The general function of an interview is to exchange information. The interviewer's role is to obtain information about the applicant and to furnish the interviewee with information about the company. The interviewee's role is to furnish information about his or her qualifications and to seek information about the company and the job being considered. Interviewing is a two-way street.

Interviews vary in format and style depending on the company involved, the type of salespeople desired, and the specific purpose of the interview (screening or selection). Each sales manager must decide which interviewing techniques work best. An important choice is between patterned or unpatterned interviews.

The *patterned,* or guided, interview is the easiest to use. First adapted to the selection of salespeople by management consultant Robert N. McMurry, this method employs a list of questions the interviewer asks to obtain the required information. The list serves as a control and helps the inexperienced interviewer cover all factors relevant to the applicant's history, qualifications, and goals. Written notes are taken of the applicant's responses. As skill and confidence are gained, the interviewer can go beyond a list of questions to explore other areas of interest.

The *unpatterned,* or unstructured, interview requires more skill and experience. In this method the interviewer has in mind the major areas in which information about the candidate would be helpful, but there is no set list or sequence of questions and the interviewer is willing to let the conversation develop in depth on any particular topic. The assumption is that the interviewee will reveal a lot about him or herself during the discussion. As a fact-finding device, the unpatterned interview is limited by the skill of the interviewer. Unless an interviewer is trained in using this sophisticated interviewing technique, one is better off with a patterned interview.

## Screening Interviews

An early step in the selection procedure is a preliminary screening interview. This has two purposes: to interest applicants in sales positions with the company and to assess these applicants' qualifications. An applicant wants to know about the company and the job; the interviewer wants to know about the applicant. The interviewer has to maintain a fine balance between generating enthusiasm for the job and investigating the ability of the applicant.

Screening interviews should be patterned and short: 30 minutes or less. The main purpose is quickly to eliminate applicants who are not interested in the job or whose qualifications do not meet the job requirements. This can be accomplished by briefly describing the job and asking the applicant a few pertinent questions. Frequent reasons for eliminating applicants at this stage are inadequate experience, unsuitable training, or an inappropriate personality.

Frequently, screening interviews are done by personnel specialists. Recruiting teams who visit college campuses are trained to prescreen applicants. Higher level sales executives will enter the selection process only after the initial screening.

Telephone interviews are frequently used to screen applicants. In these interviews, recruiters determine which applicants should continue in the selection process. Rodger Davenport, director of sales personnel development for American Greetings Corporation, has developed this telephone interview guide:[2]

---

### How to Prescreen Job Applicants by Phone

---

1. Indicate to all callers that the information they give will be held in strictest confidence.
2. Treat all inquiries equally. Ask everyone the same questions, and *all* the questions, even if you sense from the start that a particular caller is unqualified. Record all answers.
3. Follow your company's Equal Employment Opportunity guidelines when phrasing questions. Subjects you *can* ask about include:

> Name, address, and telephone
> Present employment
> Reason for applying at this time
> Past five years of work experience and reasons for leaving each job
> Salary history
> Income requirements
> Education
> Valid driver's license
> Bond eligibility
> Willingness to travel

4. Tell each caller when you will get back to him if he is selected for a personal interview.
5. Try to avoid offending any caller by reacting to anything he says.
6. Keep each conversation as short as possible so the line can be cleared for the next caller.

## Selection Interviews

After progressing through the preliminary selection steps, the applicant is interviewed in depth. The selection, or employment, inter-

---

[2]Rodger Davenport, ''Sharpening Interviewing and Selection Skills,'' *Sales and Marketing Management* (December, 1978), p. 50. Reprinted by permission from *Sales & Marketing Management* magazine. Copyright 1978.

views are usually conducted by line sales managers since the final decision should rest with the field sales manager who has the vacancy. The selection interview is a continuation of the screening and selection process. Usually, staff experts have screened applicants, and only qualified applicants are sent to selection interviews. During the selection interview, the sales manager determines whether the applicant's attitudes and personality will permit the person to become an effective member of the sales organization.

There are several techniques used for selection interviews. The most common is a background interview. The interviewer employs a structured format to discuss the experience, education, interests, and other activities of the applicant. Some sales managers prefer a discussion interview. This involves a very informal and flexible interview with no set questions. However, as discussed earlier, this approach must be used by an experienced interviewer.

Another technique is the stress interview. This involves posing a problem to the applicant and asking him or her to handle it. This puts the applicant in an unusual, unexpected situation, such as many a new sales rep will encounter. For example, the manager may select an object (such as a pen, stapler, or book) and ask the applicant to "sell" it. Or the manager may be less obvious and pose a challenge such as: "Why didn't you go out for extracurricular activities in college?" or "What do you think your major weakness is?" Sometimes stress is placed on an applicant through interruptions, criticism, or silence. By observing how an applicant responds to stress, the manager gains insight into how the person will handle new, stressful selling situations.

### Are You a Good Interviewer?

Poor interviews are a complete waste of time for the sales manager and the applicant. Nevertheless, many busy sales executives fail to give serious thought to the techniques of interviewing. James M. Black, author of a practical guide for interviewing, has identified eight types of poor interviewers.[3]

1. The *conversation capper* loves the sound of his own voice. Unfortunately, when an interviewer is doing most of the talking, he is not obtaining information.

[3]James Menzies Black, *How To Get Results from Interviewing* (New York: McGraw-Hill, 1970), pp. 9–11.

2. The *agile anticipator* thinks he knows the answers before they are given. He breaks in with his own views, thus emerging with a distorted view of the interviewee's replies.

3. The *listless listener* is only going through the motions. His mind is wandering; he hears only what confirms what he already believes.

4. The *prosecuting attorney* is conducting a penetrating cross examination of a hostile witness. By putting the interviewee on the defensive, he loses his respect and cooperation.

5. The *goodwill ambassador* is afraid to ask hard or touchy questions. Because he is unwilling to ask blunt questions, he fails to obtain needed information.

6. The *captious categorizer* thinks he has special insight into the minds of others. He classifies interviewees according to his own prejudices, even to the point of thinking physical appearance is a clue to character.

7. The *simultaneous question-snapper* is the world's busiest executive. He has calls coming in, he is signing letters, he is giving orders to subordinates, and so on, while trying to conduct an interview.

8. The *faulty-question framer* does not ask the right questions, or asks questions that are too general and vague, or he interrupts with additional questions before the interviewee can respond to his original inquiry.

The above examples suggest some of the mistakes interviewers make. Effective interviewing does not come easily. It is difficult to apply any rigid rules to interviewing since interviewing is both an art and a science. However, some general guidelines are suggested below.

## Prepare for the Interview

An interviewer must be able quickly to evaluate a candidate. To save time, prepare yourself for the interview, identify goals for the interview, determine exactly what you want to know about the candidate. As indicated earlier, the application form can be used as an aid for interviewing. Use it to prepare questions. Also, use it to eliminate areas for discussion. Asking the candidate questions that were already answered in writing is a waste of time.

## Select a Suitable Environment

Make sure the setting is appropriate for interviewing. If the interview is in your office, avoid interruptions, accept no phone calls, and postpone routine office work. If you are in the field, select a quiet room in a convenient hotel or motel and make sure you will not be interrupted.

## Establish Rapport

A pleasant, relaxed atmosphere must be established early in the interview (even if a stress question is planned for later). The interviewer and the interviewee must be at ease with one another. Perhaps the easiest way to do this is to open the interview with a topic of mutual interest. A review of the interviewee's application form often suggests a suitable opening question. Another approach is to review the steps taken so far in the hiring process with the applicant.

## Listen

Most authorities recommend that the interviewee should do about two-thirds of the talking. To make sure the interviewee does the talking, ask probing questions. Questions that can be answered by a simple yes or no don't tell you much about the applicant. Also, don't prejudice the applicant's responses by expressing approval or disapproval.

## Observe

A successful interviewer also learns through observation. You can begin to learn about an applicant as soon as the person enters the room. Does the interviewee project a businesslike appearance? Is the applicant dressed appropriately? Is the interviewee poised and confident? Alert? Observation will provide many clues about how the applicant is likely to behave in a selling situation. For instance, clasping and unclasping the hands, fidgeting, not maintaining eye contact, crossing the legs and arms are signals of nervousness, uncertainty, and lack of confidence.

## Take a Few Notes

Most interviewers need to refer to notes when evaluating an interview. However, taking notes during an interview distracts the applicant and slows the tempo of the interview. Try to develop unobtrusive methods of taking notes. Better still, use a simple evaluation form, which can be filled out after the applicant has left.

### Use Two or More Interviewers

It is unwise to rely on the results of a single interview or interviewer. With only one interviewer, a possible danger is the halo effect described in Chapter 2. A single factor may create a favorable or unfavorable impression and influence the interviewer's appraisal of other factors. Unskilled interviewers are especially likely to be unduly influenced by an applicant's appearance or personality. This danger is reduced by multiple interviews of each applicant.

### How Does the Interviewee Feel?

Think about the last time you interviewed for a job. Did the interviewer follow the guidelines suggested in this section? What could the interviewer have done to obtain more information about your qualifications?

_____

_____

_____

### Interviewing the Applicant's Spouse

More and more, companies recognize that a sales rep's spouse influences sales performance. One survey of salesmen and their wives showed that wives exert great influence over their husbands' career decisions.[4] The same is true for husbands of saleswomen. Consequently, meeting and learning something about the goals, aspirations, and attitudes of the spouse of the sales recruit is a must. They can make or break a sales rep. Moreover, husbands or wives are flattered that the company is interested in them also.

The interview with the sales candidate and the spouse should be relaxed and informal. Lunch or dinner meetings are ideal, since most people appreciate an invitation to dine out. If possible, the sales manag-

---

[4]Marvin A. Jolson and Martin J. Gannon, "Wives—A Critical Element in Career Decisions," *Business Horizons* (February 1972), pp. 83–88.

er's spouse should be included so that the candidate's spouse will feel at ease. The conversation should be unstructured. Let the spouse talk about the applicant. If travel is involved, find out how the spouse feels about the applicant being away from home at night. It is better to discover potential problems before a person is hired rather than after.

## PSYCHOLOGICAL TESTS

In her book, *Psychological Testing,* psychologist Anne Anastasi defines a psychological test as "an objective and standardized measure of a sample of behavior.[5] Industry uses tests to predict employment success. The assumption is that a test will provide a sample of a person's behavior that is a valid predictor of future employment behavior. As a sales selection technique, psychological tests are used to measure attributes that cannot be measured by other selection tools. They relate to mental ability, personality, and interest.

Psychological testing of sales applicants began soon after 1940, and since then research into what makes a good sales representative has resulted in the development of many tests. Some of the reasons for increased emphasis on testing are greater importance of selection, rising costs of selection and training, increased knowledge of psychological tests, and greater availability of tests for industrial use. Companies also report that testing reduces turnover by providing an objective means of evaluating sales recruits.

### Guidelines For Testing

To measure and predict behavior effectively, tests are constructed using four major guidelines: job analysis, reliability, validity, and standardization.

*Job analysis* will reveal the type and degree of specific qualifications required for successful job performance. Each test must match the individual to the job.

*Reliability* refers to the consistency of test results. A test is reliable if a person will achieve approximately the same score on the same test under the same conditions if this person takes the test again. If results

---

[5]Anne Anastasi, *Psychological Testing,* 4th ed. (New York: Macmillan, 1976), p. 23.

are inconsistent, it is doubtful whether the test provides a true picture of the candidate's behavior. Obviously, selection decisions cannot be based on variable results.

*Validity* refers to the authenticity of the test as a measure of behavior. A test is valid if it actually measures what it is supposed to measure. In order to predict job success accurately, a test must be valid. There are two ways to validate an employment test. One is to give the test to present salespeople and then compare test results with actual performance. If there is a close correlation, the test is probably a valid predictor of job success. The second method is to give tests to new salespeople, but withhold the test scores from interviewers. After the salespeople have been working for a while, compare their performance with their test scores. Again, the degree of correlation will reveal the validity of the test.

*Standardization* requires a uniform procedure for administering and scoring a test. Deviation from the procedure will impair the reliability and validity of the test.

## Types of Tests

There are many kinds of tests available for screening and selecting salespeople. Sales managers should seek the advice of experts when choosing tests.[6]

*Intelligence tests* determine whether an applicant has sufficient mental ability to handle a particular sales job. General intelligence tests are designed to show how well a person reasons, thinks, and understands, and as such, they provide a rough guide to the applicant's overall mental abilities. Other, more specialized tests have been designed to measure certain types of intelligence, such as speed of learning, facility with numbers, fluency of ideas, memory, and verbal skill.

*Sales aptitude tests* measure whether an applicant has the potential for selling and may be useful if applicants have had some selling experience. However, it is doubtful whether it is possible to measure a special aptitude for selling. Also, just because a person has an aptitude for selling does not mean that he or she will be successful because the applicant must also have the interest and desire to succeed in selling.

*Personality tests* have value if they indicate people who will fail in selling because of personality defects. However, personality tests are not as reliable as other kinds of tests. Since the accuracy of results of such

[6]For a list of representative tests and sources, see *Ibid.*, pp. 636–50.

tests depends on skillful interpretation, results should never be analyzed by an untrained layperson.

*Interest tests* determine if a person wants to do a job. If the information obtained is reliable, it can be quite helpful. An applicant who has little interest in selling as a career cannot be expected to perform up to potential. On the other hand, a person with strong motivation to sell may be able to overcome a lack of natural ability.

## Using Tests to Help You

Psychological tests are helpful, but there is no magical shortcut for finding good salespeople. Tests used for selecting salespeople are helpful only if they are a part of the total screening and selection program and are directly applicable to an individual company's needs.

When using tests, a manager should be aware of their limitations. Perhaps the greatest limitation is that tests are suited for group rather than individual predictions. There is no such thing as an average or normal sales rep, and tests that attempt to predict sales success based on what is normal are on shaky ground. These tests may eliminate innovative and creative people who do not conform to normal or average concepts of behavior.

A good many tests developed to predict sales success have not been scientifically and statistically proven valid for measuring what they purport to measure. Great care must be used in selecting tests. There are opportunists who have developed tests that are not based on accepted testing principles. It is doubtful whether these tests have much value in selecting salespeople.

A problem with many standard tests is that bright applicants can fabricate answers. This is especially true of interest and personality tests. Since applicants want jobs, they will answer questions as they think companies want them answered.

The best advice for sales executives is to use tests with caution. They are a tool to assist the sales executive in selecting the right person, but they should not be relied upon too heavily. In general, psychological tests are most helpful in the initial screening process.

When used with discretion and with competent professional help, tests can provide a manager with additional information that may not be available from other sources. Test results may help a manager avoid a serious error, but they must not be allowed to make the selection decision. Not infrequently, it is wise to ignore a candidate's test results and take a chance, if other factors are favorable.

## MEDICAL EXAMINATIONS

A complete medical examination is important in selecting people who sell since good health is vital to selling. A sales rep is often on the road for long periods of time, numerous calls must be made, and physical work may be involved (for example, carrying a heavy sample case). To cope with the stresses of selling, a rep cannot be handicapped by illness.

The company doctor or other designated physician is used. To assist in the examination, the company should advise the doctor of the physical requirements of the job, such as extraordinary travel requirements and physical tasks involved. The doctor makes sure that the applicant has no chronic conditions or diseases that might impair the rep's effectiveness.

To avoid problems under the equal employment opportunity laws, several precautions must be taken with the medical exam. Among these are that the job description must be specific as to the physical qualifications for the job. In addition, the company, if ever challenged, must be able to prove these qualifications are real and necessary. For example, if the job requires carrying a heavy sample bag in and out of stores, the company must be sure that a woman applicant who has been eliminated on that basis cannot, in fact, do this. Further, there must be assurance that disabled persons are not eliminated simply because of their disabilities. Finally, to comply with the law if a medical examination is required, it should be the last step in the selection process, and all recruits must take it.


## TRIAL PERIODS

Some companies try out sales recruits before permanently hiring them. It can be argued that it is wise to hire all salespeople on a trial period basis since it is easier to replace people when they are on trial than if they are permanent employees.

When salespeople are hired on trial, frequent progress evaluations should be made to determine if the employment of these new people is to be continued. The length of the trial period varies from company to company. Life insurance companies have found that a three-month trial period is usually sufficient to discover if an agent will be successful. In a large retail shoe chain, the trial period is even shorter. A month is considered sufficient.

## Case Study

We have discussed various tools used to select salespeople. These tools provide the sales manager with information about applicants, but they do not make the decision. Sales managers must use the information and their personal judgment to make a decision. To see some of the problems of doing this, study this case and answer the questions that follow.

Rogers Food Supply Company

Steve Polansky is midwestern regional sales manager for Rogers Food Supply Company, a large distributor of food products. He has 12 sales representatives who call on hotels, restaurants, and retailers to promote and sell the firm's complete line of products. A vacancy exists in the region, and preliminary interviews and other screening procedures have narrowed the selection to three people: Jim Adams, Tom Brown, and Beverly Carter. Brief descriptions of their qualifications follow.

1. Jim Adams is 24 years old, single, and in good health. He was recently discharged from the army, having served as a corpsman. Prior to military duty, he left college, where he was a biology major, at the end of his junior year and worked as an office clerk for a large retail chain. Adams shows interest in personal selling as a career, but he does not appear to have crystalized his personal and career goals. Tests show him to be self-confident, aggressive, emotionally stable, tactful, with a good sense of humor, and the ability to take charge. However, tests indicate that he thinks accurately at a rate below that for a person with his mental capacity.

2. Tom Brown is 41 years old, married with three children, in good health, and has been employed as a salesman for 20 years. He left college after two years and began selling real estate. Since then he has sold insurance, securities, and automobiles, and is now a salesman for a local appliance store. He likes his job, but the pay is relatively poor. Brown is a professional salesman and makes a good impression. He thinks this job is exactly what he has been looking for, and he wants to make a permanent change. Tests indicate that he is conscientious about his interest in selling and has exceptional sales insight. He appears to have a thorough understanding and appreciation of the methods, strategies, and techniques of personal selling.

3. Beverly Carter is a recent graduate of the state college, where she was a marketing major. Recently married, she is 21 years old and in good health. She had an exceptional record in college, where she was a dean's list student, captain of the gymnastics team, and president of her sorority. Tests and preliminary interviews indicate that she has outstanding potential. She makes an excellent impression and gives every indication of having the ability to be a successful leader. She is interested in selling, but she has her sights set on a long-range career goal of top marketing management. Carter openly admits she looks upon selling only as an apprenticeship for her marketing career.

*Evaluate the qualifications of each applicant against what you think are the requirements for a successful Rogers' sales representative.*

_____

_____

_____

*Which applicant would you choose to fill the vacancy?* _____

_____

_____

_____

*What additional information would you like to have prior to making a decision? Why?* _____

_____

_____

_____

## ORIENTATION

Orientation of new salespeople is viewed by some managers as the last step in selection and by others as the first step in training. Regardless of how orientation is considered, it is an essential activity. The sales manager must help new salespeople make the transition from recruits to employees as smoothly as possible.

It is especially important to provide a strong orientation for female or minority recruits entering a predominantly white, male sales organization. These recruits often have special problems that require extra attention during the first few months on the job.[7] The manager and other salespeople may also need some special training to adjust to having these people on the sales force.

New salespeople will be enthusiastic about their new jobs, but they will also be apprehensive. The major purposes of orientation are to:

1. Reduce anxieties.
2. Help the new sales rep become a contributing member of the sales organization.
3. Maintain enthusiasm at a high level.
4. Develop commitment to the company's sales goals and policies.

Orientation begins when the sales recruit is enthusiastically welcomed by the sales manager. After the welcome, these key activities should be part of every orientation program.

1. Make sure all employment records and forms are completed and processed. The new sales rep may have difficulty in this area, so be sure that any help that is needed is provided.
2. Give the new sales rep all the necessary employment information, especially concerning expense accounts, vacation policies, payroll procedures, and other important personnel policies and procedures.
3. Be sure new reps know the formal and informal office practices. Alert them to any special events or activities, such as office parties or gift funds.
4. Make sure the new rep's office or desk is ready and that samples and office supplies are available. If a car is provided, make sure the recruit understands the company's policies about maintenance, insurance, and personal use.
5. Introduce the new rep to the other salespeople, immediate supervisors, clerical and secretarial workers, and others with whom the rep will have contact.
6. Make a special effort to keep in touch with the recruit. Call or

---

[7]See, for example, Barbara Pletcher, "Memo to: Saleswomen Re: Problems and Opportunities," *Marketing Times* (January-February 1979), pp. 26–29, and John W. Lee and Thomas Reusehling, "Don't Whitewash the Black Sales Trainee," *Management Review* (April 1974), pp. 56–58.

stop in to ask "How are things going?" Be sure to provide feedback on job performance. Frequent feedback is especially important for inexperienced sales reps so that they do not develop bad selling and work habits.

The critical element in the new sales rep's orientation is the sales manager's own attitude and behavior. The sales manager is the role model for the inexperienced sales rep and if the manager appears indifferent to job responsibilities and his or her work habits are sloppy, the recruit will soon decide that the company's performance standards are low. On the other hand, a professional manager will show by example what is expected from a professional sales representative.

### Brain teasers

| | *Agree* | *Disagree* |
|---|---|---|
| 1. Research has provided reliable techniques for predicting whether a person will be a successful sales representative. | ___ | ___ |
| 2. Since professional recruiters are better trained in selection techniques, they should make all selection decisions. | ___ | ___ |
| 3. A well-designed application form will provide pertinent information about a sales recruit and aid the interviewer. | ___ | ___ |
| 4. References have become a less effective selection tool because of privacy legislation. | ___ | ___ |
| 5. Most personal interviews are informal and require little preparation. | ___ | ___ |
| 6. A single interview is usually sufficient to select a new sales rep. | ___ | ___ |
| 7. It is essential that a prospective sales rep's spouse be interviewed. | ___ | ___ |
| 8. Since good health is essential to a sales rep's success, a thorough medical exam should be required for all sales applicants. | ___ | ___ |
| 9. Psychological tests are most effectively used to screen sales candidates. | ___ | ___ |
| 10. Since most new salespeople are enthusiastic, there is no need to provide feedback on performance during their first few months on the job. | ___ | ___ |

## Activities

1.  *In discussing sales selection errors, a personnel researcher commented: "Many errors arise from the emphasis in current selection procedures on the abilities, experience, attitudes, or dexterities needed to perform a particular job." What does the researcher mean by this statement? What other factors must be considered when selecting salespeople?* _____

_____

_____

_____

2.  *A regional sales manager suggested to the director of sales that the company use a systematic hiring procedure employing a weighted application form, reference checks, formal interviews, and psychological tests. The director refused, with the comment: "I don't want to be bothered with all that so-called scientific selection stuff. Sales managers worth their salt know a good sales rep when they see one." How would you answer the director of sales?* _____

_____

_____

_____

3.  *A large national company has the following statement on its application form:*

    The company may request an investigative consumer report on persons making application for employment with the company. Upon written request, the company will supply you with complete disclosure of the nature and scope of the investigation it requests. The company will use any information it receives from such an investigation only for employment purposes. Under the Fair Credit Reporting Act, you may obtain information from the files of the agency that compiles the investigative report.

    *Do you think this statement provides adequate protection for the applicant and the company?* _____

_____

_____

4.  Obtain copies of your company's or another company's application forms, interview guides, and other selection tools. What improvements, if any, would you suggest? _____

_____

_____

_____

5.  The Binet-Simon Intelligence Test is based on the assumption that intelligence is a common characteristic; that is, all normal people can think, reason, and understand to some extent. The test questions are designed to find out how well a person thinks, reasons, and understands. The test is long and requires a professional to administer and interpret it. Do you think this test would be useful in selecting salespeople for your company? Why or why not? _____

_____

_____

_____

6.  Make a list of the 10 most important things you believe a new sales rep should know about selling and your company. What is the best way to make sure a recruit receives this information?

_____

_____

_____

## SELECTED REFERENCES

### Selection Process

BRUNETT, ROBIN, "How to Pick an Ace Saleswoman." *Marketing Times* (May-June 1976), pp. 7–9.

GREENBERG, HERBERT M., and RONALD L. BERN, *The Successful Salesman: Man and His Manager*. Philadelphia: Auerbach, 1972.

WOTRUBA, THOMAS R., "An Analysis of the Salesman Selection Process," *Southern Journal of Business* (January 1970), pp. 41–51.

## Selection Tools

ANASTASI, ANNE, *Psychological Testing,* 4th ed. New York: Macmillan, 1976.

BLACK, JAMES M., *How to Get Results from Interviewing.* New York: McGraw-Hill, 1970.

DAVENPORT, RODGER, "Sharpening Interviewing and Selection Skills," *Sales and Marketing Management* (December 1978), pp. 67–69.

DRAKE, JOHN D., *Interviewing for Managers.* New York: American Management Association, 1972.

ELLMAN, EDGAR S., "Reference Sheet: How to Interview an Applicant for a Position in Sales," *Industrial Distribution* (January 1978), pp. 60–61.

HECKLER, PETER D., "Interviews: Are Yours Valid and Reliable?" *Los Angeles Business and Economics* (Winter 1977), pp. 7–10.

KOTEN, JOHN, "Psychologists Play Bigger Corporate Role in Placing of Personnel," *The Wall Street Journal,* July 11, 1978, pp. 1, 18.

PHILLIPS, VAN L., "Recruiting the Sales Force: the Stress Approach," *Marketing Forum* (September, October 1969), pp. 20–21.

## Orientation

KELLOGG, MARION, "Are You a Good Manager of New Salesmen?" *Sales Management,* June 11, 1973, pp. 23–24.

LEE, JOHN W., and THOMAS REUSCHLING, "Don't Whitewash the Black Sales Trainee," *Management Review* (April 1974), pp. 56–58.

STANTON, WILLIAM J., and RICHARD H. BUSKIRK, "Assimilating New Sales People into the Organization, in *Management of the Sales Force* (5th ed.). Homewood, Ill.: Richard D. Irwin, 1978.

# 4

# TRAINING SALESPEOPLE TO SELL

*After reading this chapter, you should be able to demonstrate your learning as follows:*
- *Justify the cost of sales training to someone skeptical of its value.*
- *Design a sales training program for a particular sales force.*
- *Identify specific knowledge, skills, and attitudes that can be improved by training.*
- *Recommend which of the two training policies, conditioned or insight response, is better for a particular sales force.*
- *Know what sales training techniques should be employed in any specific training program.*
- *For a particular sales force, justify centralized or decentralized sales training by staff specialists, field sales personnel, or outside experts.*
- *Know the principles of learning that should underlie every sales training program.*
- *Know how to evaluate the effectiveness of a sales training program.*

## THE BASIS FOR SALES TRAINING

Before beginning our study of sales training programs, it is critical to remember that in sales management there are two distinct forms of training—formal and informal. Formal training in most companies involves carefully planned programs complete with schedules, lesson plans, visual aids, the use of selected teaching devices, systematic reviews, and evaluations. Formal training programs in their various forms will be the main subject of this chapter. However, we must not forget the equally important, prevalent, and continuing *informal* training activities in which all companies engage.

Continuous sales training is a prime responsibility of sales supervisors in their personal contacts with their salespeople. This involves personal work with individuals, guiding their daily activities, and advising improvements. This has been characterized as "curb side" training, informal, and on-the-spot instruction for performance improvement. Although not formal or utilizing special training plans and devices, curb side training plays a vital part in the development of sales personnel.

There are three important phases in formal sales training: designing the sales training program, managing its operation, and evaluating its success. This chapter will examine each of these phases.

## Reasons for Training

Many people assume that sales training is necessary and possible only in large companies with a big sales force and large operating budgets. This is not so. Sales training can be and is carried out successfully in small companies with only a few salespeople and on small outlays. Sales training is a universal condition in American business. There are two important, prevalent reasons for training sales personnel.

### To Develop the Right Work Habits

Salespeople will learn some pattern of work habits, however they are taught. They will learn how to cover their territory, to approach customers, in what style to live while traveling, what type of records to keep, and how to plan and execute their sales calls. They will learn how to do these things well and efficiently, or poorly and at substantial expense to the company. Salespeople must be trained so that they learn the right work habits and patterns, at the right time, and from the right learning source.

### To Offset the Effect of "Detraining"

Salespeople are constantly being detrained—taught the wrong things—by their field experience. They adopt undesirable "shortcuts," gravitate toward the easy way of selling, and often become discouraged from the constant buffeting of the competitive marketplace. They must be trained to offset this negative effect of detraining by their field sales experience, and periodically retrained for the same reason.

## Results of Training

Training pays for itself in numerous ways. Not all positive results can be precisely measured or stated in exact figures, but they are very important, nevertheless. Salespeople should be trained to:

- Improve their relationships with customers by showing them the right way to do business.
- Motivate them to develop themselves and improve morale because they see that the company is concerned with their development. Football coach Vince Lombardi characterized this as the all-important "second effort."
- Reduce the cost and lost sales that result from high turnover of sales personnel.
- Make the sales force more flexible and innovative in meeting changing competitive market conditions.
- Reduce the costs of inefficient territory coverage, poor use of company-supplied sales tools, wrong interpretation of company policy (credit terms, for instance) or operating procedures (delivery schedules).
- Increase sales volume.
- Reduce the cost of supervision: well-trained salespeople cost less to supervise because they require less supervisory attention from their bosses.
- Increase the efficiency of controlling their activities: well-trained salespeople need less direct control from supervisors.

## Application Exercise

Study these two summary reports made by the sales supervisor of a drug firm. It is his practice to travel with and observe each of his salespeople for a day each month, making notes on each in the form below.

*Salesman:* Bill Smyth
*Calls on Doctors:* Relates well to doctors. Is polite and easy in his relationship with them. Seems uncertain in presenting our new drugs; does not answer questions about them easily. Does not press nurse-receptionist for quick admission to doctor.
*Calls on Druggists:* Uses promotional aids well. Has good working

relationship with old customers. Does not approach new druggists easily.
*Condition of Car and Sample Bag:* Cluttered, difficulty in locating materials.

*Saleswoman:* Judy Wallace
*Calls on Doctors:* Gets on well with doctors. Presents new products clearly and persuasively. Answers questions clearly. Gets in to see doctor quickly.
*Calls on Druggists:* Main emphasis is socializing with druggist and employees. Seems to know everybody in every store.
*Condition of Car and Sample Bag:* Neat and orderly. Everything in its place and can be found quickly.

*Do these salespeople need any form of training? Why? What advantages would the company gain if they were trained more thoroughly? What advantages, if any, would the salespeople gain? If you think some training is required, how should it be done? Why?* _____

_____

_____

_____

In summary, we see that the net effect of training is to develop proper work habits and to offset the effect of field detraining so that sales expenses are reduced and sales volume is maximized. Both of these are critical management objectives. As the sales manager of a plastics company said, ''The company that thinks it cannot afford to, or does not need to train and retrain its sales force has just thought itself out of business.''

## THEORY OF TEACHING AND LEARNING

Before considering the design of the sales training program, we must understand the basic characteristics of the learning process. Essentially the learning problem is one or a combination of three conditions: the learner knows nothing about the subject being taught, or knows something, but not a sufficient amount, or what the learner knows is incorrect. So the mission of the sales learning-teaching process is to transmit knowledge and skills and to create positive attitudes and/or to correct these if they already exist incorrectly.

Training personnel to sell effectively and efficiently is essentially the industrial application of the basic principles of teaching and learning as they have been developed by professional educators in our schools and universities. A good training program therefore must be based on certain principles.

## Clearly Recognized Purpose

It would be a poor trainer who did not clearly recognize the purpose and mission of the training program. But this is not enough. The trainees must have a clear understanding of why they are being trained, toward what goals their instruction is directed, how they will use what they learn, and how they will personally benefit from the instruction. Training can never be successful if trainees feel they are simply "walking through" the program because it is company policy. This aspect of sound sales training underlines the value of a carefully planned pretraining indoctrination period in which the trainees are shown the purposes and benefits of the training and are allowed to raise any questions of purpose and method that may be unclear. In addition, it is useful during the course of the training program to remind the trainees of the purposes and uses of their training.

## Clarity of the Training Program

Often because the trainers know the company, industry, products, sales problems, and technical jargon of the business so well, they forget that trainees do not, and that trainees are likely to become lost when the trainer uses language or refers to concepts and procedures that are unfamiliar to them. The training material must be simple and clear and presented in terms that are understandable to the trainee.

## Planned Repetition

In learning we seldom fully grasp a new idea or procedure the first time we are exposed to it, no matter how clearly it is presented. This is especially true if the idea or procedure is complicated, or varies in form, or application between different selling situations. In addition, repetition is necessary if the trainee is trying to unlearn some incorrect notions or techniques.

To overcome this difficulty, the good trainer carefully plans restatement and repetition into the program. Important subjects are repeated at appropriate intervals in the training program, either in their original form or in a different form. In this way trainees can reinforce their understanding of the point and see it in several different applications. Trainers should not be reticent about planned repetition of key points for fear that it will bore trainees. Planned repetition is a necessary characteristic of good learning and training, and it will be welcomed by trainees.

## Systematic Review

Reviewing, going back over and highlighting material already covered, has several advantages. It allows trainees to check their understanding of what has been covered. It shows them what they have failed to learn and where, therefore, they must improve their knowledge by extra work. And if they have been applying themselves, a review bolsters morale because it demonstrates what they have learned. Finally, periodic review sets the stage for training material that is to follow.

## Orderly Development of Material

The major difference between learning by experience and learning by training is that training is *orderly* and can be repeated, while experience is *random* and uncontrolled. To illustrate this point: You need to teach trainees how to deal with a particular objection that is often raised by customers. If they learn how to handle this objection only by experience, they might make dozens of calls before they encounter objections of any kind and many more before encountering the particular objection you want them to be skilled at handling. Even then, experience alone is not likely to indicate how well the objection was handled. Orderly training shows how to manage this objection, demonstrates the proper handling of it, and allows practice in the proper response.

The training program should be designed so that the learning has a logical and meaningful sequence; it flows from one topic to a related topic, it does not skip randomly from one subject to another. In this way the trainees are not confused by being asked to study what appear to be unrelated topics, and they are able to relate individual steps or activities to those that logically precede or follow. For example, the subject is how to prospect for and acquire new customers. The logical order or flow of this topic would be: (1) how to locate new potential customers, (2) how to identify the buyer to be visited, (3) how to arrange to meet the buyer, (4) how to plan the introductory call, (5) how to open a continuing relationship with the buyer, and (6) how to follow up.

## Paced to the Trainees' Capacity to Learn

People learn at a different rate of speed. It is important to remember that, excepting the genius mentality, the rate of speed at which people learn has no relationship to how well they retain and use what they learn. Fast learners can be quick forgetters or poor users of what they have learned. It can also be that slow learners remember what they have learned for long periods of time and use the information well. This means that the trainer must be sure that the training is not proceeding at a pace too fast for slower learners and that the fast learners are retaining the information they absorb so quickly. One way to check these conditions is periodic tests, verbal or written, during the training program. These tests should cover not only the material recently learned, but earlier material as well.

## Trainee Participation

Research in learning has shown that we retain relatively little of what we see or hear. But we retain a greater proportion of what we see, hear, and do. Implementing or performing what we are learning reinforces the message that the memory at first receives only by sight or sound. For a long time, golf professionals, surgeon-teachers, law professors, and other skilled trainers have been practicing this concept. First they explain, then they demonstrate, and then they have the student perform what is being taught. Skilled sales trainers realize the importance of reinforcing oral and visual instruction by action, and they devise ways to have trainees participate in their own training. A later section on teaching aids suggests ways this can be accomplished.

## DESIGNING THE SALES TRAINING PROGRAM

We have noted the substantial benefits of good sales training and we have studied the basic conditions of learning and teaching. We turn now to the design of the formal sales training program, based on the principles of learning.

Clearly, the benefits of sales training outlined previously cannot be attained unless the program is well designed to fit the particular company's needs. In this light, the design of a sales training program involves answering four critical questions for each sales group:

- Which salespeople should be trained and when in their careers?
- What should the training program cover?
- What should be its form and organization?
- Who should do the training and at what location in the company organization?

These questions are our topics in this section, and before we discuss them, it would be useful for you to write down your answers to the questions for your company or for one you know well.

_____

_____

_____

_____

_____

## Which Salespeople Should Be Trained and When in Their Careers?

### Training New Sales Personnel

When should they be trained? This is a difficult question for most companies because its resolution is based on a dilemma. On one hand, training is more efficient and meaningful if the sales recruit has some firsthand selling experience. Consider the example of a beginning sales rep for a hardware manufacturer. The training is more interesting, efficient, meaningful, and economical if before it begins, the rep knows the language of the trade, industry and competitive problems and practices, objections commonly raised by customers, and other pertinent company and market information.

But on the other hand, providing selling experience for untrained sales personnel is difficult and risks losing sales volume and damaging relations with customers because of their inexperience. As a result, in most cases, only a modest amount of field selling experience is provided for sales recruits before they are given at least basic sales training.

### Retraining Experienced Reps

Frequently situations arise that make it necessary to retrain experienced salespeople. Examples of these situations are when:

- New products are to be introduced.
- New kinds of customers are to be solicited.
- Rep is to be put in a new territory.
- New reporting or other new sales operating procedures are introduced.
- Rep is promoted to a supervisory position.
- There is evidence that the sales force has adopted improper selling habits.
- Competition, economic conditions, governmental regulations, or other environmental conditions change in such a way as to affect selling operations drastically.

When these or similar conditions arise to change substantially the required knowledge, skills, and attitudes of experienced salespeople, retraining is usually needed.

### What Should the Training Program Cover?

Successful sales reps for any company, regardless of size or industry, must know their product and company policies and procedures; possess the necessary sales and territory management skills; and have a positive, constructive attitude toward their products, customers, job, company, and themselves. The basic questions of training program content are: In what should salespeople be trained and when in their careers do they need this training and retraining? The answers to these questions are shown in Figure 4-1.

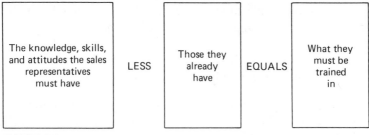

FIGURE 4-1

For example, in one company, experienced salespeople know the technical specifications of all products; new hirees do not know them. Therefore, they must be trained in product specifications. The same sort of analysis applies to all people who sell, regardless of the extent of their experience.

## Limitations on Training Programs

The question arises whether the formal training program should undertake to impart all of the necessary skills, attitudes, and knowledge to all of the sales reps. The answer is: not necessarily. It depends on prevailing conditions. The reasons for this follow.

### Not All Skillls and Attitudes
### Can Be Trained

Some are fixed when a person is hired. For example, perseverance and honesty are ingrained in one's background and personality, and no external force can have much influence over them. In other cases, required skills or knowledge can be trained, but no company can afford to do it. An example is the electronics company that requires its salespeople to have graduate level electrical engineering training. When certain required skills, attitudes, or knowledge cannot be trained by a formal program, or when the company cannot afford to train them, the sales recruiting and selection system must deliver new hires who already possess the desired qualities.

### Success Requirements Vary
### Between Sales Groups

To succeed, sales reps selling different products in different industries and under different competitive conditions require different skill-knowledge-attitude "mixes." Therefore, the content of training programs vary. No single program can fit all selling conditions, as we saw in the discussion of the job description in Chapter 2.

### Individual Sales Training Needs Vary

In broad classes of sales recruits, we can assume a certain consistency of background. For instance, all graduates of reputable business schools have had at least elementary accounting. We can safely presume that broad classes of sales recruits require the same content of their training. But frequently individual training needs vary by individuals, and, therefore, we must individualize training to the greatest degree possible.

## Informal Training Can Accomplish Much

As pointed out earlier, a major responsibility of sales supervision is continuous informal, "curb side" training. Much of the knowledge, skills, and attitudes that successful sales reps must possess need not be included in the formal training program, but can be imparted on-the-job by the supervisor's informal instruction.

## Case Study

At various points in this chapter we will apply what we have learned to this real-life company training situation.

The Pacto Company

Pacto, a manufacturer of mechanical and electrical typewriters, calculators, and related office equipment, regularly hires men and women sales recruits from high schools and junior colleges. Their job is to call on office managers of business firms, banks, insurance companies, and retail establishments in their assigned territories to sell the company's full line of products. They are expected to provide simple servicing for machines already sold. More complicated repair jobs are handled by a crew of repair specialists.

This field sales force of 450 works out of 20 district sales offices nationally. The sales force turnover is about 8 percent per year, which is average for the industry.

Pacto, with national headquarters in New York, is the third-ranking company out of six in the industry. Both of the leading companies are much larger and have more complete product lines than Pacto.

*Specifically what should the training program for new Pacto sales-people cover?* _____

_____

_____

_____

*To be successful, do Pacto sales representatives need anything that cannot be trained? If so, what? If not, why not?* _____

_____

_____

## Optimum Content
## of the Formal Sales Training Program

Designing the content of a formal training program for a particular company is a matter of analyzing the knowledge, skills, and attitudes that are required for sales success in that company. The following checklist is useful in answering these questions about the content of the sales training program.

Product knowledge

1. How much and what kind of technical knowledge do the sales reps need to have about their products: how they work, what they will and will not do, how they are made, their expected life? What do they not need to know about their products?
2. What do they need to know about how their products fit into the customer's technology, production, use, or resale process?
3. What do they need to know about competitors' products, strengths and weaknesses, characteristics, use features?

Knowledge of company policy and procedures

1. What must the people who sell know about internal policies and procedures: expense accounting, retirement and sick leave, vacations, transportation?
2. What must they know about the market policies and procedures: credit, terms of sale, delivery, product guarantees, advertising and promotion support, service and technical assistance?
3. What must salespeople know about marketing operations: order and report forms, territory coverage, personal records?

Required selling skills

1. Must salespeople know how to prospect for customers?
2. Must they be able to plan each call?
3. Must they know how to handle customer objections?
4. Must they be skilled in identifying customer needs and matching them with product features and benefits?
5. Will they need to entertain customers?
6. What social skills are required?

7. What communications skills (letters, telephones, and such) will they need?

Attitudes

1. What positive attitudes must sales reps have toward customers, company, job, supervision?
2. What kind of relationship will they have with their customers (cooperative, abusive, or some other) and what attitudes will this require?

This step-by-step analysis against the job description will show specifically what each sales groups' training requirements are and what the skill, knowledge, and attitude content of the training program should be.

*Now that you have studied the checklist, go back to your answers to the Pacto Company case. Would you change any of your answers? Add any more? Why?* _____

_____

_____

_____

*What are the training needs of your company's sales force? What should your program contain?* _____

_____

_____

_____

## Learning Basis, Training Policy

The next consideration in designing the formal sales training program concerns the learning basis or training policy to be employed.

Sales training as it is performed by American companies is based on either of two basic education or training philosophies: conditioned response and insight response. The type of policy for a particular sales group depends on the specific conditions of: type of sales reps involved, characteristics of the customers, products, markets, and competition.

Both policies are well suited to certain conditions and are ineffective in others. The first policy discussed is the historical basis for sales training; the second policy is relatively new on the business scene.

## Conditioned Response

Under this policy, sales personnel are trained *in advance* in the proper response to any and all problems, conditions, and objections that they may encounter. The selling job is carefully analyzed—prospecting for new customers, the approach, the sales presentation, meeting objections, the close and follow-up are carefully synthesized into a general model representing *all* selling situations. Then experts provide instructions for every phase of the work and responses for all sales problems. The sales reps are required to learn set instructions and responses and to adhere to them strictly.

Under a carefully worked out conditioned response program, no sales reps ever find themselves in situations that have not been anticipated and for which they are not fully prepared with memorized reactions. All salespeople in a conditioned response sales force react to the same problems in the same way. Conditioned response is generalized response, and the training program is designed to transmit this response.

## Insight Response

The opposite policy expects reps to respond to selling problems on the basis of their personal analytical insights into the nature of each individual selling situation. The training is aimed at helping them develop their insight and analytical skills. Insight response is individualized response.

### Application Exercise

Which is the policy to adopt? Which training policy is better for a particular sales group? For yours?

Following is a list of products and services. Opposite each indicate whether you believe the product or service is better adapted to conditioned response or insight response selling and note the reason for your decision.

To understand which training policy is best suited for a particular sales group, it is useful to consider two completely different selling situa-

| PRODUCT OR SERVICE | CONDITIONED OR INSIGHT RESPONSE? | REASON |
|---|---|---|
| Encyclopedias sold door-to-door | _____ | _____ |
| Internal office communication systems | _____ | _____ |
| Low cost, term life insurance | _____ | _____ |
| Travel tour package | _____ | _____ |
| Cosmetics sold direct to women in their homes | _____ | _____ |
| Refrigerators sold in department stores | _____ | _____ |

tions. When you do so, criteria will begin to develop that will help you decide between the two policies. For example, with atomic power generation equipment, the selling situation is complex and highly technical. Customers are knowledgeable and their requirements are varied. Salespeople are highly trained and sales force turnover is generally low. At the other extreme, door-to-door selling for example, the selling job is fairly simple and nontechnical. Customers know little about the products and their requirements are standard. Sales reps are not highly trained and sales force turnover is high.

In these examples, we see that in the first selling situation insight response is indicated, and conditioned response is favored in the second. The basic questions in any particular selling environment are:

1. *Is it feasible to condition the reps' response?* In complex, changing sales situations involving knowledgeable buyers with various requirements, it is not possible effectively to condition the proper responses, because the customer's individual needs and requirements are so varied that it is impossible to anticipate them. When these conditions are reversed, conditioned response is possible.
2. *Is it desirable to condition the sales response?* The kind of customers, their knowledge, and desires dictate the answer to this question. Is the customer best persuaded by a conditioned or an insight approach?

In the two selling situations mentioned above, the choice between the two training policies is not difficult. But the selling conditions of a great many companies place them between these extremes. Their situation is neither clearly conditioned nor insight response. For these in-between companies, the decision involves weighing the advantages and disadvantages of the policies.

---

### CONDITIONED RESPONSE

ADVANTAGES

Expert experience and directions are brought to bear on all of the problems the salespeople encounter.

No sales problem, procedure, or situation is overlooked; there are no surprises.

Training is economical once the response program has been developed.

All sales reps in the group react in the same way, making it easy to transfer them between territories within the same company.

All information the seller wants the customer to have is supplied.

DISADVANTAGES

The reps may overlook particular interests or problems of individual customers while adhering to the conditioned response pattern.

Salespeople are not allowed to adjust to unique selling conditions.

Customer may resent standardized selling process as manipulation or high pressure tactic.

Some sales reps may resent absence of initiative and opportunity, thus affecting morale.

---

### INSIGHT RESPONSE

ADVANTAGES

Salespeople are flexible to adjust to new, changing market and customer conditions.

Their selling focus is on an individual situation, not on generalized situations.

Customers' individual conditions and problems are the focal point of sales calls.

Sales reps' morale may be raised by active participation in their own work.

DISADVANTAGES

Training is slow, difficult, and expensive.

Each sales group must analyze the pros and cons of these two training policies very carefully. As we have shown, each policy has advantages and disadvantages in regard to cost, the rep's morale, flexibility, and customers' reactions. Which policy is better for the Pacto Company? Why?

_____

_____

_____

## Teaching Instruments and Techniques

Sales training has adopted a variety of teaching devices and techniques from education. Each has its own special purposes and applications. Most companies use a combination of these devices and techniques in formal sales training rather than relying on a single one.

### Visual Aids

These include films, tapes, flip charts, chalk and flannel boards, film strips, closed-circuit and playback television, and overhead slide projection. The advantages of visual aids are that they add color, motion, and drama to the training. They can be repeated as often as necessary for review and reinforcement of the message and for rechecking by the trainees. Since visual aids are prepared in advance, their form, content, sequence, and organization can be completely preplanned and controlled. There need not be any unrehearsed presentation mistakes. The main disadvantage of visual aids as a training device is that usually they should be prepared by experts and so are expensive to use. However, a company's advertising agency may be able to provide the necessary artistic talent and technical competence to produce effective visual aids for training salespeople. In addition, there are a number of firms that specialize in this activity, deriving their income from the planning and production of made-to-order visual training aids for specific clients.

### Lecture

This is the formal, structured, verbal presentation of information and fundamentals to trainees by expert trainers and company executives.

This technique is economical of trainee time and makes top-flight trainers and executives available for training efficiently and at low cost. It is a very effective method of transmitting straight factual information. The difficulties inherent in the lecture method of training are that unless lectures are carefully prepared, planned, and rehearsed, the trainees will "shut off" the lecturer because of boredom or antagonism. In addition, because lectures must necessarily be generalized, the method is poorly adapted to the transmission of changing information, and the treatment of dynamic, dissimilar selling conditions.

### Discussion

Under the guidance of a skilled conference leader, trainees discuss a common problem, procedure, company policy, or case history. This training technique is well suited to indoctrinating trainees in selling problems that involve individual judgment, personal decision, and adjustment to specific selling situations. It has the further advantage of directly involving the trainees in their own training. A study of training methods showed that sales managers believe discussion is the most productive technique. A limitation on discussion in sales training is that it requires skilled and experienced conference leaders. Such people are in short supply. Skill and experience are required so that the session does not degenerate into a bull session or, at the other extreme, a "hidden" lecture.

### Role Playing

A problem situation is stated and several trainees play the important roles in the problem. Other trainees, trainers, and experts observe and later make suggestions and offer constructive criticism. The advantages of this training technique are that it adds realism and interest to the training and increases the trainees' skills and confidence in reacting immediately to selling problems in a face-to-face situation. The weakness of the technique is that trainees sometimes feel awkward and embarrassed "play acting" in public and so the quality of role play sessions is apt to vary. This condition can detract from the effectiveness of this training device.

### Panels

Each member of a small group of trainees, experts, or a combination of them, under a chairperson, makes a short, prepared presentation on a training topic, followed by questions from other panel members and the trainee group. Advantages are that panels make experts available to trainees economically; trainees can ask individual questions; trainers can observe what trainees are uncertain about from their responses to the panel; adds interest through the give-and-take between panelists and between panelists and trainees. One weakness of panel discussions is that different opinions and points of view may be presented by panelists and this may confuse trainees. In addition, it is sometimes difficult to control the interchange between trainees and panelists to ensure a consistent message. This is especially true when one panelist monopolizes the presentation or the question-and-answer period.

## Observed Sales Calls

The trainer makes field calls with the trainee, observing the sales techniques used, and later provides coaching for improvement. The advantages of this training technique are that it provides a highly realistic learning experience along with immediate alteration of bad selling habits and techniques. However, it is expensive and the selling situations encountered (and therefore the learning experiences) are random; they cannot be preplanned or fitted into any sort of predetermined sequence of trainee experience.

## Programmed Instruction

The total body of knowledge that the trainees are to learn is broken into segments, each consisting of explanatory material and questions covering it; these are presented to the trainee in sequence either by a teaching machine or in a text. The trainee answers a set of questions on each module of the work and is directed either to redo the explanatory material and take the test again or to proceed to the next "lesson." The advantages of this technique are several: it can be used by a single trainee, no class of trainees is necessary; it does not require a trainer to be present; the trainee can progress at his or her own rate of learning. The drawbacks of this training technique are that a programmed instruction plan must be written for a specific company and industry, and this is expensive. In addition, the results of this technique are hard to evaluate.

## Live Dramas and Skits

A script is produced that highlights the training points to be emphasized. Actors in the appropriate stage setting and with the appropriate props act out the script before the trainee audience. The advantage of this technique is that it can be used to introduce a change of pace and add interest to the training program. It facilitates learning and allows the trainees to associate themselves with members of the cast of actors. Dramas can be used to introduce humor, criticism, and satire that are useful for training, but might not be acceptable to the trainees in lectures or discussions. It can be used to lighten the training atmosphere while still imparting a useful message. The disadvantage of dramas and skits as training devices is that they are difficult to design and are, therefore, expensive. It requires a specialist to prepare a script that is interesting and entertaining and, at the same time, gets the message across. Usually such specialists must be engaged outside the company. All of this adds to the cost of this training activity. In addition, the actors should be professionals. Company personnel as amateur actors are a risky proposition! There are companies specializing in planning, producing, and putting on training dramas and skits for individual clients.

### Business Games
### (Also Called Simulation Exercises)

A business or sales problem is presented to trainees, either competing individually or as teams; a series of decisions are made, which are scored against the "moves" of competing units; after a series of moves, one unit emerges as the "winner" when judged by profit, return on investment, penetration of new markets, or other standards. Advantages are that this technique is realistic, interesting, and gives the trainees a genuine sense of competition in the market. Further, it allows the exposition and demonstration of business and selling problems that cannot always be easily shown by other teaching methods. It is, however, an expensive technique, and management games applicable to some industries and selling situations are not available unless specially prepared for them.

### Application Exercise

*For each of three of the topics you considered important for Pacto sales recruits to learn, which teaching techniques do you think would be best for each topic and why?*

_____

_____

## WHO SHOULD TRAIN SALE REPS AND WHERE?

Having considered general learning theory, the content of the formal sales training program, training techniques and methods to be used in a particular company, we will now consider where training should take place and who should teach in the formal sales training program.

### Ability to Sell and the Ability to Train

A basic principle of education and training is that the skills of *teaching* are different from the skills of *performing* the subject being taught. There is a popular fallacy that anyone who does something well is automatically an outstanding teacher-trainer of those same skills. In practice, this is not true because *doing* skills, such as selling, are completely different from the skills of teaching or training.

Some skilled salespeople and sales managers are top-flight trainers, but others are very poor. Some mediocre salespeople are good trainers. Some professional sales trainers were or would be poor salespeople, others, excellent. There is no necessary connection between a person's selling or sales management abilities and his or her skills as a teacher of selling. Consequently, a prime consideration in deciding who should do the sales training is the individual's competence as a teacher-trainer.

### The Sales Trainers and the Training Location

On the question of who should train sales reps and the training location, most companies, except the very smallest, must choose between a combination of alternatives. The alternatives are: training specialists, field sales managers and experienced salespeople, or outside training specialists. On the problem of where training should take place, it can either be centralized in a single location or decentralized to the field sales installations. Thus, a number of combinations are possible. For instance, sales training can be conducted by training specialists in a centralized location, by sales managers in the field, by outside experts in the field, or by field personnel in a centralized location.

For the majority of companies, only three of the many alternatives are possible because of the excessive costs in time and money of the other alternatives. Field sales personnel cannot generally afford the time away from their sales work for extensive participation in centralized training at another location. Outside training experts are too expensive to be employed in decentralized training at a number of different field locations. As a result, these alternatives are unrealistic for most companies.

Most companies choose between sales training by company training specialists in a central location, training by outside experts in a central location, and training by field sales personnel at the field sales locations. Each of these alternatives has its merits and its limitations.

---

### TRAINING BY COMPANY TRAINING SPECIALISTS AT A CENTRAL LOCATION

| MERITS | LIMITATIONS |
|---|---|
| Provides specialized training know-how and experience. | Adds overhead costs for training staff, special equipment, meeting rooms, etc. |
| Does not take line salespeople away from their work or distract their attention from their sales job. | Difficult to relate training to real-life selling situations and problems. |
| Training is the main purpose of the operations; no dilution of the training activity by the pressures of selling problems. | While in training, the trainees learn nothing about the market they will be working in. |
| | When the trainee is sent to the field after training, a manager may belittle centralized training as "ivory tower" learning and unrelated to real market conditions. |

---

### TRAINING BY OUTSIDE EXPERTS AT A CENTRAL LOCATION

This alternative shares all of the merits and limitations of training by company training specialists at a central location, with another advantage and two additional potential limitations.

| MERITS | LIMITATIONS |
|---|---|
| Provides ideas and techniques from training in other industries and companies; broader experience and viewpoint. | May not know or be able to master important problems or conditions unique to the particular company; may not "speak the language" of the company. |
| | Possible danger of leaking company trade secrets to the outside training experts. |

## TRAINING BY FIELD SALES PEOPLE AT FIELD SALES LOCATIONS

| MERITS | LIMITATIONS |
|---|---|
| No added overhead cost for training personnel, since line salespeople who do the training are already on the payroll. | Does not provide specialized training know-how and experience. |
| Training can be related to real selling situations. | Takes line salespeople away from selling and managing. |
| While in training, trainees learn about conditions in the market they will be working in. | Training emphasis likely to be diluted by the pressures of everyday sales activities. |
| Field salespeople themselves are involved in the training and so are less likely to deny its value or downgrade it. | |

## Compromise Plan

Frequently used is a combination plan in which training is done in the field by field salespeople who are assisted in a staff capacity by training specialists from headquarters. In such instances, the functions of the training specialist are to help plan the training program with field trainers, to participate to some extent in the program, to counsel field trainers, and to assist in evaluating the program. While this is not necessarily the ideal solution, it does have all of the merits of training in the field by field people, and to some extent it lessens the problems of the lack of special training know-how and the diversion of salespeople from their selling jobs.

### Outside Sales Trainers

Smaller companies often have special problems in regard to outside sales trainers. They cannot afford to maintain their own sales training staff, but there is a need for sales training. How can you locate outside sales training experts? How can you find out if they are effective?

To contact outside trainers, possible leads include your trade association, business friends, the National Society of Sales Training Executives, companies with sales training staffs, Sales and Marketing

Executives International, your bank, the Small Business Administration, and the faculties of business colleges.

How do you evaluate outside sales trainers? Ask them to give you a list of their clients and check the experience these companies have had with them. Does their proposal fit *your special* needs? If possible, observe them at work in a training program, their approach, materials, and methods. Talk with their people. Check your local Chamber of Commerce and Better Business Bureau.

## Making the Decision on Trainers and Location

We can summarize the preceding discussion in the form of an analytical model to be used by an individual sales group to decide what combination of training personnel and location is best for them. In the analytical model that follows, these abbreviations are used for the three alternatives for training location and personnel:

CCS = centralized location by company training specialists
COX = centralized location by outside training experts
DFS = decentralized location by field sales personnel

Each sales group must use the kind of analysis summarized in this model to decide the optimum training location-personnel choice for them. This requires weighing the relative importance *for them* of one program training need against the others in light of the capabilities of each alternative summarized in the model. For instance, decentralized training by field personnel reduces expense, adds realism to the training, indoctrinates the trainees in their future territories, safeguards company trade secrets, and focuses on company problems and procedures. But this alternative does not provide specialized training skill and experience, does not utilize full-time trainers, and is not likely to be particularly creative.

## Application Exercise

*Using the Pacto Company's sales force, analyze their training needs and enter your conclusions in the two blank columns in the following analytical model.*

*Now assess your conclusions by comparing the training program requirements against each other. What is the relative importance of each requirement? Which are critical, less important, not required?*

| SALES TRAINING PROGRAM SPECIFICATION | PACTO TRAINING PROGRAM REQUIREMENTS | | LOCATION AND PERSONNEL ALTERNATIVES | |
|---|---|---|---|---|
| | Must Provide This Specification | Need Not Provide This Specification | Accomplishes Well | Accomplishes Poorly |
| **TRAINING SPECIFICATION** Provide specialized training experience, know-how. | | | CCS COX | DFS |
| **TIME COST** Not take field salespeople's time away from selling. | | | CCS COX | DFS |
| **EMPHASIS** During training, emphasis strictly on training. | | | CCS COX | DFS |
| **PROGRAM EXPENSE** Keep training costs at minimum. | | | DFS | CCS COS |
| **REALISM** Training directly related to real-life conditions. | | | DFS | CCS COX |
| **MARKET INDOCTRINATION** Trainee shown conditions in the territory. | | | DFS | CCS COX |
| **PROGRAM CREATIVITY** Provide new ideas, concepts, training techniques. | | | CCS COX | DFS |
| **SECURITY** Safeguard company trade secrets. | | | CCS DFS | COX |
| **FOCUS** Directly and exclusively on company problems, procedures. | | | CCS DFS | COX |

## FOLLOW UP AND EVALUATION, RECYCLING OF TRAINING

We have seen that the purpose of formal and informal sales training is to transmit required knowledge and skills and to create a positive attitude by the sales reps to their company, products, and jobs. On one level, evaluation of the success of the training program is not difficult. We can easily evaluate if the program has succeeded in giving the necessary factual information to the trainees. We can simply test them, for instance, to see if they know the facts about products, company policies, and sales operating procedures. However, in the areas of sales skills and personal attitudes, the evaluation of sales training is difficult and inexact for a number of reasons.

- Skills and attitudes are difficult to observe and to evaluate objectively.
- We can never be precisely sure what changes are caused by training as opposed to what may have existed in the trainees before they were trained.
- After training we cannot be absolutely sure what skills, attitudes, and knowledge the reps learned from sales experience as opposed to those imparted by the training program itself.

Evaluating the effectiveness and efficiency of sales training can never be made in completely accurate measurements. Sales training is an educational undertaking and, like all education, beyond the level of the simple transmission of information, it is inexact and only semi-measurable. However, if training dollars are to be spent well and efficiently, the training program must be subject to constant evaluation and, if necessary, revision. Methods for evaluating the continuing effectiveness of sales training programs range from very sophisticated, therefore expensive, to fairly simple and inexpensive. Consider the example that follows of a complex training evaluation program.

Shell Oil has developed an extensive system for evaluating the training program for experienced salespeople.[1] How they developed this system and how it works are summarized here.

[1]C. E. Hahne, "How to Measure Results of Sales Training," *Training and Development Journal* (November 1977), pp. 3–6. Reproduced by special permission from the November 1977 *Training and Development Journal*. Copyright 1977 by the American Society for Training and Development, Inc.

The first step was to set *specific* and *measurable* objectives for sales training. These are:
1. Increase sales volume.
2. Improve the performance of the sales reps.
3. Change the sales reps' behavior (better communicators, persuasion skills, improved sales strategies, more insight into customer's needs, etc.).

Next, the decision was made to use outside training programs and personnel rather than training in-house. The process of selecting which outside program to use included:
1. Identify all of the potentially useful outside training programs.
2. Contact sales training people in other companies for their evaluation of these programs.
3. Evaluate each program's content, materials, and personnel against Shell's training objectives.
4. Review the testimonials and critiques of each program.
5. Observe programs in action and talk to the trainers.
6. Enroll a few Shell salespeople in selected programs as a trial.

Then, one of the outside programs was chosen. This program was selected for three reasons:
1. The training related directly to the daily problems of Shell sales reps.
2. Training results were measurable.
3. Trainees' supervisors become involved in a continuing "training partnership" with their reps.

To evaluate the effectiveness of the program, Shell began by asking the questions: "What do we need to know? How can we get this information?" The decision was that evaluation depended on the answers to three questions.
1. At the end of the program, do the trainees believe they have learned things they can *apply* to their own sales problems? An unsigned questionnaire is used to gather this information.
2. After 2–3 months, have the trainees' results improved? Trainees' supervisors provide the answers here.
3. Have the specific personal selling problems the trainees worked on in the program been solved? Again the supervisor is asked for a report.

Obviously, Shell's program for the evaluation of sales training is sophisticated and expensive, and so beyond the needs and financial capability of many companies. This does not mean, however, that less expensive evaluation techniques cannot be used to provide some insight into the effectiveness of sales training programs. Some of these are discussed below.

### Observe the Reps at Work

After training, skilled observers who know the training program and its objectives accompany recent trainees on their sales calls. They observe how the trainee is or is not applying what was taught in the program in order to evaluate the techniques used in the training program and to improve them.

### Sound Out Customers

Customers are contacted personally or by mail for their opinions about the sales rep's performance after training. In some instances, customer's reactions indicate strengths or weaknesses in the sales training program.

### Review Sales Performance Against Standards

Some companies establish one set of performance standards, such as new accounts opened or promotions arranged with customers, for salespeople without training and another set of performance standards for those who have been through the training program. By comparison, some evaluation of the training program is achieved.

### Interview Trainees

Carefully planned, pre-training interviews when compared with post-training interviews with the trainees can indicate what effect training has had on their attitudes, skills, and knowledge levels. A version of this evaluation device is to employ written tests of the trainees before and after their training.

### Seek Management Opinion

The supervisors of salespeople who have been through training can be a useful source of information about the value of the program. Do the newly trained people have a positive, constructive attitude, the necessary selling skills, company and market information? Their immediate supervisors can supply valuable information on such questions and thereby indicate the strengths and weaknesses of the training program.

### Application Exercise

*What might the following evidence indicate about the effectiveness of the formal sales training program for a company that manufactures hardware products sold by company sales reps to retail hardware stores?*

*Retailer to sales supervisor: "Your salesman Levin did a bang-up promotion job for us last month! He set up a floor display of one of your products and arranged local advertising and more than doubled our usual volume."* _____

_____

_____

_____

*Recent trainee to supervisor: "They told us in training that the calls-per-day column in the sales activity report form was to be for the month. Now I get a nasty letter from the controller asking me for weekly figures. What gives?"* _____

_____

_____

_____

*Supervisor's report: "Salesman Bonner consistently neglects to use the sales promotion materials we provide."* _____

_____

_____

_____

*Retailer to supervisor: "Your Linda Sloan must be the busiest rep you have. Don't see her but about twice a year and when she does come, she runs out as quick as she can."* _____

_____

_____

_____

*Sales manager to rep's supervisor: "Before he went through the training program, your man Hunt was the worst salesman this company ever had. Now I see he's third in your territory."* _____

_____

_____

_____

*Observer's report on calls with a recent trainee: "Rushes calls, ill at ease, nervous."* _____

_____

_____

_____

*Retailer to sales supervisor: "Your regular products are okay. They're good and I can explain them to customers when they ask questions about them. But those new items you've brought out—I don't know the first thing about them."* _____

_____

_____

_____

## Recycling the Sales Training Program

What happens if the various forms of evaluation of the sales training program indicate that it is inadequate? Or if evaluation shows that the reps are not being indoctrinated in the proper attitudes, or their product, company, or industry knowledge is insufficient, or they lack the required selling skills? In this unhappy event, it is necessary to recycle, to redesign the training program. To do this we must start at the beginning, as we did in this chapter, with a reexamination of training objectives, program content, teaching methods, location of the training, and training personnel.

But if evaluation of the sales training program indicates that it is a good one, satisfactory in all respects, should we continue the expense and bother of regular evaluation of the program? Absolutely! As we have been reminded previously, the marketplace is in a constant state of change. Competitors introduce new products, new uses for the product appear, new competitors enter the market, economic conditions change, new customers appear, and old customers disappear—the only thing we can be sure about the market is that it will change. Nothing is so sure as change. Consequently, the skill, knowledge, and attitude requirements for successful selling are also in a constant state of change. The form and content of sales training is always subject to change. Therefore, when evaluation shows a training program to be satisfactory, evaluation must continue at regular intervals because training that is good today may become inadequate as the market changes.

At some time, market and economic changes will necessitate the recycling and redesign of even the best training programs. We must continue to evaluate sales training programs in order to know when they must be redesigned. To find out too late is likely to be disasterous.

### Brain teasers

|  | Agree | Disagree |
|---|---|---|
| 1. It is usually easier and less expensive to train sales reps in the right habits at the start than to retrain them out of bad habits later. | ____ | ____ |
| 2. "Good salespeople are born, not made." | ____ | ____ |
| 3. The training needs of individual members of a sales force are likely to be different. | ____ | ____ |
| 4. The reps' attitude toward their company and job cannot be influenced by training. | ____ | ____ |
| 5. Conditioned response training is generally indicated when the product is standard, nontechnical, and buyers know little about the product. | ____ | ____ |
| 6. All sales training programs should have the lecture and discussion techniques as their major basis. | ____ | ____ |
| 7. To be a good sales trainer, a person must be, or have been, a top-flight sales rep. | ____ | ____ |
| 8. When a particular sales training program has been carefully evaluated and found to be efficient and effective, it is a waste of time and money to continue to evaluate it. | ____ | ____ |
| 9. It is difficult to evaluate accurately a sales training program. | ____ | ____ |
| 10. Repetition should be avoided in the training program plan. | ____ | ____ |

## Activities

1.  Comment on this statement: "Only large companies with large sales forces need sales training." _____

    _____

    _____

    _____

2.  Either for your company or for one you know well, write a list of the skills, knowledge, and attitudes the salespeople must have that cannot be trained. _____

    _____

    _____

    _____

3.  For the sales force you used above, list the product knowledge, company knowledge, selling skills, and attitudes the sales reps must possess that are trainable. _____

    _____

    _____

    _____

4.  For a company you know well: (1) Make a detailed list of the skills, knowledge, and attitudes the people who sell for this company must have; (2) opposite your list, indicate which teaching technique (visual aids, lecture, etc.) is best suited to training each skill, knowledge, or attitude, and (3) indicate your reasons for your answers to (1) and (2). _____

    _____

    _____

    _____

5.  Contact a sales executive who is involved in sales training. Interview this executive concerning what that company does to evaluate the effectiveness of their sales training. What is your appraisal of their evaluation activities? What would you suggest that they do to improve them? What are your reasons for this?

    _____

    _____

    _____

6. *Secure the outline of a sales training plan. To what extent does this plan follow the training principles discussed in this chapter?* _____

_____

_____

_____

## SELECTED REFERENCES

### The Basis for Sales Training

BURR, ROBERT B., "Training and Development of Salesmen," in *The New Handbook of Sales Training,* ed. Robert Vizza. Englewood Cliffs, N.J.: Prentice-Hall, 1967, pp. 35–40.
FALVEY, JOHN J., "Myths of Sales Training," *Sales and Marketing Management,* April 3, 1978, pp. 40–43.
SELWITZ, ROBERT, "Training for Effect," *Industrial Distribution,* (July 1977), pp. 33–37.

### Theory of Teaching and Learning

SKINNER, B.F., "The Science of Learning and the Art of Teaching," *Harvard Educational Review,* 24, (Spring 1964), 86–97.
STILL, RICHARD R., and EDWARD W. CUNDIFF, "Training Salesmen," in *Sales Management: Decisions, Policies and Cases* (2nd ed.). Englewood Cliffs, N.J.: Prentice-Hall, 1969.
STROH, THOMAS F., "Sales Training Methodologies," in *Managing the Sales Function.* New York: McGraw-Hill, 1978.

### Designing the Sales Training Program

HOPKINS, DAVID S., *Training the Sales Force: A Progress Report.* New York: The Conference Board, 1978.
"Sales Training and Motivation, Special Report," *Sales and Marketing Management,* December 12, 1977, pp. 65–96.
STANTON, WILLIAM J., and RICHARD H. BUSKIRK, "Developing and Conducting a Sales Training Program," in *Managing the Sales Force* (5th ed.). Homewood, Ill.: Richard D. Irwin, 1978.

STROH, THOMAS F., *Training and Developing the Professional Salesman.* New York: Amacom, 1973.

"Training to Reach New Heights," *Sales and Marketing Management,* August 9, 1976, pp. 43–54.

# 5

# LEADERSHIP AND SUPERVISION IN SALES MANAGEMENT

*After reading this chapter you should be able to demonstrate your learning as follows:*
- *Distinguish between cause, direction, and motivation in sales reps' behavior.*
- *Distinguish between primary, secondary, rational, and emotional needs in the motivation of people who sell.*
- *Explain Maslow's hierarchy of needs and its relationship to the motivation of salespeople.*
- *Understand the relationship between the degree of a rep's cooperation with the supervisor and his or her sales effectiveness and value as a company employee.*
- *Identify the several supervisor-leader "roles."*
- *Understand the underlying basis for cooperation between the manager-leader and the sales follower.*
- *Observe the quality of leadership as demonstrated by a particular manager and suggest means for improvement.*
- *Know what followers demand of their supervisor-leaders.*
- *Know what human relations skills in management encourage ardent cooperation by subordinates.*

The most difficult task any manager faces is the supervision of subordinates. Sales managers' supervision jobs are exceptionally complex: they cannot assume sales reps are strongly motivated day in and day out; the reps may be scattered across a large geographical area; they may offer a broad product line to serve diverse markets; the selling task is often technical and highly competitive; and the business expenses they control are large. However, failure to identify the needs of your salespeople and to provide effective leadership will result in increased turn-over, lower productivity of the sales force, and unnecessary selling expense.

In this chapter we will expand our understanding of what sales executive leadership and supervision are so that you will better understand why sales reps do or do not follow their supervisors well. To lead people effectively, a thorough understanding of human behavior, the concepts of motivation, and how to apply them is needed. We will also identify the important human relations skills of good sales leadership and indicate how these skills can be improved for greater efficiency and lower cost in sales force operation.

## UNDERSTANDING BEHAVIOR

Human behavior and its causes are complex. In a classic compilation of scientific findings, the authors observe:

> . . . Human behavior itself is so enormously varied, so delicately complex, so obscurely motivated that many people despair of finding valid generalizations to explain and predict the actions, thoughts, and feelings of human beings—despair, that is, of the very possibility of constructing a science of human behavior.[1]

But as complex as it is, sales managers must master the fundamentals of human behavior if they are to have any chance at all of being good leaders and supervisors.

### Elements of Behavior

Despite the barriers to understanding, behavioral scientists have developed some useful generalizations about human behavior. Industrial psychologist Harold J. Leavitt suggests that three major assumptions are inherent in all theory of human behavior:[2]

[1]Bernard Berelson and Gary A. Steiner, *Human Behavior: An Inventory of Scientific Findings* (New York: Harcourt, 1964), p. 3.
[2]Harold J. Leavitt, *Managerial Psychology*, 4th. ed. (Chicago: University of Chicago Press, 1978), p. 8.

1. Human behavior is *caused,* or influenced, by outside forces, primarily the environment and heredity.
2. Human behavior is *directed;* it is pointed toward a goal or desire.
3. Human behavior is *motivated;* some form of "push," "need," or "motive" underlies all forms of behavior.

Behavior results from a need, tension, or discomfort within a person, and one acts to satisfy a need or relieve the tension or discomfort. For instance, a pebble in your shoe will be uncomfortable. Removing your shoe and taking the pebble out is the behavior needed to relieve this discomfort. In this example, the pebble is the *cause* of your behavior, your actions are *directed* toward eliminating your discomfort, and physical comfort is the *motive* for your behavior.

The principles of causality, motivation, and direction apply also to more complex forms of behavior than in the simple example above. For instance, the successful rep is able to relate the features of the product to the customer's needs and buying motives. This is purposeful behavior. From a management perspective, we must recognize that the effectiveness of a person's performance is related to the extent to which performance achieves a goal or is a means to attaining a goal. The role of sales managers is to influence reps' behavior by providing them with a stimulus, or cause, for acting. Figure 5-1 shows this relationship.

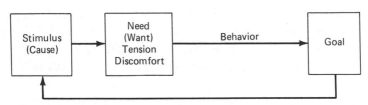

FIGURE 5-1

Reprinted from *Managerial Psychology,* 4th ed., by Harold J. Leavitt by permission of The University of Chicago Press. © 1958, 1964, 1972, 1978 by The University of Chicago.

## MOTIVATION

Motivation is the heart of sales management. It is simply the "how to" of getting salespeople to do their jobs well. Motives are the "whys" of behavior and a sales manager must understand the "whys" of the sales reps' behavior before any actions can be taken to lead and motivate them. Incentives, or stimuli, must be developed to fit their specific needs.

## Theories of Motivation

Before reading further, think of an important purchase you recently made. Did the sales rep identify your needs? Was he or she able to relate the product's features to your specific needs? Did other causal factors (advertising, personal recommendations, and so on) influence your decision? What were your motives for buying this product? What does this exercise tell you about the relationship of motivation theory to personal selling?

PURCHASE _____  _____

CAUSES: _____   NEEDS: _____   GOALS: _____

_____   _____   _____

_____   _____   _____

How can you identify the specific motives of your people when each person's needs and life goals are unique to him or her? Fortunately, there is general agreement that all human needs fall into a general pattern.

## Primary and Secondary Needs

Psychologists differentiate between primary and secondary needs. Primary needs are physical needs that must be satisfied immediately. Hunger, thirst, and protection from excessive heat or cold are examples of primary needs. Secondary needs are those that can be satisfied at a later time. Frequently, secondary needs are psychological or have been learned from others. The needs for recognition and love are secondary needs.

## Rational and Emotional Needs

Another useful distinction is between rational and emotional needs. Rational needs are based on reason. A person's desire to purchase a Volkswagen Rabbit because of its economy of operation illustrates the dominance of a rational buying motive. On the other hand, another person's purchase of a Cadillac may result from an emotional need for status and prestige. It is frequently difficult to identify exactly which of our needs are based on emotion and which are based on reason.

## A Hierarchy of Needs

Professor Abraham H. Maslow of Brandeis University, a prominent student of behavior, has developed a theory that arranges needs in order of their importance.[3] He shows us that needs on the lowest level must be satisfied before higher level needs become important motivating forces. When a need is essentially satisfied, it ceases to be a motivator of behavior.

For instance, a man lost in the desert for several days without food has only one thing on his mind. He is hungry and will do anything for food, even eating a rat or snake, which would otherwise repell him. Once his desire for food has been satisfied, other needs become important, such as the desire for sleep and shelter. Likewise, a sales rep who has been on the road for several days is concerned only with getting back home. However, after the weekend, the rep will be ready to resume making calls. Once satisfied, a need is no longer a motivator of behavior.

Each of us has a personal hierarchy of needs. For an ambitious young male executive, personal achievement may be the dominant driving force. He may neglect his family, his private social life, and even his health to get ahead. However, his wife's needs may be quite different. Her goal may be social status. She might want to be a member of the country club and have her children go to the "right" schools.

Often an individual's needs are in conflict. Polly Rice wants advancement and recognition as an outstanding sales rep. But to do this, she must outperform her fellow reps with whom she is very friendly and enjoys a satisfying social relationship. Polly must choose between her conflicting desires for advancement and satisfactory social companionship. Bruce Lukas wants to make more money, which means making calls on weekends, holidays, and evenings. However, his son is a star Little League baseball player, and Bruce wants to see all of his son's games. Bruce also has to choose between conflicting desires—the material satisfactions of additional income or the inner satisfactions of watching his son play ball.

Maslow's hierarchy of needs is in five levels. As a theory of motivation, its contribution is to identify and rank the motivating forces. In the order in which they must be satisfied for the next level to become an effective motivator, these need levels are: physiological, safety and security, social, ego, and self-fulfillment.

[3]Abraham H. Maslow, *Motivation and Personality*, 2nd ed. (New York: Harper, 1970).

### Physiological Needs

These include the basic requirements for food, clothing, shelter, and the like. Also called the "tissue" needs, these are built-in needs required for normal functioning of the body. As the first level in the need hierarchy, these needs must ordinarily be satisfied before those needs above will significantly influence a person's behavior. Praise of a salesperson's performance (an ego need) has no motivating power if the rep is not earning enough to feed the family at a satisfactory level. However, physiological needs are not a motivating force when they are totally satisfied.

### Safety and Security Needs

Protection from threat, danger, and deprivation can be primary motivating forces. These are activated when people are uncertain or fearful for their well-being, that of their family or their job. In today's fast-paced world, many working people are especially concerned with being prepared for what the future may bring. Life insurance, pension plans, health and accident policies are a few of the incentives that appeal to this level of needs.

### Social Needs

These are satisfied by meaningful relationships with other people. We are social animals. We all have a desire to belong, to be accepted, to give and receive friendship and love. Company bowling teams, plant picnics, and the like serve to enhance the social aspects of a job.

### Ego Needs

These are directed toward enhancing or gratifying one's ego or self-image. One ego need is the desire for self-esteem, self-respect, self-confidence, and achievement. A person wants to feel that he or she is "somebody." We all desire the esteem of others. That is, we want status, recognition, and appreciation from our peers. Status in an organization may be conveyed by a person's title, office size and furnishings, and special privileges and responsibilities.

## Self-actualization Needs

The final level of needs is defined as those desires for self-fulfillment. This is the wish to succeed simply for the sake of accomplishment, not for material gain or recognition. Because other needs take precedence, very few people are strongly driven by self-fulfillment needs. Marie Curie, Leonardo da Vinci, and others are the exception rather than the rule.

Maslow's hierarchy is a useful means of analyzing human motivation. It shows us that a need is an effective motivator only when it is activated; that frustration of an activated need acts negatively on productivity and morale; and that satisfaction of an activated need acts positively on productivity and morale.

## Case Study

To apply what we have learned so far, study this sales leadership situation.

Saturn Drug Company

Recently Stanley Bates was promoted to district sales manager and transfered to the Atlanta district of the Saturn Drug Company. His 11 sales representatives cover metropolitan Atlanta and the surrounding area for about 300 miles.

Saturn manufactures and distributes a wide line of perscription and over-the-counter drugs. Sales reps call on doctors, hospitals, drug retailers, wholesalers, and chains. Calls on doctors are to introduce new products and to remind them of old items with the objective of having the doctor prescribe Saturn brands. With retailers, wholesalers, and chains, the reps check inventory, introduce new products, and sell promotions. The reps are paid a straight salary plus a commission on all sales over their individual quotas.

There is a liberal expense policy. The reps are reimbursed for all business-related travel expenses and their costs for overnight lodging, entertainment of customers, telephone, postage, and telegraph. The reps are supplied with a substantial stock of samples to give to doctors on their calls.

The performance of sales reps is evaluated primarily on the sales in their territories. However, consideration is given to the number of calls per day, number of products presented per call, the supervisor's assessment of their work, and their success in following the current sales promotion plan.

The reps can improve their sales results on these criteria primarily in two ways: increase the number of calls they make each week, and improve the quality of their relationships with their doctors, wholesalers, retailers, and chains. Two examples: (1) Some doctors are in their offices on Saturday mornings and previously scheduled presentations are possible in hospitals on Saturdays and holidays; and (2) wholesalers and retailers can be helped by advice on their particular inventory and promotion problems and activities.

In addition to their selling and promotion responsibilities, Saturn's reps frequently carry out market research in their territories. The company has what is recognized as one of the best market research programs in the industry. One important basis for this program is the frequent and detailed individual reports the reps provide on competitive conditions in their territories.

When Bates took over, he familiarized himself with his predecessor's policies and procedures. He found that the reps were expected to submit detailed sales activity reports monthly and expense accounts weekly. The reps met regularly every six weeks in the Atlanta office for lunch and an afternoon conference. He noted also that the previous manager's policy was to travel a day a month with each rep, writing a detailed critique of the rep's performance. One copy of the critique was sent to the rep and another retained in the rep's personnel file.

Bates noted the following information about three of his reps:

| SALES PERSON | AGE | MARITAL STATUS | SERVICE WITH COMPANY | LAST YEAR'S EARNINGS |
|---|---|---|---|---|
| Rita Collins | 24 | S | 2 yrs, 6 mo. | $14,500 |
| Charles Sebastion | 31 | M, 2 children | 9 yrs, 3 mo. | $20,800 |
| Hugh Evans | 62 | widower, no children | 37 yrs, 2 mo. | $25,900 |

| SALES PERSON | POTENTIAL CUSTOMERS IN TERRITORY | CUSTOMERS SOLD TO LAST YEAR | REP'S LAST YEAR'S SALES VOLUME |
|---|---|---|---|
| Rita Collins | 450 | 175 | $181,250 |
| Charles Sebastion | 520 | 240 | $260,000 |
| Hugh Evans | 510 | 300 | $323,750 |

In addition to the preceding information about Collins, Sebastion, and Evans, their personnel files contained notes by the former sales manager, dated shortly before he was transferred.

*Rita Collins:* Bad family problems; both parents have serious health conditions and big medical expenses they can't pay themselves. Rita pays a lot of these. Good rep, works *very* hard, will make it big with us.

*Charles Sebastion:* Last four years his sales have come up big. Good rep! Gripes about a lot of little things—why don't we have a district newsletter, why don't we challenge another district to a sales contest, let's have district picnics. But he's good!

*Hugh Evans:* Long-time guy. Never be a manager because he doesn't want to; likes to say he could be a manager if he wanted to, but he doesn't. Talks a lot about the old days and his consistently fine sales record. A good sales rep. None better.

*Using Maslow's theory of the hierarchy of needs, on what level of need satisfaction do you think the manager's sales reps probably are now? Your reasons?*

*Rita Collins*        *Probable Need Level:* _____

*Your reasons:* _____

_____

_____

_____

_____

*Charles Sebastion*        *Probable Need Level:* _____

*Your reasons:* _____

_____

_____

_____

_____

*Hugh Evans*        *Probable Need Level:* _____

*Your reasons:* _____

_____

_____

_____

_____

## Motivation Theory and Management

List in order of importance what you feel are the major factors motivating you in your job.

1. _____

2. _____

3. _____

4. _____

5. _____

6. _____

Let's compare your list to what the experts say are the reasons we work. The results may surprise you. The surprise comes from the fact that the work ethic or philosophy of American business is subtly but drastically changing. In American business today we are witnessing the coexistence of two different kinds of salespeople and managers who, for sake of simplicity, we might characterize as the *traditional* and the *new generation.*

The "traditional" people have the *economic* view of business and selling. For them the only business of business is business, the only goal of business is profit, and a career in business supersedes virtually all other personal activities. Success for the company is measured by growth and profit; for the individual it is measured by personal income and organizational status. For these people, various forms of monetary incentives—increased take-home pay, fringe benefits, seniority rights—are still important motivators, although they are also influenced by nonmonetary motivators.

The "new generation" has a *social* view of business. For them business has significant social responsibilities, the accomplishment of which is as important as the production of profit. They believe that a successful business career is only one important element in a person's life, others being a happy family atmosphere and participation in community affairs. For these people, the various forms of monetary incentives are less important. The important motivators are internal drives related to the challenge of the job, participation in organizational decision making, and the relationship between the individual and the company.

Now let us examine specific aspects of incentives in sales motivation.

## Challenging Job

Whether a person's job is challenging and interesting is one key to motivation. It is very difficult to motivate people who find their jobs dull, boring, and endless. Fortunately, the challenge of selling is an effective motivator for sales reps. Being competitive, most salespeople rise to the competitive aspects of selling. They are motivated by factors intrinsic to the job: achievement, responsibility, growth, enjoyment of the work, and earned recognition. These job-content factors appeal to the ego and self-fulfillment needs.

## Participation

One means of providing sales reps with a challenging job is to encourage them to take an active part in decision making. Involve your people in decisions that affect them. When they are allowed to participate, they are more willing to accept management decisions. They feel important when allowed to express their views. For example, many managers believe that each rep should have a part in setting his or her quota or other performance evaluation standards. The reps' performance is related to the particular conditions in their territories and since reps are familiar with their territories, they should be involved in setting their performance standards in that territory. Also, since they help set the goals, they will be more anxious to achieve them.

Active participation by field salespeople will have another major benefit. Problem solutions will be improved. The old adage, "Two heads are better than one," is true. By encouraging participation, the sales manager will bring the collective thinking of several people to bear on the sales problems.

## Being a Part of the Company

Equally important in motivation is making the sales reps an integral part of the company. To be motivated, they must be sold on the company, their colleagues, customers, and the products or services they sell. If they understand their role in the company, they will make the company's goals their goals and think in terms of "my company." They are tied to the total company, not just to the field sales office.

## Morale

Morale and motivation are closely related. Morale relates to the reps' attitudes toward their jobs: the total of their feelings toward their supervisor, pay, fellow employees, and other job-related factors, and the total of their attitudes toward themselves. Factors contributing to morale are such conditions as company policy and administration, work conditions, pay, relationships with peers, and the rep's personal life. Although not powerful motivators, these factors may lead to job dissatisfaction. As an example, in Ralph Austin's territory the weather is especially humid. He requests an air conditioner for his company car, but company policy prohibits this. Although an air conditioner won't motivate Ralph greatly, the lack of one is significant. He expresses dissatisfaction with his job, makes fewer calls, and spends more time at home. His sales are beginning to suffer.

As Austin's situation indicates, successful selling performance depends on good morale. His sales manager will find it difficult to motivate him until the question of the air conditioner is resolved. Morale has a two-way impact. Creating good morale will not necessarily motivate sales reps. However, unless they are generally content with their jobs, they will not be receptive to attempts to motivate them.

At this point, re-examine your list of motivating forces. Which of these are true motivators? Which are related to morale?

---

---

---

Before leaving the subject of sales reps' motivation and morale, fill out the following morale and motivation audit for your manager or some other you know.

## MORALE AND MOTIVATION AUDIT

How does the sales manager you chose rate on each of these points?

|  | EXCELLENT | FAIR | POOR |
|---|---|---|---|
| 1. Pays wages that compare favorably with those paid for similar sales jobs. | _____ | _____ | _____ |
| 2. Lets each rep reach as many decisions as possible about his or her work. | _____ | _____ | _____ |
| 3. Holds sales meetings to discuss the company's benefit program. | _____ | _____ | _____ |
| 4. Takes every opportunity to be personally friendly with each rep. | _____ | _____ | _____ |
| 5. Sets quotas and goals with the reps, not for them. | _____ | _____ | _____ |
| 6. Encourages salespeople by praising them for a good job done, even to the point of being lavish. | _____ | _____ | _____ |
| 7. Gives the reps every possible responsibility consistent with their experience and ability. | _____ | _____ | _____ |
| 8. Has an attractive program of fringe benefits (vacations, insurance, pensions, etc.) | _____ | _____ | _____ |
| 9. Strives to provide opportunities for advancement for all salespeople regardless of age, length of service, etc. | _____ | _____ | _____ |
| 10. Makes sure that every rep gets some recognition or praise occasionally. | _____ | _____ | _____ |

## Learning Exercise

*The new Atlanta District Sales Manager for Saturn Drug, Stan Bates (discussed earlier), wants to apply motivation theory to the supervision of his 11 sales reps. For example, he is concerned about how to motivate them to make more calls on Saturdays and holidays. What specific things can he consider doing? What are your reasons?*

_____

_____

_____

_____

## SALES MANAGEMENT LEADERSHIP AND SUPERVISION

To this point we have been concerned with the motivation and morale of sales reps. We turn now to a closely related condition, the sales supervisor as a leader of people who sell. We will deal with such critical questions as:

- What determines the degree to which sales reps cooperate with their supervisors?
- What are the conditions under which the supervisor must be an effective leader of people?
- What "roles" must the sales supervisor play in leading?
- Why do some sales reps follow their supervisor-leaders enthusiastically and to the best of their capabilities, while others are stubborn, reluctant, and unproductive?
- What are the results of poor leadership by the sales supervisor?

### The Basic Condition of Sales Supervision

Most sales supervisors rise from the ranks of sales reps. When they are promoted to supervisor, their job changes completely. Salespeople are evaluated and rewarded or punished on how they do—how they sell, cover their territories, service customers, and so forth. In short, they stand or fall on their own personal sales performance record. But sales managers are evaluated and rewarded or punished, not on how well they themselves sell, but on how their sales reps perform. The job of the rep is to sell; the job of the sales manager is to supervise the selling activities of people. If they do a good job, the sales manager is successful. If they do a poor job, the manager has failed. *A critical element in the success or failure of a supervisor's sales reps is the quality of the manager's leadership.*

### The Critical Importance of Sales Reps' Cooperation

In leading and supervising people who sell, the degree to which they cooperate with their sales supervisor is of critical importance. What difference does it make whether the reps cooperate fully or only partially with you as their sales manager? Isn't this matter of cooperation an idealistic question more suited to ethics and religion than to hard-headed, profit-seeking business? After all, aren't salespeople paid to do their jobs, to cooperate? What is the reason for this concern about cooperation in sales executive leadership? Why must reps be led instead of simply directed? Let us imagine a line that measures the degree of cooperation a salesperson gives to a manager. The line would extend from zero (no cooperation at all) to 100 percent (complete cooperation). Somewhere on the line will be a cut-off point. This is the absolute minimum amount of cooperation that the sales supervisor will tolerate. If a person does not cooperate at least to that degree, he or she will be fired. Our cooperation scale and cut-off point is shown in Figure 5-2.

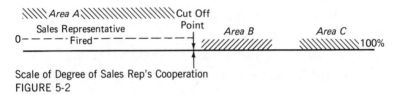

Scale of Degree of Sales Rep's Cooperation
FIGURE 5-2

If the person in question cooperates to any degree in area A below the cut-off point, you will fire him or her. If the person cooperates to any degree in areas B or C, the rep will be retained. But there are two important observations in Figure 5-2 that show us why the degree of cooperation in either area B or C is so critical.

1. In the area B-C (above the cut-off point), it is largely the sales rep who elects the degree to which he or she will cooperate.
2. Where in area B-C the rep elects to cooperate is importantly a result of the quality of the leadership of the sales manager.

In summary, in every sales supervisory situation, there is a point at which salespeople will be fired if they do not produce a minimum degree of cooperation with the sales manager, but above that point they are free to choose the degree of cooperation they will deliver. This choice is importantly determined by how well they are led and supervised by the sales manager. When properly supervised, salespeople will *want* to do the things that will achieve the company's goals.

### Costs of Less Than Complete Cooperation by Sales Reps

Since reps may choose the degree to which they will cooperate with their sales manager (above the cut-off point), does it make any real difference if they elect a low or a high level of cooperation? If there is no dollar-and-cents difference between minimum and maximum cooperation, do we need to concern ourselves with leadership and supervision as an important determinant of the level of cooperation?

When sales reps elect to operate at a low level of cooperation because they are poorly led and supervised, they generate real costs that could be avoided by good leadership and supervision. When they choose to cooperate in area B rather than area C, they generate the costs of:

– Lost business.
– Damaged customer relations.
– Impaired corporate image.
– Increased sales expenses.
– Poor quality competitive and market intelligence.
– High personnel turnover.
– Lowered morale.
– Theft of corporate property.
– Absenteeism.
– Customer complaints.
– Work done late.

In short, anything less than 100 percent cooperation by salespeople lowers sales, increases costs, and cuts profits.

### Learning Exercise

Refer to the Saturn Drug Company, page 125.

*In what specific ways could the sales reps for Stan Bates generate avoidable costs if Bates does not provide good supervisory leadership?* _____

_____

_____

_____

_____

## CONCEPTS OF SALES LEADERSHIP AND SUPERVISION

Since the degree of the sales rep's cooperation with his or her supervisor is, above the cut-off point, a matter of personal choice, and since a low level of cooperation generates costs that can be avoided by good leadership and supervision, we must understand the nature of the leadership process. Therefore, let us look at the basic concepts of good sales executive leadership.

### Essence of Sales Leadership

Some authors and researchers of executive leadership claim the ability to prescribe formulas or "golden rules" of leadership that are applicable to any and all supervision problems. But sales leadership problems are essentially unique unto themselves. No two sales supervision problems are exactly the same. Consequently, no leadership "principles" are applicable to every leadership problem. The real basis for understanding leadership and for developing this skill is:

- An understanding of why sales reps follow (or do not follow) to the full extent of their capacity.
- Mastery of the skills of creating and maintaining cooperative followership, which are the human relations skills of leadership.

As a result, our discussion of sales leadership and supervision will not be concerned with propounding formulae or rules, but rather with understanding the nature of cooperative followership and the human relations skills of encouraging such followership.

### Conditions of Sales Management Leadership

The sales manager must exercise leadership under two kinds of conditions—routine and emergency. In leading and supervising your reps under routine conditions, you must deal with day-to-day, repetitive situations. Customers must be called on, orders written and submitted, customer service must be provided, reports filled out. This is the daily, undramatic, repetitive business of sales supervision.

In other circumstances you must lead in emergency conditions. A competitor springs an unexpected new product or cuts the price, a storm or flood damage a field sales installation, a government agency passes a ruling that challenges your price schedule. These are sudden, unexpected, nonrepetitive, dramatic conditions. That sales executives must lead and supervise their people under both routine and emergency conditions places several important requirements on the sales supervisor as a leader. Good supervisors must have certain specific qualities.

### Differentiating Routine
### from Emergency Conditions

Of course, many emergency sales situations are quickly and dramatically known. It requires no special insight to realize that when a competitor cuts the price 20 percent, an emergency exists, requiring prompt and effective retaliatory action. However, not all sales management problems are so obvious and dramatic. Frequently, what appears to be a normal and routine situation in fact hides an emergency. A serious case of indigestion may only be the result of overeating (routine), or it may be the first signs of an ulcer or appendicitis (emergency). A change in a competitor's advertising theme may simply be an effort to improve communication with customers (routine), or it may be the first step in the introduction of a new product (emergency). The leader must be skilled at recognizing what is a true routine situation and what is a seemingly routine situation that is hiding an emergency.

### Managing Routine Operations

To an important extent, the management of routine selling operations is a rehearsal or a training exercise for effective reaction to emergency conditions. If routine, day-to-day sales leadership is done properly, the "right way of doing it" becomes unconscious habit, requiring no special thought or attention by the supervisor or the reps. In addition, it demonstrates to the manager's followers that the supervisor-leader knows his or her business. Consequently, when an emergency strikes, the supervisor and the reps are prepared to cope with it since their experience under routine conditions has prepared them for effective reaction to emergency. It is for this reason that the skillful football coach has his team practice (routine) goal-line stands so that when the team encounters this emergency in a game, they are technically and emotionally ready to cope with it.

## Saving Reps' Efforts for Real Emergencies

Physically and psychologically, the human body and mind have special emergency systems built into them. Under conditions of true emergency, we generate extra physical energy, mental keenness, and attention. In emergencies we can do things we would never believe ourselves capable of: the 98-pound woman who lifted a stalled automobile from her child, the computer engineer-salesman who worked 36 straight hours to repair a customer's equipment so the payroll could go out on time. But in these emergency systems, like the storage battery in an automobile, there is only a certain amount of "juice." When it has been used up, the battery is dead. The skillful supervisor-leader recognizes this fact and conserves followers' extra efforts for true emergencies. The good sales supervisor does not try to look like a hero to the boss by constantly driving the reps under trumped-up emergency conditions.

## Leading Under Routine Conditions

Leading under routine conditions is extremely difficult. Normally, emergency conditions involve penalties on followers that compensate for a considerable amount of poor leadership. But routine conditions do not usually contain such penalties. Two examples illustrate this. In Company A sales are down and management had decided that unless sales can be substantially increased, retrenchment in the sales force will be necessary. Some salespeople will have to be laid off. To be sure, in this situation the sales manager must exert leadership, but the situation itself contains penalties for the reps (loss of their jobs) that will compensate for a considerable amount of poor leadership by their supervisor. On the other hand, in Company B every rep on the sales force has exceeded the quarterly quota by at least 10 percent, and there are three weeks remaining in the quarter. This situation requires considerably more leadership skill from the supervisor than the first because there is no built-in penalty for poor followership.

## Roles of the Sales Manager as Leader

In management leadership there is no such thing as "the leadership role." Rather, leadership is multiroled. The supervisor must be capable of playing one of several roles depending on what the situation requires.

Before discussing the leadership roles, we must make it clear that role playing in executive leadership is not unfair, unscrupulous, or double dealing. Quite the contrary, it is the honest and responsible way for a leader to behave. Consider a parallel example. What roles do parents play for their children? You would say they must play many roles: disciplinarian, encourager, loving stabilizer, an example of what it is to be an adult, provider, advisor, educator, and perhaps several more. Note these are all *different* roles. Is it wrong for parents to play these several roles at different times and under different conditions? Is it immoral, unethical for parents to shift from one role to another as the occasion demands? Of course not. In fact, when you consider the matter carefully, it would be wrong for parents not to play these several roles, not to shift from one to another as the situation requires.

So it is with the sales manager in the leadership of sales reps. If one of your people wants advice on how to increase volume with a big account, should you refuse to play the role of advisor? Or if another is discouraged, should you refuse to try to cheer him up? Another is having serious personal financial difficulties. Should you refuse to help her find remedies? Should you refuse to play these and other roles with your reps? Of course not, no more than parents should refuse their children.

It is this legitimate and necessary role-playing aspect of sales management leadership that we are concerned with here. When particular conditions require a particular leadership role response, the leader must play that role and play it well. The major roles the sales manager must be able to play are discussed here.


### "Super Doer"

This is the professional, super-performance, competence dimension of leadership. Since the supervisor knows a great deal about selling, the salespeople respect his or her orders and advice. When you suggest what they should do, they cooperate fully because they know they are receiving instructions or directions from a professional. "Joe, your selling story should emphasize our service policies more than it does now." "Louise, the man who makes the buying decisions for that customer is John Lewis, not Bill Carter whom you have been spending so much time with." "Chris, you'd do a lot better if you brought out our promotion materials earlier in your presentations." When guidance and advice comes from a "super doer" supervisor, the rep tends to cooperate fully and willingly.

### Hero-Inspirer

In this role, the sales manager is the emotional catalyst for the reps, the "spark plug" that makes it all work. This enables followers to attach themselves emotionally to a person and company. Visualize, for example, a medium-sized or large company; an organization of many thousand employees, perhaps a dozen plants, and as many or more warehouse and sales installations—sprawling, faceless, impersonal. How does a person become emotionally attached to such an organization so that he or she is personally motivated to give the last ounce of ability? The answer is through the supervisor in the role of hero-inspirer.

### Innovator

In this role the leader is the source of problem-solving ideas for followers: how to win the big account, how to cover the territory more effectively, how to reduce expenses, how to make better use of promotional materials. When necessary, reps look to the supervisor to play this role for them. "Boss, how should I do it?" The sales manager must answer, or at least help the reps discover their own answers.

### Parent Image

In this role the sales manager is the embodiment of what reps think a parent should be: kindly, loved, respected, fair, but arbiter, judge, and disciplinarian. In this role the manager holds the world steady for followers so they can learn about it: what the rules are, how people are judged, how success is attained, and what constitutes failure.

### Guardian of the Status Quo

In this role the manager speaks for and represents the company to reps and subordinates, and is the source of information about company history, policy, procedures, and "our way of doing things." When necessary, the manager explains and enforces these things.

### Application Exercises

Below are three short leadership problems involving Stan Bates of Saturn Drug. They are incomplete and do not furnish you with the amount of information you would like to have. However, try to decide in each case:

> 1.  *What role does the rep seem to be requesting from Bates?*
> 2.  *What role does Bates seem to be playing?*
> 3.  *What response would you expect from the rep? Why?*

1. Bates has traveled all day in the territory with Tony Belli, whom he sees regularly twice a month and irregularly between times. They are having a drink together in the early evening before the manager returns to Atlanta.

BATES: Well, tell me, Tony, what's your overall impression of how things are going in your territory?

BELLI: I guess I shouldn't complain.

BATES: (smiling) But you are. Is that it?

BELLI: Hell, Stan, you get the reports. You know how it's going! I've tried every trick I know—but it's no good! I'm working evenings, Sundays, and holidays. I'm using all of the promotion material you send out from the office. I'm calling on customers almost twice as often as I used to and nothing seems to work. I still can't get the old sales figure up to quota!

BATES: Well, you know, Tony, how I sweat over those quotas in the office to get them just right, to get them on-target and reasonable. Why, I bet I spent 500 hours revising them on the advice of you field people. It's like our president says: if the quotas are unrealistic, our whole business is based on a fallacy.

2. Steve Malone has called Bates on an urgent matter. The following phone conversation takes place:

MALONE: Look, Stan, I just called to talk to you about a real urgent matter. I've just come from Ace Drugs, and their people say that if we shave just a half cent off our price for "Creon", they'll buy 100,000! That's almost our total for last year! Can we do it?

BATES: Just half a cent? Why, Steve boy, that should be duck soup for a salesman like you! Put on the old charm! Get in there and sell our research, delivery, and credit story! Make 'em see how it's worth far more than a measly half cent a pound to do business with the leader of our industry.

3. Mary Toller has come in to see Bates, and the following conversation takes place:

TOLLER: Last month you said—and I agreed—that Pinecrest Hospital should be ready to buy a slug of our targeted delivery products. Well, I got an appointment for a special presentation to their senior staff, and I cooked up a great presentation for them, down to the last detail of quality, reliability, and performance. Emphasized our product research base. They all said our line was great. Now I find out their pharmaceutical committee has turned us down—and that's that.

BATES: I'm glad you brought this up to me, Mary. I like to know that you feel free to take me into your confidence, to share your troubles with me. When I first started selling with the company, my supervisor was a real hell-for-leather salesman, but not much of a manager. You couldn't get to first base talking out your problem with him. He just told you to go out and solve it yourself. I want to be in on my rep's problems!

## Significance of the Multiroled Nature of Leadership

What did you decide? In the first case did you decide that Tony Belli wanted a parent image response to reassure him, or an innovator to help him solve his problems? What did you decide he received from Bates? Do you think Belli will feel reassured or frustrated?

In the second case was Steve Malone asking for an innovator or some other role? Was he getting back the hero-inspirer, or parent image? If you were Malone, how would you feel after this exchange? Why?

In the third case, did Mary Toller want an innovator or some other role? Was she getting the guardian, parent image, or something else? What do you think the results will be?

These problems are not presented here because there is a right or a wrong answer to them. To be sure, there are better and worse answers. But their purpose is to underline the leadership requirements that follow from the fact that the supervisor-leader must play several roles. We turn now to those critical requirements.

## Multiroled Leadership

As we have seen, there is no such thing as ''the leadership role.'' The sales supervisor must play several roles, changing them as the situation requires. Furthermore, as the preceding exercises demonstrated, determining the proper leadership role in any given situation is a difficult task. Adopting of the improper role can have serious effects on the sales rep.

## Role Action and Reaction

Whether the salesperson recognizes it, when he or she deals with the supervisor, the rep is always requesting *some* role response from the boss. On the other side, the supervisor is always playing *some* role in his or her relations with the rep. The interaction of the role requested by the rep and the supervisor's role response will always produce a result: anger, satisfaction, frustration, pleasure, and so on. We can visualize the relationship as shown in Figure 5-3.

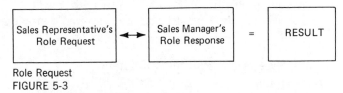

Role Request
FIGURE 5-3

This makes role analysis, discussed later, a particularly critical leadership skill because of two conditions:

1.  For the sales manager, the rep's role request is a given; the manager has to accept it as it is; the manager cannot say to the rep, ''Don't give me that problem, give me another one.''
2.  The good manager has a *specific* result in mind to come from the interaction of role request and response.

So, the manager's problem then is: ''I want this specific result out of this interaction. I can't change the request. So then, what response to the given request has the best chance of achieving the result I want?''
A real event from the sports world illustrates this relationship.

The coach of a professional football team was having difficulties with a star player. Although the player had the physical attributes and skills to be truly outstanding, the coach judged that he was not going "all out." This is the *given* in the role situation; the man was performing at less than full capacity. Obviously, the *result* the coach wanted was all-out performance by the player. What response by the coach is most likely to produce the result he wants? The coach reasoned that the man was not playing to his full capacity because he believed he was so exceptionally skilled that his position on the first team was secure even without his full effort. The coach benched him at the start of several games in a row (role response). After four games, the coach was well satisfied that the player was consistently performing to full capacity.

### Role Skills

Good manager-leaders are skilled in executing all of the leadership roles. However, each of us is particularly skilled in one or another leadership role. Some roles just "come naturally" because of our personality, upbringing, and experience. We can all identify leaders we know who are naturally great parent images or innovators. But by the same token, other leadership roles do not come naturally to us. For example, a supervisor who is naturally a good guardian of the status quo is quite likely to be a poor innovator. This being the case, we must carefully analyze each of our leadership role strengths and weaknesses and deliberately work to improve performance in those roles that are not natural to us.

## THE NATURE OF "FOLLOWERSHIP"

Why do salespeople cooperate fully with good supervisor-leaders? We saw earlier that salespeople can choose the degree to which they cooperate with you as the manager at any level above the minimum cooperation point, at which they will be fired. We also saw that if they choose to cooperate at less than full capacity, they generate costs that could be avoided if they were well led. This raises two basic questions. What determines the degree of cooperation a salesperson chooses to deliver to the leader-manager? How does leadership affect the degree of cooperation? The answers constitute the subject of this section.

## A "Contractual" Relationship

A contract is, of course, an agreement between two or more parties under which each receives and gives something of value. In this sense the leader-follower relationship is a contract. It is not a written contract, nor is it sometimes even consciously recognized, but it is, nevertheless, a contract under which the leader and the follower each give something of value in return for receiving something of value. This concept of the contractual nature of the leader-follower relationship is critical in understanding why the follower chooses the degree of cooperation he or she does; why the rep generates or avoids the costs of low cooperation.

## What Salespeople Give
## under the Followership "Contract"

In the contract of leadership and followership, the things the sales reps give that the supervisor values are: their time, energy, skills, attention, loyalty, interest, extra effort, imagination, knowledge, devotion, and—sometimes—physical discomfort. These values can be given completely or partly withheld (short of the cut-off point) at the reps' discretion. In a very real sense, these are the qualities and activities the follower "has for sale" under the "contract."

## The Follower's "Prices"
## for Complete Cooperation

If the reps give you the values they have to offer under the "contract" and do not receive what they require in return, they are frustrated, dissatisfied, produce at a low level, generate avoidable costs, and often quit. If, however, they receive a full measure of what they require in return, their job satisfaction and productivity are high, and they do not generate the avoidable costs of less than complete cooperation. What the rep requires of the leader in order to deliver complete cooperation is discussed here.

### To Be Understood

As human beings we all demand to be understood by those whose opinions we value, but understanding is difficult because each of us is a complex bundle of physical, psychological, and economic desires and drives. Furthermore, the understanding we desire from various people is not the same kind. We want many different kinds of understanding. For example, salesman Joe Klein wants to be understood by his wife, by the tax man who handles his returns, by his children, and by you as manager. But he does not want the same kind or degree of understanding from each. The understanding that sales reps want from supervisors is most like the understanding they want from their spouses. This is the kind of understanding that can overcome the treacheries of communication, surmount their own inability to understand themselves and occasionally their own deliberate efforts to hide feelings and meaning. They want the kind of understanding from their leader that can translate words into meaning; that when the rep *says* about an important customer, "That damn old grouch! Always giving me problems. I'm fed up!", what the rep *means* is, "He's a tough customer, but I'm going back again next week!" Sales reps want the kind of understanding that when they ask, "How'd we do last quarter?", they really mean, "If you have any pats on the back, I could use one right now."

## To Be Valued

If the sales rep is to cooperate to the fullest extent, one "price" is that the manager should value two elements—the rep as a person and the rep's work. Ideally, the sales manager values both. This is not always possible due to personality differences, but if the supervisor does not at least value the person's work, the rep should be fired.

## To Contribute

To follow to the fullest extent of their capacities, salespeople must know, or be shown, how they contribute to the work of the company and the sales force. On the surface this requirement for ardent followership appears too obvious to require special attention. You might say: "It should be no mystery to salespeople what they contribute. They contribute sales income to the company." But we must remember the nature of the command hierarchy and the information system in a company. The command hierarchy is a pyramid or a triangle, as shown in Figure 5-4.

At the top resides the most power, and at this level there are the fewest people (ultimately in most companies just a single person). At successively lower levels of the hierarchy we find more and more people, with less and less power, until we reach the lowest level where the sales

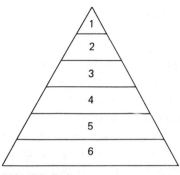

FIGURE 5-4

reps are located. But if we consider the company's organization structure not as a command and power hierarchy, but as an information system, we would have another pyramid or triangle. However, it would be inverted as in Figure 5-5.

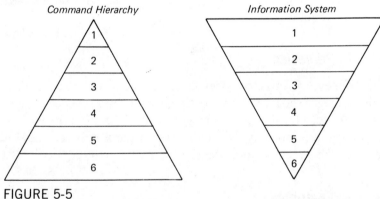

FIGURE 5-5

The information system diagram shows us that the most information about the company's policies, prospects, plans, and operations resides at the top and the least information exists at the bottom. In addition it shows us that less and less information is known at progressively lower levels in the organization.

Applying this analysis to the problem of the need for salespeople to contribute and the need for them to know how and why they contribute, we find that the leadership problem is less simple than we might have first thought. When orders and directions for the sales rep's participation pass between levels in the command hierarchy, they also pass between information levels as in Figure 5-6.

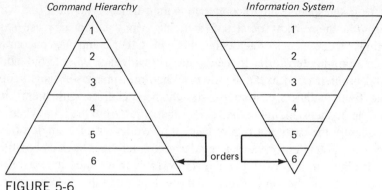

FIGURE 5-6

Therefore, orders or directions for the rep's participation that are sensible and obvious on the basis of the information available to you on level 5 may make no sense at all on the basis of the information available to the reps on level 6.

Never assume that, on the basis of information available to them, salespeople recognize how what they are asked to do contributes to the overall sales results, simply because it is apparent to you on the basis of the information you possess. Their contributions must be explained clearly to them at all times.

## To Belong

As Maslow observed, humans are social animals. We crave companionship and satisfying social intercourse. In fact, our society has three degrees of severity of criminal punishment. The second most severe punishment is solitary confinement. People have gone mad in solitary confinement.

At first it might seem that providing sales reps with satisfactory social relationships is not a particularly difficult task. After all, it could be argued, the essence of their job is to work with people and to interact socially with customers. But this is not the case, because the kind of social interaction the rep requires as a human being is not the buyer-seller relationship, no matter how friendly a rep may be with a particular customer. In essence the selling relationship is competitive, not social. The customer "wins" by getting the best product and the most service at the lowest possible price. The salesperson "wins" by getting the highest possible price at the least cost.

If salespeople are to cooperate to their fullest, you must find ways to provide them with social satisfactions. Many companies use sales meetings as one means of achieving this end. Other companies encourage reps in adjoining territories to meet regularly with each other to talk about mutual problems and exchange ideas. When the supervisor visits people in the field, calls on customers with them, socializes with them after hours, he or she is adding to the social satisfaction from the job. When, as is frequently the case, a group of sales reps works out of a single office, there is the potential for various regular group activities such as bowling, golf, bridge, or poker. But whatever form it may take, it is a prime responsibility of the supervisor, to the extent possible, to see that the salespeople are able to relate themselves to some satisfying social group.

## To Be Buffered, Protected

The last "price" for followers' full cooperation that we will discuss is the demand that their leader protect them from unnecessary pressures and diversions, or at least that the supervisor pass these pressures on to them in the proper amount and at the proper time. They want their leader to act as a screen, not as a magnifying glass.

All organizations, and business is no exception, generate diversionary pressures on operating people. These diversions distract their attention from the work they are doing. Some of these diversions, such as special market intelligence reports from field reps, are necessary, but many, such as intemperate criticism by a superior to a rep's supervisor, are unnecessary.

Salespeople require the supervisor to plan the impact of these diversions on their selling work. They require that the supervisor not pass on to them diversions that they do not need to know or participate in. They expect a supervisor to make them aware of these pressures only at a time when they need to know about them.

The supervisor should not magnify the diversions. "Headquarters wants the reps to make a two-page report on the competitor's new product. Just to be sure, I'll tell them to submit 10-page reports." Or, "The big boss gave me 10 degrees of hell about Jim's poor work during the last month. I'll give Jim 50 degrees of hell about it!" This is magnification, not buffering.

Reps are not asking their supervisors to sabotage higher management or to withhold necessary information and assignments. They are asking their leader to protect them from unnecessary diversions, not to magnify them when they are transmitted, and to plan carefully when and how the reps will be informed of them.

### Learning Exercise

*Consider once again Stan Bates and Saturn Drug. How could Bates go about providing his reps with the "prices" they require for their complete cooperation? Be as specific as you can.*

_____

_____

_____

## HUMAN RELATIONS SKILLS IN SALES LEADERSHIP

The preceding section explored "followership," what encourages salespeople to cooperate with their supervisor to the fullest extent of their capacities, and thereby avoid the dollar costs of less than complete cooperation. We saw that the leadership-followership relationship is an unwritten "contract." The degree of followers' cooperation is importantly determined by how well or how poorly they judge the supervisor is abiding by the "contract": by how well they are led. We now turn our attention to a consideration of how the supervisor-leader "pays" the "prices" that the followers place on their full cooperation.

### Human Relations Defined

The supervisor pays the prices of full cooperation by expert use of the skills we call the human relations skills of executive leadership. Human relations is the art of creating and maintaining organizational cooperation for maximum efficiency, low cost, and high personal job satisfaction.

In this section we will study six of the more important human relations skills: management by objectives, perception, conceptionalization, delegation, communication, and self-awareness. We will also suggest ways to develop and improve these skills.

## Management by Objectives

Followers' "prices" that we have just discussed are the basis for one of the most recent developments in supervision—management by objectives or MBO. For many this popular term is frightening, but it should not be because it simply describes a commonsense approach to achieving the cooperation of subordinates by good leadership techniques.

MBO began as a management planning and decision-making process at the very top levels of a few large companies. In this form it is indeed very complex. But now MBO has sifted down to the supervisory level and is widely used in industry. Here it is useful and easy to understand.

For the sales supervisor at any level, MBO involves:

1. Careful study of the history and operations of the sales unit in question.
2. Identification of specific objectives for the unit and personal objectives for each rep over a specified period of time, for example, increase market share by 5 percent in the next fiscal year; reps participate in setting these goals.
3. Translation of the objectives into definite target activities, for example, increase our market share 5 percent by adding 200 new retail customers.
4. Assignment of the target activities to the various units of the sales organization (sales districts, regions, and so on), for example, sales representative Billingsley will add five new customers, Krum will add 15.
5. Communication of the objectives, target activities, and timetable to the salespeople so that they understand specifically what is required and that their performance during the period will be evaluated against these standards.
6. During the MBO cycle, the sales manager provides feedback and guides, coaches, and encourages the reps on attaining their specific objectives and target activities.
7. At the end of the cycle, the sales reps are evaluated against the original objectives that were established.

There are two important payoffs for MBO. First, salespeople must look at themselves and their activities against specific goals they have helped to set. Second, during the MBO cycle, sales managers and reps have specific guidelines for their activities and established performance measures.

The disadvantages of MBO are that it is expensive and time-consuming. However, the experience of many companies shows that the advantages are well worth the costs of this procedure.

## Perception

The executive leader must be skilled at perceiving the meanings and causes of individual and group behavior. In short, perception is the ability to look *and* see, to listen *and* hear. Without perception the supervisor cannot understand and value his people, cannot show them how they contribute and belong to a social group, cannot buffer them. The supervisor can pay none of the prices for their complete cooperation unless he can perceive them.

To the perceptive supervisor everything has potential meaning that may explain individual and group behavior, no matter how trivial the evidence may seem. The perceptive supervisor's radar is always in motion. He has sandpapered fingers. Nothing that might possibly be useful to perceive his people is overlooked. To quote Shakespeare, "He hears sermons in stones and songs in trees."

But what is most critical: the perceptive supervisor perceives meaning and evidence from the things that are normally expected to transmit meaning, *as well as from those things that are not normally expected to contain messages.* For instance, letters, reports, phone calls, telegrams, and special studies are expected to transmit meaning to help the supervisor understand the meaning and causes of individual and group behavior. But here the nonperceptive supervisor stops: the perceptive leader looks elsewhere for meaning other than simply from those media that are normally expected to transmit messages. Perceptive managers study rumors, mistakes, accidents, facial expressions, and tones of voice, noting what is *not* said or written, as well as what is. They seek meaning in new or changed behavior patterns. They gauge their reps' morale from perceptive meanings.

## Conceptual Ability

Conceptual ability is the process by which we relate and understand everything that happens to us. It is the way we decode and unscramble experience. Conceptual ability is the means by which you understand who you are, who your people are, what your company is, what selling is, why your company is in business—indeed, how you understand everything around you. We all must have a conceptual scheme. Without one we would have to invent the wheel every time we faced a transportation problem. There are two critical aspects of conceptualization in high-quality, sales executive leadership: the mutual understanding of conceptual schemes between individuals and the relative accuracy and reality of your own conceptual scheme.

First, there must be mutual understanding by the leader and the follower of the conceptual scheme on which they are each working. That is, are they both decoding their experiences in the same or different ways? Unless they are on the same wave length (conceptual scheme), there can be no effective working relationship, communication, rapport, or leadership. For example, if someone tells you that $2 + 2 = 6$, you will say that this is wrong. But if the person goes on to say that $4 + 4 = 10$, you can answer when the person asks you what $6 + 6$ is, because you have come to understand the particular conceptual scheme on which he or she is working. And you will have recognized that it is different from the conceptual scheme you are using. Your concept is that $X + Y = Z$. The concept of the person who gave you the problem is $X + Y$ *plus 2* $= Z$. Now you decide which of the two conceptual schemes to use and together you can solve any similar mathematical problem. But without a mutual understanding of the conceptual schemes on which you are working together, you are helpless to cooperate with each other.

Now let us consider an example from selling. An important customer has drastically cut back a large order with only vague and evasive explanations. The sales rep's diagnosis (conceptualization) of the cause of the problem is price. But the supervisor sees (conceptualizes) the situation as a step in the customer's planned product line changeover to higher quality. Neither the rep nor supervisor explains to each other their conceptualizations of the problem, but they try together to seek a solution. Since they are working on two different conceptual schemes, they are wasting their time, and no practical solution is possible.

The second problem is the degree of reality of the conceptual scheme as it relates to effective executive leadership. As the previous discussion indicated, everyone must have some conceptual scheme by which to decode and arrange experience and life data. Without such a scheme, we are helpless to understand anything or take any action, except by completely random, toss-of-the coin reactions. But the effectiveness of the leader's and followers' actions is also the result of the realism of their conceptual scheme, that is, the accuracy with which the conceptual scheme reflects the real world.

When a person's conceptual scheme is totally incapable of explaining reality, we judge the person to be neurotic or insane. The paranoid has a conceptual scheme; he or she decodes everything that happens as a threat to life and safety. In its extreme form, this conceptual scheme is so strong that we put such people under confinement because they become a threat to themselves and others.

In a less dramatic, nonetheless critical, manner, the sales manager's conceptual scheme is pivotal to leadership. The accuracy with which the conceptual scheme reflects the realities of the supervisory situation and that of the reps importantly determines the manager's effectiveness as a leader.

One commonly encountered manifestation of an unrealistic conceptual scheme occurs when a sales rep is promoted to a supervisory position and thereafter fails to recognize that market conditions have changed since he or she worked the territory. Consequently, the new manager manages the reps, evaluates their activities, issues them instructions, and interprets what they are doing against conditions that existed when the manager was a sales rep, not against conditions as they are now.

People are imperfect, and no one's concepts can ever perfectly reflect the real world. But supervisor-leaders must constantly question their concepts of themselves and their reps to ensure that to the greatest degree possible they are realistic and meaningful. You must ask such questions as:

- Why do I work? Why do my reps work?
- Are the quick and easy answers to those questions the right answers?
- What is the function of sales in my company?
- Why does my company exist? What do I really do? Should I be doing these things?
- Do my people and I see (conceptualize) events in the same way? Could we improve our mutual conceptualizations? How?
- What do our customers really want from us? Are we providing these things? How?
- What are the real conditions in our market?

By constantly asking questions such as these, the supervisor-leader ensures that his or her concepts of self, job, role in the company, and of the reps are as close to reality as possible.

## Delegation

Many people believe that "if you want something done right, do it yourself." This notion has no place in good supervisory leadership! The people who sell are evaluated importantly on how well they sell. Sales managers are evaluated on how well their reps sell. This makes it necessary for sales managers to *delegate* many of the responsibilities for territory management and sales performance to their subordinates.

Delegation is a hard skill for new managers to learn and especially so if the new manager has been a successful sales rep. Often these people do not delegate because:

- It is risky. The manager is evaluated on the reps' performance and they may foul up.
- Within the company's broad guidelines, delegation means that sales reps manage their territory in their own way; the manager may feel their way is not the best way.
- The manager does not understand or trust the information system that is designed to keep him or her informed of market developments and rep performance. The manager believes that only personal observation and active participation in the reps' work will provide the necessary operating information.

But the sales manager *must delegate*. There simply is not enough time for the manager to take on all of the reps' sales problems and at the same time do a good job of managing them. There are at least two steps the manager should take to make delegation more effective and less risky:

- Constantly coach, train, and counsel reps on sales techniques and good territory management; help and encourage them to become effective problem solvers on their own.
- Study the company's sales information system carefully. Does it furnish the facts you need, in the necessary detail and at the proper time? Do you completely understand and trust the system? Are you using it effectively?

No one can deny that there is an element of personal risk for the manager in delegation. Some reps may foul up, making the manager look poor to the boss. But the essence of management is getting things done *through people,* and this demands the development of the management skill of delegation.

## Communication Skills

The leadership skills of communication are the abilities to recognize the differences in individuals and in meanings and to use this recognition to transmit and receive messages accurately.

Without the ability to communicate effectively, a manager cannot execute the required roles of leadership—"superdoer," innovator, parent image, and so on. Without the ability to communicate, the manager cannot transmit to followers that they are valued, contribute, and belong. In short, without the ability to communicate, the leader cannot lead.

It is important to recognize two major aspects of leadership communication. First, communication takes place through several media and the supervisor must be skilled in the use of all of them. The manager communicates by various written media: reports, letters, memoranda, or telegrams; also verbally, face-to-face, with reps and customers and by telephone. *But equally important, supervisors communicate by behavior,* by a smile or a frown, by tone of voice, by a pat on the back, by the firmness of a handshake, by how they conduct themselves in the presence of others, by what they do and do not do.

Second, effective communication is *consistent communication:* one message must not contradict another. For example, a memo is sent out to all salespeople, directing them to reduce their expenses, but when the sales manager travels with them, they are taken to the most expensive restaurants in town and the supervisor travels short distances by taxicab. The various media of communication between the sales manager and reps must reinforce, not contradict, each other.

## Self-Awareness

This is the leader's ability to recognize that he or she is an integral part of the management and leadership process. The traditional way of explaining and understanding management and executive leadership is that it is the responsibility of the manager to decide what must be done, to direct that it be done, and to check that it is done. The subordinate is expected to follow orders. This is the "mechanistic" concept of management. It conceives management and executive leadership as if they were like driving a car. If the automobile is in proper working order, the engine starts when the ignition key is turned on, it backs up when put in the proper gear, and accelerates when the correct pedal is pressed. It does not matter who is driving the car. So with the mechanistic concept of management—when followers are directed to do something, they do it.

But, as we developed earlier, this is no longer a realistic way to understand executive leadership and management. Sales management is not an objective process like driving a car or doing a crossword puzzle. *Sales managers are an integral part of their own leadership.* Sales executive leadership does not take place at arm's length. It is not simply a matter of turning the key in the ignition or filling in the right words in the right spaces in the puzzle.

The skilled sales manager not only realizes this critical requirement for management, but welcomes it and is skilled at managing it. He or she realizes that the followership conditions and problems with sales reps are what they are because the manager is involved with them. Skilled managers are self-aware. They do not insist on leading at arms length. They are willing and able to be a part of their reps own leadership, playing the leadership roles well and delivering the required motivations to their reps so they will follow to the complete extent of their abilities.

## Brain teasers

|  | Agree | Disagree |
|---|---|---|
| 1. Turnover of sales reps is independent of motivation. | ____ | ____ |
| 2. All human behavior is pointed toward a goal. | ____ | ____ |
| 3. Most people will satisfy their social needs first. | ____ | ____ |
| 4. Unless a sales force has high morale, it will be impossible to motivate the salespeople. | ____ | ____ |
| 5. If sales managers know the few basic rules of supervisory leadership, they are equipped to handle any leadership problems they may encounter. | ____ | ____ |
| 6. It requires no particular skill for the supervisor-leader to identify emergency leadership conditions. | ____ | ____ |
| 7. There is no such thing as a supervisory leadership role. | ____ | ____ |

8. The supervisor-leader should always respond with the role the sales rep requests.          _____  _____

9. Because the leadership role requested and the response delivered will inevitably have some result, the leader must choose the role response carefully.          _____  _____

10. In executive leadership it is useful to consider the corporation's formal organization as both a command hierarchy and an information system.          _____  _____

## Activities

1. *Think about a close friend or coworker. Do you really understand the person? What are his or her needs? Does Maslow's need hierarchy give you a better understanding of the person's behavior?* _____

_____

_____

_____

2. *George Patton, the colorful World War II general, once said: "I don't want them (his troops) to like me, I want them to fight for me." Does this statement have any meaning for sales management? Why, or why not?* _____

_____

_____

_____

3. *Analyze a recent important action that you have taken. What factors influenced your behavior? What were your goals? What motives guided your actions?* _____

_____

_____

_____

4. *In the first few months of his new job, Stan Bates encountered these sales personnel problems. How do you think he should handle them? What are your reasons?*

a) *Jeff Dobson was married a little over a year ago. Since his marriage, he has gone deeply into debt for clothing, furniture, and household appliances. Several installment payments are due every week and he has trouble just keeping his books straight. His sales have begun to suffer, and he has come to Stan Bates for help. He claims his many creditors and charge account obligations are taking his mind off his work.*

_____

_____

b) *Betty Watson has been guilty of several violations of sales ethics. She has misrepresented the company's products, made false delivery commitments, or been rude to some customers. Whenever a customer or doctor complains about mistreatment or she is caught in an inaccuracy, Watson attempts to explain her action with half-truths. A customer has just refused to accept one of her orders. Watson insists the factory made a mistake, but the factory's original copy of the order indicates that she was wrong again.*

_____

_____

c) *Bob Shelton is an aggressive young salesman who has a remarkable sales record. For the three years he has been with the company, he was the top rep in his district and one of the top 10 in the country. Six months ago, his district manager was promoted to a home office position, and Stan Bates was appointed to succeed him. Since then Shelton's sales have slumped, and he is now closer to the bottom than to the top of the district.*

_____

_____

5. *Identify a poor salesperson you know. What avoidable costs does this individual probably generate?* _____

_____

_____

6. *Have you or your company ever experienced a situation that seemed to be a routine problem, but which actually turned out*

to be an emergency? Why did you at first consider it to be routine? What alerted you to the fact that it was an emergency?

_____

_____

7. Consider a sales manager you know well (perhaps yourself). What sales management "role" does this manager play best naturally? What role or roles does he or she not play so well? How could this manager improve?_____

_____

_____

8. Identify a particular order or direction given by a supervisor to a subordinate. As best you can, make two lists: one of the background information the supervisor possessed concerning the order, the other of the information the subordinate had. Do the two lists match? If not, why and what result would you anticipate because the two sets of information do not match?_____

_____

_____

## SELECTED REFERENCES

### Understanding Behavior

BERELSON, BERNARD, and GARY A. STEINER, *Human Behavior: An Inventory of Scientific Findings*. New York: Harcourt, 1964.

KOLASA, BLAIR J., *Introduction to Behavioral Science for Business*. New York: Wiley, 1969.

LEAVITT, HAROLD J., *Managerial Psychology* (4th ed.). Chicago: University of Chicago Press, 1978.

### Motivation Theory and Management

HERZBERG, FREDERICK, "One More Time: How Do You Motivate Employees?" *Harvard Business Review* (January-February, 1968), pp. 53–62.

MASLOW, ABRAHAM H., *Motivation and Personality* (2nd ed.). New York: Harper, 1970.

McGregor, Douglas, *The Human Side of Enterprise*. New York: McGraw-Hill, 1960.

## Sales Management Leadership and Supervision

Hanan, Mack, and others. "How to Motivate Your Sales Force," in *Take-Charge Sales Management*. New York: Amacom, 1976.
Jolson, Marvin A., "The Salesman's Career Cycle." *Journal of Marketing* (July 1974), pp. 39–46.
Markin, Rom J., and Charles M. Lillis, "Sales Managers Get What They Expect," *Business Horizons* (June 1975), pp. 51–58.
Mossian, Herbert, and Eugene H. Fram, "Segmentation for Sales Force Motivation." *Akron Business and Economic Review* (Winter 1973), pp. 5–12.
Newton, Derek A., "Get the Most Out of Your Sales Force." *Harvard Business Review* (September-October, 1969), pp. 130–43.
Stanton, William J., and Richard H. Buskirk, "Sales Force Morale," in *Management of the Sales Force* (5th ed.). Homewood, Ill.: Richard D. Irwin, 1978.

## Basic Human Relations Skills

Brown, Ronald, "Effective Communications," in *From Selling to Managing*. New York: Amacom, 1968.
Scanlon, Burt K., *Management 18: A Short Course for Managers*. New York: Wiley Professional Development Programs, 1974.
Stroh, Thomas F., "Sales Management Communications," in *Managing the Sales Function*. New York: McGraw-Hill, 1978.

# 6

# SALES FORCE INCENTIVES AND COMPENSATION

*After reading this chapter, you should be able to demonstrate your learning as follows:*

- *Considering the needs of salespeople, identify specific incentives to motivate them individually and as a group.*
- *Against specific sales objectives, select and plan incentives to encourage sales personnel to achieve each objective.*
- *Given a sales compensation plan, evaluate the plan and suggest improvements.*
- *With a specific sales job description and the company sales objectives in mind, design a sales force compensation plan.*

In Chapter 5, we explored the role of the sales manager as a leader. Through day-to-day contacts, the field sales manager is perhaps the most effective motivator of his or her people. The manager sets the style and tone for their relationship with the company. However, personal supervision is limited by the time available to the manager for this activity. Other incentives, including compensation, are required to motivate people who sell.

The first task is to discover what each individual on the sales force needs or wants. A manager cannot motivate salespeople unless he or she understands their desires. Part of this task is to develop an awareness of human behavior. The theories and concepts of motivation presented in the preceding chapter provide this background. But a general awareness of motivation is not enough. The sales manager must also identify the individual needs of salespeople. Tom Reynolds has four children and a mortgage; he is concerned with security. Rose Page is single; she wants to meet new friends and have an active social life. Obviously, Tom's needs and Rose's needs are different. The incentives used to motivate them must be different.

The special cases of sales trainees and older salespeople present special motivation problems. It is hard to motivate sales trainees who must undergo long breaking-in periods before they are productive. It is difficult to give them a feeling of accomplishment. Older sales personnel present a different challenge. Sometimes there are limits on what they can earn or they may feel that their personal growth is restricted. Often, older salespeople feel that their occupation lacks prestige and acceptance within the company. They no longer see a clear opportunity for advancement.

Talking with and observing your people will provide insights into their behavior. The sales manager must then choose the proper incentives to motivate sales personnel. The manager must provide the conditions for motivation: opportunities for growth, achievement, participation, responsibility, and recognition. Also, the sales manager must ensure that the basic conditions for good morale are provided: adequate pay, satisfactory working facilities, and social opportunities, as discussed in Chapter 5.

## Case Study

Before we consider the various types of incentives for salespeople and the kinds and characteristics of good compensation plans, it will be helpful for you to have a base from which to consider these topics. To do this, think about the salespeople you know personally. Read the Corelli Realty Agency case and answer the questions that follow. These are the kind of people we are trying to motivate by effective incentive and compensation plans. Keep these people in mind as you study the topics that follow.

### Corelli Realty Agency

Corelli Realty employs 12 full-time sales representatives and specializes in residential properties in and around a large eastern city. The agency has been in business for 30 years under the management of Andrew Corelli.

Recently, Corelli began to wonder how effective his compensation plan is in motivating his salespeople to achieve their maximum sales potential. After considerable study and thought, he retained a consultant and asked her to decide "if our reimbursement plan is the best way to bring out the maximum potential of our salespeople."

Real estate industry practice in sales compensation varies somewhat from agency to agency; however, the plan Corelli uses is quite common in the industry. Corelli's salespeople are paid on straight commission. The agency's total commission is seven percent of the selling price of the property. The seven percent commission is divided in this way: 27.5 percent to the listing salesperson, 27.5 percent to the Corelli salesperson who makes the sale, and 45 percent to the agency for profit and overhead expenses, such as advertising, office space and taxes. The listing salesperson is the individual who secured the original registration of the property with Corelli. Salespeople perform both listing and sales functions. It happens sometimes, therefore, that the listing and selling person are the same for a particular property.

As part of her study, the consultant interviewed four salespeople whom Corelli identified as typical of the force. In these informal interviews, the consultant wanted to find out what the sales reps thought of their jobs and their remuneration. Some conversations from these interviews follow.

*Susan Makepeace* (age 23; seven months with the agency): "I'm just beginning to find out what this business is all about. I'm beginning to make enough so that at least I can start to enjoy some of the things I want, like ski weekends, neat posters for my apartment, and clothes that aren't just left over from college. I could get to love the real estate business!"

*John Tavonini* (age 37; four years with the agency): "To be honest, basically I want to make money, a lot of money! Not for money itself, but for the good things money can get for me and my family, security, a few extras, things like that. I've worked my tail off since I came with Corelli, but that's okay because now I'm beginning to rake it in. And I like that!"

*Barbara Caldwell* (age 47; fifteen years with the agency): "I took this job when my husband died and I had two kids and no money. I hated it, but it paid the bills. When my last child got married three years ago, it was just me and this job. I decided to see if I really liked it, or I'd quit. The last few years I liked it. It's not really a business, it's helping people buy what they really want and need. You don't sell houses like you sell used cars. You help your clients by giving them information they need, counseling and advising them. You're a professional, not a huckster."

*Sol Morse* (age 60; thirty years with the agency): "I've been with Andy Corelli since he set up shop. I was his first salesman. We've seen a lot of ups and downs together. But looking back, it's been fun. Sometimes though, I think it was better in the old days. You know, milk and crackers in the back room for lunch, and all that. Now we got electric typewriters, a computer terminal, sassy secretaries, and carpets on the floor."

As another part of her investigation, the consultant asked Corelli to explain his philosophy of motivating salespeople. Part of what he said was: "Salespeople work for the money. They always have and they always will. That's how I got started in this business in the first place. I'm hoping you'll come up with a plan to put more zing in our compensation plan without putting the agency into bankruptcy."

*What seem to be the prime motivators or job interests of the four salespeople the consultant interviewed?* _____

_____

_____

_____

*Do you think Corelli's philosophy of sales motivation is correct? What are your reasons?* _____

_____

_____

_____

*Without adding very much to sales costs, what additional motivational activities could Corelli consider for his salespeople?* _____

_____

_____

_____

## INCENTIVE PLAN OBJECTIVES

The first step in designing or re-evaluating an incentive plan is for the sales manager to have a clear idea of the specific objectives to be achieved and, if the manager has more than one goal in mind, the relative importance of each objective. William L. White, a specialist in sales force incentives, suggests that there are typical objectives for financial as well as nonfinancial incentive programs.

- Attain assigned sales volumes (sell volume or unit quotas).
- Reduce selling costs (increase profits by cutting controllable selling expenses).
- Add new accounts (produce accounts that purchase more than an assigned minimum during a time period).
- Sell high margin products (increase profits by selling products with maximum gross margin).
- Sell new products (make the added sales effort necessary to introduce new products to the market).
- Sell products in oversupply (make added efforts to clear heavy inventories).
- Cultivate territory more intensively (obtain a greater portion of the business of present accounts).
- Participate in a team effort (group selling).
- Perform nonselling functions (contribute to the achievement of other marketing objectives).[1]

## TYPES OF INCENTIVES

In addition to personal supervision, there are two other major ways to motivate people who sell: financial and nonfinancial incentives. Like leadership, their purpose is to stimulate salespeople to use their energies and resources more effectively. They may provide a special effort incentive or a continuing incentive. A sales contest is an example of a special effort incentive since a contest is designed to achieve a specific, short-term goal. On the other hand, compensation and promotion are related to the achievement of continuing, long-term objectives.

### Nonfinancial Incentives

Nonfinancial incentives for people who sell include a variety of techniques used for specific, special-effort situations. Sales conventions

---

[1] William L. White, "Incentives for Salesmen: Designing a Plan That Works," *Management Review* (February 1977), p. 26.

and meetings, sales contests, honors and recognition, and communication are the major forms of nonfinancial incentives.

These incentives are usually designed to achieve one or two specific, short-range objectives. However, they must be coordinated with the company's long-range marketing goals and overall motivation program. For example, if your company has an overall goal of balanced sales between the various products, it would be foolish to introduce a sales contest that encourages the salespeople to emphasize a specific product line.

### Financial Incentives

Business organizations provide two forms of financial rewards. Financial incentives may be direct monetary payments (salaries, wages, and such), or they may be indirect monetary rewards. Indirect rewards, commonly known as fringe benefits, include paid vacations, insurance plans, and pension programs.

Financial incentives are the most widely used and misunderstood means for motivating sales personnel. Some sales managers feel strongly that money is the only way to motivate their people. They are wrong, Financial remuneration is an important motivator, but nonfinancial incentives cannot be ignored. In particular, money as a motivator decreases in importance once a satisfactory level of earnings has been reached. However, up to that point, salespeople will strive hard to reach and maintain a satisfactory standard of living.

Financial incentives have changed in recent years. Many more sales reps are now paid through a combination of salary and commission or bonus than used to be. Such plans provide stability of earnings and a direct incentive. Also, fringe benefits have become a more important part of the average income of people who sell. These and other trends will be discussed in a later section on compensation.

### SALES MEETINGS AND CONVENTIONS

Almost every sales manager is involved in planning and conducting sales meetings or conventions. Local meetings attended by salespeople from one sales office or district are usually held weekly or monthly. Conventions, which are held once or twice a year, are national or regional gatherings of sales personnel.

As a means of motivating salespeople, sales meetings and conventions should be designed for specific purposes. For example, a sales meeting or convention can emphasize training material, such as explaining the firm's advertising campaign, assisting sales personnel to improve their sales techniques, and providing new product information. Or a meeting can be used to communicate changes in company policies or information on current market trends.

Authorities agree that poor sales meetings are one of the most common and important mistakes that field sales managers make. Effective conventions and meetings are strong motivators, but poor meetings are a waste of everyone's time and the company's money. The keys to a good meeting are planning and participation.

### Planning

The first step in planning a sales meeting is to specify the objective for the meeting. The objective must be set in conjunction with the company's overall marketing and sales objectives. Major automobile manufacturers, for instance, orient their annual dealer meetings toward the goal of introducing the new models to dealers and the press. Once the objective for the meeting has been established, the sales manager must decide on the theme, the time and place for the meeting, the agenda, timetable, and the administrative arrangements.

### Theme

Every sales convention should have a theme. This serves as a guide in planning the agenda and stimulates enthusiasm. For the salespeople, the theme indicates the basic purpose of the meeting. It is not necessary that each individual weekly or monthly sales meeting have a distinct theme. However, a general theme for the month or quarter can provide a useful orientation for the regular sales meetings.

Themes for sales conventions are almost unlimited. Frequently, sales conventions are run in conjunction with sales contests, and a joint theme is used for both. Sports, college life, current events, and exotic places are commonly used themes for sales conventions. For example, Sales and Marketing Executives International's Graduate School of Sales Management and Marketing uses a college theme. The faculty director is the dean, executive participants elect class officers, athletic competition is held between classes, and a graduation ceremony is conducted.

## Time and Place

It is essential that arrangements be made far in advance so that a sales convention will not conflict with other activities. It is best to schedule meetings at times when they will not seriously interfere with normal selling activities. In addition, most good hotels and meeting facilities are booked months, even years, ahead. Consequently, forward planning is required to make sure the desired facilities are available when you want them. Annual conventions should be held when business is slack, perhaps during the summer or during the Easter or Christmas seasons.

Selecting a meeting place involves many considerations. For example, the location of the meeting can indicate the relative emphasis of the meeting as between work or pleasure. The size of the group will be a major factor in selecting the type of facility. It is often important to get the sales force away from their normal surroundings. This rules out company facilities. Other considerations are convenience, type of accommodations desired, equipment and meeting rooms, food service, and reputation of the facility. Airport motels are especially popular as meeting places because of their easy accessibility and their interest in catering to business groups.

## Agenda and Timetable

The agenda and timetable establish the basic structure and sequence of the meeting. It is essential that a written agenda and timetable be developed during the planning stages. As plans progress, these will be revised.

The final agenda and timetable serve as the program for the meeting. Topics, speakers and discussion leaders, times and places of sessions, and recreation activities are included. It is a good idea to give the salespeople a printed program in advance so they will know exactly what they will be doing.

## Administrative Arrangements

There are many details to attend to when planning and conducting a sales convention. If the manager has prepared well, many of these details will automatically be taken care of. Space arrangements, food, speakers, and recreation facilities must all be considered in advance.

Usually the meeting planner should visit the facility prior to the meeting. Establishing effective communications with the staff of the facility is critical. They need to be informed of your requirements. It is especially important to inform the convention site's sales and catering staff of any special services, personnel, or facilities that will be needed. During the meeting, the sales manager should continue to work closely with the staff of the convention facility.

One effective method for handling these details is a checklist. Charles L. Lapp and Jack R. Dauner present several useful checklists and planning charts in their guide, *Conducting Sales Meetings.*[2] Below is a meeting room checklist.

- Availability of room.
- Size: length and width.
- Ceiling height.
- Ventilation.
- Lighting.
- Acoustics.
- Availability to food and beverage service.
- Location of rest rooms.
- Location of coat room.
- Electrical outlets.
- Public address facilities.
- Accessibility.
- Labor union considerations.
- Quietness (inside).
- Location of telephones.
- Availability of blackboards, lecterns, easels, etc.
- Storage facilities for props.
- Seating arrangements.

### Participation

The second key to a successful sales meeting is participation by the salespeople. It is important for them to have an active part in the meeting. An exchange of ideas and experiences is vital. Unless they feel that they are free to express their ideas, they will not become actively involved in the meeting.

There are many ways to effect participation from sales representatives. One technique is to have them prepare special presentations in advance. A machine tool manufacturer has its top sellers prepare and talk about how they closed the most difficult sale of the year, the most unusual sale of the year, or the most important sale of the year. The presentations are made to the entire sales force at the national sales meeting, and

[2]Charles L. Lapp and Jack R. Dauner, *Conducting Sales Meetings.* (New York: Sales and Marketing Executives International, 1963), p. 20.

humorous gifts are awarded to the presenters. For this company, the opportunity to tell their personal success stories is a potent motivator for the sales force.

Other techniques for obtaining participation are skits, panel discussions, debates, case studies, and role playing. Each of these techniques makes the salespeople feel they are a part of the meeting. They also provide a flow of ideas that may not be forthcoming from a formal presentation: for example, a role-playing session with chain saw sales reps, where the participation of an older salesman proved informative. This man was an excellent salesman, but he was closed-mouthed about his sales techniques. When he was put in the role-playing situation, he clearly demonstrated why he was an outstanding salesman.

### Evaluation of Meetings

Think about the last sales conference you attended. Was it an educational and stimulating experience? Were you able to share experiences and ideas with other sales representatives and sales managers? Were you exposed to top executives and leading outside speakers? Did you rekindle your enthusiasm for your company and products? If so, the conference was probably worth your time and the company's money.

However, if your replies were negative, the conference was a costly experience for both you and the company and served no purpose. Sales conventions and meetings are expensive. Transportation, accommodations, entertainment, speakers, and the costs of planning for large numbers of salespeople involve major expenditures. Also, meetings take sales representatives away from selling. Unless the conference results in improved sales effort, the time spent on it will be a waste.

## SALES CONTESTS

Sales contests are an established technique for stimulating the sales force. They are most common in firms specializing in consumer goods, such as food and drugs, and less frequently used by companies selling "big ticket" items to industrial buyers. The type of sales contest will depend on the job to be done. Sales contests will vary according to prizes awarded, methods of determining winners, and themes.

Sales contests help attain company goals by satisfying some of the personal goals of the salespeople: recognition from their peers, awards for performance, personal esteem, and respect of their families. However, sales contests must do more than "increase sales." Management must set specific goals. Some of the more precise sales objectives for contests include opening new accounts, selling cooperative advertising, emphasizing high profit items, reducing expenses, and recruiting new salespeople.

### Planning the Contest

Planning sales contests requires expertise, and unless the sales manager has this specialized knowledge and experience, it is wise to seek outside help when developing a contest. Sources of help can be the company's sales promotion manager, advertising manager, or advertising agency. In addition, there are sales premium representatives and major companies that have a premium organization. In recent years a number of sales incentive firms have emerged, specializing in helping the sales manager develop a contest program that fits the company's goals and is designed for the particular company's sales force and market. Any of the previously mentioned sources should be able to put you in touch with one or several of these firms.

The major factors to consider in developing a contest are: theme, prizes, duration, and promotion.

### Theme

A good sales contest theme is necessary to provide the play element, sharpen competition, and enhance promotion of the contest. Sports themes are often used since they provide the contest with a competitive atmosphere. Themes with the flavor of big winnings, such as poker or roulette, are also effective.

### Prizes

Prizes are frequently the key to a successful contest. Money is still used extensively, but there is a growing trend toward noncash incentives. Merchandise catalogs offer the winners a choice and appeal to all members of a salesperson's family. Trading stamps do the same thing and have the additional advantage of an immediate payoff at a redemption center. A large appliance manufacturer increased sales 400 percent when it rewarded sales reps with trading stamps for selling accessories on service calls.

Travel is a good prize because it has a strong appeal to the spouse and is easy to dramatize. A building materials producer boosted sales 20 percent during a slow season by giving top salespeople and their spouses a trip to the builders' convention in Las Vegas. Trips to exotic places are particularly popular.

Also gaining popularity are prizes that offer more practical rewards. For major contests, several companies are offering a college scholarship for the winning sales representative's child. Life insurance policies are also a popular prize. Finally, honors can and should be used in conjunction with tangible prizes.

### Duration

Sales managers disagree on the best length for a contest. In general, it should last long enough for every salesperson to make a complete cycle of their territories. This will vary, but most sales managers feel that three months is sufficient. Peak excitement can be maintained for only so long. After three months, enthusiasm may diminish.

### Promotion

A sales contest should be launched with fanfare. It must immediately generate excitement and enthusiasm. For this reason contests are often introduced during a national sales convention or at regional sales meetings. Follow-up promotion is also necessary; the excitement cannot be allowed to taper off. The sales reps should be sold continuously on the prizes. Those who are behind should be reminded of this. Winners should be recognized.

## Criticisms of Sales Contests

As a sales stimulation technique, contests have received much criticism. Some of these criticisms are aimed at poor management of sales contests; others are concerned with the value of contests as a motivating device.

### Poor Contest Management

Sales contests fail because the sales manager has not carefully planned the contest. The timing may be off, the wrong prizes may be offered, and the goals may be unrealistic. Too often, sales contests offer only a very few prizes attainable by only the top sales representatives.

Sales contests should allow every participant who reaches reasonable goals to earn some prize. All salespeople must have a chance to win or morale will suffer. When they compete for a limited number of top prizes, there are only a few happy winners and many unhappy or apathetic losers.

Another reason for failure is inadequate promotion of the contest. Poor internal communication results in sales representatives not knowing all they should know about the contest. The contest must be well publicized to everyone involved.

## Value of Contests

The problems mentioned above can be overcome by careful planning. A more serious concern is the question of the value of sales contests as a sales stimulator. A frequent complaint is that sales contests distort the normal sales pattern. It is argued that a contest does not really raise sales over the long run. Rather, the sales contest merely provides a short-term shot in the arm.

An example will illustrate this criticism. An oil company ran a sales contest to increase sales of oil to motorists. During the contest period, sales rose substantially. However, at the end of the period, sales were about what they had been the year before.

A second criticism is that contests distract the sales force from their main job of selling. They are encouraged by the contest to concentrate on winning prizes. For example, one company ran a contest aimed at encouraging salespeople to set up dealer displays. The contest was successful; displays were placed in stores. Nevertheless, sales did not increase accordingly because many neglected their selling and service responsibilities.

## Why Contests Work

Despite the qualms of some sales managers, contests are widely used. And they work for most companies. A number of studies reveal that the vast majority of companies using special sales contests consider them an effective motivating force. Contests work because they provide recognition, excitement, and rewards.

### Recognition

Everyone wants recognition. Salespeople want to feel important; they want status. A sales contest provides them with an opportunity to earn recognition.

### Excitement

Most of us will play harder than we work. A sales contest puts a game element into what may otherwise be just a job. The contest is a challenge to which salespeople will respond. It provides new excitement and helps to overcome the routine of selling.

### Rewards

The prize is an effective motivator by itself. If all sales representatives feel they have a chance of winning, and they should, the prize is usually a reward worth striving for. This is particularly true if the prize is something a person would not normally buy.

## HONORS AND RECOGNITION

Special honors and awards are inexpensive and have considerable appeal to people who sell. Frequently, honors are given in connection with tangible rewards. They provide the recognition salespeople desire.

There are many types of honors and awards. These include trophies, plaques, certificates, membership in honorary organizations, such as the Sales Advisory Council, and titles, such as "Sales Representative of the Year." Salespeople can also be honored through news releases to local papers and trade magazines. The life insurance industry's "Million Dollar Roundtable" is a widely publicized honor.

Recognition can be given through special privileges. One manufacturer of consumer durables has the top people in sales arrive a day before the national sales meeting. They meet with market researchers and research and development personnel to discuss new product ideas. They are recognized for their achievement by being asked to express their opinions. The company also gets the added benefit of receiving their ideas, which are based on extensive contacts with customers.

## COMMUNICATION

Although communication was discussed earlier, it is important to emphasize the role of communication as a motivating force. Sales representatives may be out in territories that are hundreds of miles from the home office. They need frequent recognition and reinforcement. Continuous communication can be maintained through written correspondence, phone calls, meetings with field sales managers, and visits to salespeople in the field.

Personal contacts are the most effective form of motivation. But continuous personal contacts are impossible. A field sales manager cannot be with every sales representative at the same time. Planned phone calls are an acceptable substitute. One sales manager keeps in touch with her salespeople by calling at least once a week. She carefully plans these calls and writes down the main points to cover. The calls usually include praise for some worthwhile accomplishment.

Bulletins, announcements, letters, and other forms of written communication are also useful in motivating sales personnel. A congratulatory letter from the boss may be remembered longer and valued more highly than a routine monetary reward. The sales bulletin is an ideal place to use honest praise. Contest winners should be spotlighted in sales bulletins and company publications. Salespeople know that their colleagues and the home office are aware of their accomplishments.

Listed below are a number of typical sales objectives. Indicate which form of nonfinancial incentive you would suggest to encourage achievement of the objective by members of the sales force.

OBJECTIVE                              INCENTIVE

1. To encourage dealers to use
   more cooperative advertising.       _____
2. To improve selling techniques.     _____
3. To introduce a new product.        _____
4. To achieve greater coverage in
   present channels of distribution.   _____
5. To familiarize sales reps with
   product changes.                    _____
6. To induce dealers to use
   special display materials.          _____
7. To reduce selling expenses.        _____
8. To help recruit qualified
   new sales personnel.                _____

## Learning Exercise

*Consider the Corelli Realty case discussed earlier in this chapter. What specific sales objectives should Corelli set for his salespeople? Could he use nonfinancial incentives to encourage them to attain these goals? Why or why not?* _____

_____

_____

## COMPENSATING PEOPLE WHO SELL

A sound compensation plan is essential to successful management of the sales force. However, there is confusion and disagreement about the role of financial incentives as motivators. One point of view is held by sales managers who feel that people are motivated strictly by financial considerations. They are unwilling to recognize other needs. At the other extreme are the proponents of internal growth needs. They argue that people are entirely concerned with factors related to the job. Financial compensation is relatively unimportant as a true motivator of behavior.

The correct role of money as a motivator lies somewhere between these two extremes. Financial compensation has several functions in motivating sales representatives. It is the determinant of their purchasing power; it is a symbol of status; it is an indication of equitable treatment.

Further, an inadequate compensation plan can adversely affect all aspects of sales force operation. Depressed pay rates create dissatisfaction and lead to low morale. Turnover of salespeople is often directly related to low compensation. Other symptoms of a poor sales compensation plan include rising field sales expenses, declining sales, growing number of customer and sales representative complaints, and excessive loss of old accounts.

On the other hand, an effective sales compensation plan can be an important motivator. Sales are stimulated by a well-conceived compensation plan. In part, this is because compensation is more than simply a payment for services rendered. Financial rewards and recognition are closely related. A salary or commission payment is a reward, but it is also a form of recognition for a job done well.

### Trends in Sales Compensation

Compensating the field sales force is more difficult than paying factory and office workers. The conditions under which they work are less standardized and less easily controlled. Because of this, sales compensation plans are continuously undergoing change. Several studies reveal three major trends in compensating sales reps.

#### Shift to Combination Plans

Fewer companies are paying salespeople on the basis of salary or commission alone. The use of incentives, commission, and/or bonus payments, to supplement their salaries has grown rapidly since the end of

World War II. Studies show that roughly 90 percent of American companies now use some form of salary plus incentive compensation to pay salespeople.

Combination plans are used more because they provide greater flexibility. The modern sales job is more complicated. Salespeople must be problem solvers as well as sellers of goods and services. Incentives can be related to the accomplishment of specific marketing objectives and sales volume. In addition, combination plans satisfy the salespeoples' desire for some stable base income.

### Emphasis on Profitability

Many companies are now trying to relate sales force compensation to some measure of profitability. For instance, compensation is tied to gross margin. The goal is to motivate sales personnel not to sell just volume, but profitable volume. Sales compensation is keyed to the more profitable products. Unfortunately, there is no easy way to do this. Most companies try to reach this objective through some kind of combination plan.

### Fringe Benefits

The third major trend in sales compensation is the increased availability of fringe benefits. Even salespeople on straight commission are eligible for such benefits as pensions and insurance.

Changes in the nature of selling and sales personnel are largely responsible for this trend. Salespeople are no longer considered self-supporting free agents. They have closer ties with their companies. Companies have to offer a range of health, welfare, and pension benefits to attract good people. A tire company executive states: "These days fringe benefits are prerequisites. To compete for good sales talent, a company can't exist without them."

People who sell receive "hidden income" from fringe benefits. Usually, those benefits that are available to nonsales personnel are now available to the sales force. Most companies provide paid vacations. Group life insurance, hospitalization, and major medical insurance are provided for salespeople. Pensions are now accepted as normal, as are paid holidays.

In many firms, fringe benefits amount to as much as one-third of the sales reps' total financial compensation.

## CRITERIA FOR A SOUND COMPENSATION PLAN

Designing a sound sales compensation plan is difficult. We must remember that there is no "best" compensation plan even for companies with similar product lines, markets, and size. A good compensation plan for a particular company must be developed from careful analysis of *that particular company's* capabilities and requirements.

A sound sales compensation plan will consider the needs of both the company and the sales force. From the company's standpoint, the basic consideration is to get the sales force to do what management wants done as efficiently as possible. But salespeople's compensation is a major selling expense. The dilemma for sales management is how to stimulate sales personnel to maximize profitable sales volume and yet keep sales expenses to a minimum.

On the other hand, the main concern of salespeople is to maximize their earnings. They want an adequate income, a level of compensation they feel is fair when compared to the incomes of their fellow sales reps, other company employees, and the relevant labor market. They also want a balance of security (a steady income) and payment for extra effort (incentive income). Achieving the proper balance presents a dilemma for sales management.

An effective compensation plan represents both points of view. General characteristics of a good plan are described here.

### Incentive

Financial rewards are an important form of motivation. A sound compensation plan will stimulate salespeople to achieve the firm's goals. In particular, it must motivate them to generate net profit rather than simply sales volume. A good plan will encourage them to accomplish what management wants done.

### Simplicity

An effective compensation plan is easily understood and relatively simple to operate. Sales personnel should be able to calculate easily what their income will be. A plan that they cannot understand loses its value as a motivator. Further, a plan should not attempt to motivate salespeople to achieve more than two or three important selling objectives at the same time. Incentive components must be based on measurable, clear factors. Complex sales compensation plans simply do not work.

## Fairness

An essential element for any sales compensation plan is equity. The plan must be fair to both the company and its salespeople. The company should be able to keep selling costs in line with volume. The compensation plan should also protect against windfalls to sales reps in abnormal times.

Salespeople expect a plan to reward ability and productivity. This requires constant scrutiny and a willingness to revise the plan if necessary. Special care must be taken to remove inequities resulting from territorial differences.

In the matter of the fairness of the sales compensation plan, we should remind ourselves of the various government regulations concerning equal employment opportunity that were outlined in Chapter 2. As applied to sales compensation, these regulations boil down to: There can be no discrimination in any form of pay or other rewards because of race, creed, color, sex, or age. In the administration of the sales compensation plan, the sales manager is well advised to keep these government provisions in mind.

## Flexibility

A plan should be sufficiently flexible to take into account the rapidly changing needs of the company and its sales personnel. Changes in the supply of sales reps, products, customers, and the competitive situation will require changes in sales compensation. For instance, a good plan will operate effectively through the ups and downs of the business cycle.

## Control

Salespeople tend to do what they are paid to do. The sales compensation plan provides control and direction over their activities. A sound plan will strengthen the sales manager's supervision. However, no compensation plan can ever take the place of a good sales manager. A manager cannot expect the compensation plan to be a substitute for leadership.

## Competitive

The level of compensation must be competitive. As the payment for services rendered, sales compensation must be adequate. Attractive pay is needed to attract, keep, and develop effective salespeople. Early in the modern era of selling, Peter Drucker, a leading management consultant, commented: "To attract and hold the kind of people we need in selling requires, above all, ability to pay what they can earn in competitive jobs which are easier and less demanding than selling."[3]

## DEVELOPING A COMPENSATION PLAN

Rarely are field sales managers called upon to design a sales compensation plan from scratch. However, they are usually responsible for administering the plan. They may also be asked for recommendations when a plan is being revised. For these reasons, it is important for the field sales manager to understand the process by which a compensation plan for sales reps is developed. The basic steps in this process are:

1. Review the selling job.
2. Determine specific objectives.
3. Establish the level of compensation.
4. Choose the method of compensation.
5. Implement the plan.

### Job Review

The first step in designing or revising a compensation plan is to carefully review the sales job. The preparation of the job description was discussed in Chapter 2. It is sufficient at this point only to reemphasize the value of the job description as a planning tool. Careful analysis of the job description will reveal what a company must pay to acquire and satisfy the salespeople it wants.

For example, education and experience are two prime qualities that will require above-average compensation. If a college education is a requisite for a sales job, compensation must be competitive with other college level jobs. Likewise, if a company must hire experienced sales

---

[3]Peter Drucker, "How to Double Your Sales," *Nation's Business* (March 1967), p. 80.

personnel because it lacks a sufficient training program, it must be prepared to pay more for experienced people.

### Establish Objectives

Sales compensation objectives must be related to the company's sales and marketing goals. They have to be realistic. One cannot expect the sales compensation plan to overcome basic weaknesses in sales supervision.

The objectives will indicate what the plan is expected to accomplish. There are two characteristics common to all good sales compensation plans.

1. The plan encourages salespeople to do their jobs in the way management wants them to; it discourages or penalizes them for not doing the job in the right way.
2. The plan provides sales representatives with a satisfactory income; at the same time it keeps selling costs down and profits up.

Specific objectives will depend on each company's resources, needs, and marketing goals. Developing new accounts, minimizing sales expenses, full-line selling, meeting quotas, and developing new territories are a few examples.

### Level of Compensation

Compensation should be set at a level sufficient to attract, retain, and stimulate the type of sales rep desired. This usually involves paying about average in relation to what other firms are paying for similar selling jobs. However, a smaller company may be forced to pay a premium to attract competent salespeople. This is especially true if the smaller company has a limited sales training program and must hire only experienced sales personnel.

The level of sales compensation depends upon several factors. Pay must be attractive enough to appeal to sales recruits. There must be a fair correlation between sales compensation and the pay of other employees. Competitors' pay plans must be examined as must the company's own past history of sales compensation. Finally, careful attention should be given to the relationship between sales compensation and profits. Management must estimate what sales force compensation will cost the company. Overpaying or underpaying must be avoided.

## Overpaying Dangers

Although many companies overpay their people, this is a bad practice. One result is the adverse effect on company profits. Sales force compensation is usually the largest single element of selling cost. Pay levels that are too high will unnecessarily reduce profits.

Personnel problems are also created by overpaying salespeople. The morale of sales managers will suffer since they resent their sales reps earning more than they do. Further, it is difficult to persuade top salespeople to take management positions. They are reluctant to leave field sales when they are making more than their supervisors.

## Underpaying Dangers

It is also important to guard against underpaying the sales force. Two conditions may result if this is done. First, the company may attract only poor reps, and poor performance will result. Second, if good people are hired at low pay, there will be excessive turnover. They will be vulnerable to pirating by other firms.

## Method of Compensation

The major methods for paying people who sell are salary, commission, and bonus. Although some companies still pay salespeople a straight salary or straight commission, most firms now use some type of combination plan. The basic plans and the extent of their use are shown in Figure 6-1.

It should be noted that in this survey no companies reported paying their salespeople by straight commission. This is due to the nature of the sample used in the survey. Some companies do pay their sales forces on straight commission, but the number is so small that this sample did not pick them up.

Whatever the method of sales compensation, it is just as important as the level of compensation. In fact, many sales managers feel that it is the method of compensation, not the level, that influences the performance of salespeople. When choosing a method of compensation, three factors must be considered: motivation, control, and cost.

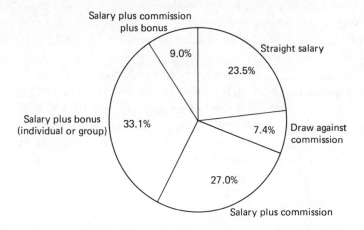

METHODS OF COMPENSATION

Salary plus commission
plus bonus

9.0%

Straight salary

23.5%

Salary plus bonus
(individual or group)

33.1%

7.4%

Draw against
commission

27.0%

Salary plus commission

Source: American Management Association,
Executive Compensation Service, 1977

FIGURE 6-1

## Motivation

Different methods of compensation will stimulate sales reps in different ways. Commissions and bonuses provide a direct incentive to achieve, while salaries are less directly related to sales performance.

## Control

Each method of compensation also provides a different form of control. When the sales force is on straight salary, they are directly responsible to the company for their actions. A sales manager has direct control and can ask his people to perform extra nonselling duties. The commission form of payment has the opposite effect. The salespeople consider themselves more independent and often perform only those activities that are immediately related to sales success. The bonus form of compensation provides control by inducing salespeople to point their efforts toward a particular goal.

## Cost

The method of compensating the sales force affects selling costs differently. Salaries are a fixed expense; commissions and bonuses are

**183**

variable expenses. When business is good, salaries will provide higher profits. However, in a business slump, fixed selling expenses may cause losses. With commissions and bonuses, selling expenses vary with performance. They will be high when sales are good and low when sales are poor.

Figure 6-2 illustrates this relationship. Assume this company has a choice between paying its 100 salespeople an average salary of $15,000 a year or a commission of 5 percent of net sales. If sales are $30 million or less, the company will minimize selling expenses by paying the sales force on commission. If sales are more than $30 million, a salary form of compensation will minimize selling expenses.

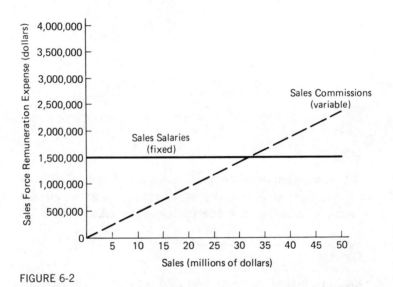

FIGURE 6-2

A word of caution is in order, however. Cost is an important factor, but it is not the only consideration. Sometimes the least expensive method of compensation may not be the best. Motivation and control are equally important. For instance, if the present projection of sales level in Figure 6-2 is $45 million, it may be wise to still use a commission form of payment. The greater selling effort generated by a direct financial incentive may increase sales substantially above $45 million.

Now let us examine each of the major methods for paying people who sell.

## Salary

A salary is a fixed sum of money paid at regular intervals. A sales rep might be paid $288 a week, $1,250 a month, or $15,000 a year. The amount paid is related to time rather than to the work achieved.

A straight salary is used when the earnings of salespeople are not directly related to sales volume or other quantitative measures of productivity. This is often true when they are expected to perform many nonselling activities, such as market investigation, customer problem analysis, servicing, and sales promotion. The salary compensates them for these nonselling duties. Salary level is based on many factors: length of service, living requirements, general performance, and competitive salaries.

Straight salary plans are also found in companies and industries in which engineering knowledge and skills are needed for selling, such as aerospace and industrial chemicals. Salary is indicated because of the extended time required to close complex industrial sales. Salary also encourages the sales rep to emphasize continued service after the sale.

Salaries are appropriate when a new product is introduced, a new market is developed, or new salespeople are being trained. These situations are all characterized by uncertainty for them. A salary provides a steady income while they get their feet on the ground.

The prime advantage of a straight salary is direct control. Salespeople can be required to perform activities that do not result in immediate sales. There is also more flexibility for management because it is easier to switch customers and territories. Finally, salaried compensation is simple to operate and easy for the sales force to understand.

These advantages are often outweighed by the disadvantages associated with the lack of a direct financial incentive. Only routine motivation is provided by a salary. This may lead to limited individual initiative and drive.

## Commission

A commission is a payment for the performance of a unit of work. Sales reps might be paid 3 percent of net sales, 5 percent of gross profits, or $1.25 for each 100 pounds sold. Straight commission plans are used mainly by firms in the real estate, leather products, furniture and fixtures, and apparel industries.

Straight commission plans are based on the principle that the earnings of the sales force should vary directly with performance. They are paid for results. Usually, commission payments are based on dollar or unit sales volume. However, more companies are beginning to compute commission rates as a percentage of gross profit.

Direct motivation is the principal advantage of commission compensation. Strong incentive is provided to increase productivity. Salespeople are encouraged to think and conduct themselves as if they were in business for themselves. Strong performers are attracted and encouraged; marginal performers are weeded out.

Loss of control over the sales force's activities is the major limitation of the straight commission. The strong incentive to sell more may encourage overstocking, misrepresentation of goods, and other bad selling practices. Customer service and good will may be neglected. Another weakness is the insecurity sales reps may face, since commission income is irregular and unpredictable.

There are several modifications of the straight commission method designed to overcome these disadvantages. Three of the most popular are commissions with drawing accounts, sliding commissions, and varied commissions.

The trend is toward providing salespeople who work on commission with a drawing account. Money is regularly advanced to them and is later deducted from their earned commissions. This gives them some of the security of a salary and gives management more control over their activities. The major problem arises when a salesperson fails to earn enough commission to repay the draw. When this happens, the person may quit or be fired, and the company must absorb the loss.

Sliding commission plans use a changing rate. In a progressive plan, earnings increase more than proportionately with increases in sales volume. For instance, Martha Adams is paid 5 percent of net sales for sales from 0 to $150,000, 6 percent for sales from $150,000 to $300,000 and 7 percent for all sales over $300,000. This type of commission is a strong stimulus to increase sales.

A regressive plan works in reverse. Earnings decrease proportionately with increases in sales volume. For example, Russ Lucci receives 1.5 percent of net sales from 0 to $100,000, 1.0 percent for sales from $100,000 to $150,000, and 0.5 percent for all sales above $150,000. This plan gives a strong initial incentive to increase sales and encourages good-will activities.

Varied commission plans promote sales of the most profitable items. Higher commissions are given for sales of products with high gross profitability and lower commissions for products with less profit. Although this plan is not as simple as a straight commission, it is more flexible and it is a way to relate selling expense to profitability.

### Bonus

A bonus is a payment made at the discretion of management for a particular achievement. It is usually a reward for special effort and provides direct motivation. However, in contrast to commission payments that relate directly to some measure of sales performance, usually sales volume, bonuses are only indirectly related to sales volume. They are considered an additional incentive rather than part of the basic compensation plan.

Attainment of sales quotas is used frequently to determine eligibility for bonus payments. A steel manufacturer developed an incentive plan based on quotas. Quotas for four product categories were established. Then incentive payments were set up for sales in excess of quotas. These incentives emphasized sales of the most profitable products rather than sales volume alone. To encourage balanced selling, salespeople receive a bonus only if they meet quotas in three of the four product groups. If they meet quotas in all four categories, bonuses are doubled.

Bonuses are also paid for other forms of extra effort related to the company's sales goals. These include bonuses based on number of new accounts opened, performance of certain types of promotional work, and reduced expenses. For example, Barbara Rice receives $100 for each new customer ordering over a certain minimum volume and $10 for setting up a floor display.

Usually bonus payments are in cash, but merchandise and other nonfinancial rewards are used. A pharmaceutical manufacturer has a plan that pays bonuses in company stock. The goal is to create a common interest in profitability by making the sales force stockholders. They are offered shares of stock if district sales forecasts are met and individual quotas are achieved. Regional and district sales managers are also eligible for stock bonuses if their performances exceed expectations.

### Combination Plans

Most people who sell and sales managers prefer a compensation plan that combines the security of a fixed base and the stimulation of incentive payments. We know, for instance, that a very high percentage of all salespeople want at least 50 percent of their income to be a fixed salary.

But it is critical to remember that the proportion of incentive pay to base salary depends on the company's objectives, the nature of the selling job, and the kind of people management wants on the sales force. When the perserverance and skill of salespeople are the keys to sales success, the incentive part of their pay is high. But when the product has been presold and salespeople are little more than order takers, the incentive share of their income is small. For example, companies selling specialty goods, such as furniture and household appliances that are relatively high priced and keenly competitive, usually pay their sales forces a small guaranteed salary plus a commission based on sales volume. On the other hand, cigarettes are largely presold by advertising, and the selling job requires less incentive than in the previous example.

Combination plans often fail because they provide too little financial incentive for the salespeople to achieve the desired objectives. As a general rule, at least a quarter of the average salesperson's gross income should be in the form of incentive pay. If it is not, the sales incentive plan will not be truly effective.

Sales incentive earnings are paid annually, semiannually, quarterly, or monthly. In general, the shorter the time interval between performance and payment of the reward, the stronger the stimulus is for them. However, payment of earned incentives may sometimes be deferred for several years. The standard life insurance compensation plan, for example, pays the agent half of the commission when a policy is sold and the rest in regular payments over the next 10 years.

There are many forms of sales combination pay plans. One variation is a point system. Points, or credits, are given for selling various products, for performing special duties, or for intangible contributions, such as cooperativeness, interest in the job, and initiative. At the end of the month, quarter, or year, the points are converted into monetary values and a bonus is paid to each salesperson who qualifies.

Another variation is to give seniority increases. One manufacturer provides a gradual increase in the incentive rate each year a sales rep stays with the company. After 25 years of service there is a 25 percent larger incentive income for the same performance as for salespeople just joining the company. This way of doing it provides incentive rewards for loyalty and persistence.

## Implementing the Plan

Implementation of a sales compensation plan involves pretesting the plan, selling it to the sales force, and evaluating the plan.

### Pretest

A new or revised compensation system must be pretested. One method is to apply the new plan to the historical performance of selected individual sales reps and sales districts. If the results of this test are satisfactory, the system can be tested further by introducing it in one or more sales districts. The results should be carefully reviewed to determine if any modifications are required before the plan is introduced to the other sales districts.

### Sell

It is essential that a new or revised compensation method be properly introduced to the sales force. This is a change and there is always resistance to change, especially one as vital as a change in compensation. The success of the plan as a motivator will importantly depend on how it is introduced.

Introducing the plan is a selling job. One must keep in mind the guidelines for good salesmanship. Most importantly, management must be customer-oriented. Emphasis must be on the benefits to the salespeople. However, it is better to go slowly and understate the benefits rather than overstate them. Sales reps will not expect too much and then be disappointed in the future.

### Evaluate

Once the plan has been sold and put into operation, it must be evaluated. The field sales manager should have major responsibility for administering the plan. A careful periodic appraisal of each sales rep's activities and performance under the plan is of major importance. Although drastic changes should not be necessary, minor adjustments may be required.

### Learning Exercise

*Refer to the Corelli Realty Agency case discussed earlier. How well do you think Corelli's compensation plan matches the standards we have studied? Why?* _____

_____

_____

## SALES EXPENSES

We turn now to the important matter of reimbursing sales reps for their expenses while they are on company business. The expenses of sales people have a significant impact on their morale and effectiveness and the company's profits. From their viewpoint, sales expenses are part of their real income. They think of expenses and compensation as similar since they both affect their financial status. A poorly administered expense plan will hurt their morale, especially if they feel the plan reduces their income.

### Need for Control

Sales expenses are a major cost factor. Studies reveal that the average cost of a sales call made by a sales rep is almost $100. There is every indication that selling costs will continue to rise.

Too often, management regards sales expenses as unwanted costs, a "necessary evil." This is unfortunate because sales expenses are an investment. Their purpose is to generate sales in the same way any promotional expenditure does. Salespeople's expenses must be properly supervised, but they must also be liberal enough to permit them to do their job effectively.

Another management concern is federal corporate income tax laws. Recent laws have cracked down on many abuses associated with business expenses. Although these laws are mainly concerned with limiting excessive entertainment and business gift expenses, they also require more detailed recording of expenses. The major impact of the law on companies has been more detailed recordkeeping and closer managerial control over sales expenses.

## Current Practices

Most companies operate on a liberal sales expense policy. Studies show that a large majority of companies pay all "reasonable" expenses under a top limit. Expense items that companies usually pay for include travel, automobile mileage and upkeep, lodging and meals away from home, job-related entertainment, promotional expenditures, telephone, telegraph, and postage. However, few companies will pay for borderline expenses, such as telephone calls or telegrams home, personal entertainment, laundry, valet service, and shoeshines.

Like compensation, the sales expense plan must be fair to both the sales reps and the company. There should be no net gain or loss to either party. The expense plan must not hamper selling activities in any way. It should be simple and economical to operate and should provide an effective means of controlling expense accounts. One way to do this is to have the sales force use credit cards. This gives the company better records of sales expenses and salespeople do not have to carry large amounts of cash.

Another successful method is to provide sales reps with a supply of predated blank checks, which can be written and cashed at the end of each week. This gives them immediate reimbursement for sales expenses. Of course, proper safeguards must be established to protect the sales reps and the company.

### Brain teasers

| | Agree | Disagree |
|---|---|---|
| 1. Individual needs are unimportant in the selection of sales incentives. | ____ | ____ |
| 2. Sales conventions should be planned strictly to motivate sales personnel. | ____ | ____ |
| 3. A sales convention should be built around a specific theme. | ____ | ____ |
| 4. Each sales rep should have a chance to win a sales contest. | ____ | ____ |
| 5. A sales contest may distract salespeople from their main job of selling. | ____ | ____ |
| 6. Compensation is unimportant as a true motivator of sales performance. | ____ | ____ |

7. Compensation for selling should be related to profitability.    _____   _____
8. Determining specific objectives is the first step in developing a compensation plan for sales personnel.    _____   _____
9. Direct motivation is an important advantage of the commission method of compensation.    _____   _____
10. Sales expenses are unimportant to salespeople.    _____   _____

## Activities

1. *You have been asked to plan a sales convention to introduce your company's new advertising campaign to the sales force. Prepare a proposal for this convention.* _____

   _____

   _____

   _____

2. *Have you ever participated in a sales promotion contest as a consumer? How did the objectives of this contest differ from those of a contest for sales representatives?* _____

   _____

   _____

   _____

3. *You are a district manager for a medium-sized insurance company. Your company has been having difficulty recruiting qualified agents, and you have been asked to develop a contest to encourage your agents to recruit new agents. Prepare a plan for this contest.* _____

   _____

   _____

   _____

4. *Suggest the method of sales compensation that would be appropriate for the following companies. Explain your answers.*
   a) *manufacturer of men's and boys' apparel*
   b) *manufacturer of machine tools*

    c) *furniture wholesaler*
    d) *beer distributor*

_____

_____

_____

5. *The Green Manufacturing Company has recently changed from a straight salary compensation plan to a salary plus commission plan. Although it is expected that most sales reps will soon earn more under the new plan, they have strongly resisted the change. What do you think are the reasons for this resistance? What can Green's sales manager do now to ensure the success of the plan?* _____

_____

_____

_____

6. *Obtain a copy of your company's compensation plan for salespeople. Does it meet the criteria established in this chapter? Why or why not? What changes, if any, would you make? The plan is, or provides:*

    *Incentive* _____
    *Simple* _____
    *Fair* _____
    *Flexible* _____
    *Control* _____
    *Competitive* _____

## SELECTED REFERENCES

### Nonfinancial Incentives

"Eight Keys to Motivation: A Star Salesman Game," *Sales Management,* November 3, 1975, pp. 45–56.

KAUFMAN, Z., "Seven Steps to Better Sales Contests," *Sales Management,* September 10, 1967, pp. 18ff.

LAPP, CHARLES L., and JACK R. DAUNER, *Conducting Sales Meetings*. New York: Sales and Marketing Executives International, 1963.

LEWELLEN, WILLIAM H., "It's Time for a New Look at Sales Contests," *Sales Management,* September 10, 1968, pp. 22–25.

PRUDEN, HENRY O., WILLIAM H. CUNNINGHAM, and WILKE D. ENGLISH, "Nonfinancial Incentives for Salesmen," *Journal of Marketing (October 1972), pp. 55–59.*

"Sales Meetings As a Communications Medium," *Sales and Marketing Management,* November 8, 1976, pp. 53–72.

SCANLON, SALLY, "Want Better Incentive Results? It's Simple," *Sales and Marketing Management,* September 19, 1977, pp. 44–47.

## Compensating People Who Sell

GONICK, JACOB, "Tie Salesmen's Bonuses to Their Forecasts," *Harvard Business Review* (May-June 1978), pp. 116–22.

JOLSON, MARVIN A., "Compensating Sales Personnel," in *Sales Management: A Tactical Approach.* New York: Petrocelli/Charter, 1977.

"Sales Force Compensation, Special Report," *Sales and Marketing Management,* August 23, 1976.

SMYTH, RICHARD C., "Financial Incentives for Salesmen," *Harvard Business Review* (January-February 1968), pp. 109–17.

STANTON, WILLIAM J., and RICHARD H. BUSKIRK, "Compensating the Sales Force," in *Managing the Sales Force* (5th ed.). Homewood, Ill.: Richard D. Irwin, 1978.

STEINBRINK, JOHN P., "How to Pay Your Sales Force," *Harvard Business Review* (July-August 1978), pp. 111–22.

WEEKS, DAVID A., *Incentive Plans for Salesmen.* New York: National Industrial Conference Board, 1970.

# 7

# EVALUATING SALES PERFORMANCE

*After reading this chapter, you should be able to demonstrate your learning as follows:*

- *Be able to justify the value of a properly designed sales evaluation program for your company and to state what the characteristics of such a plan should be.*
- *Know the obstacles to designing a good evaluation program and how to avoid them, or how to work around them.*
- *Set out the steps of designing a good evaluation program or reviewing one already in use.*
- *Be able to select relevant performance standards from among the many available to evaluate the performance of particular salespeople.*
- *Be able to administer an evaluation program and to appraise its operation.*

In this chapter we are concerned with the evaluation of sales performance, especially with formal evaluation programs. In particular, we shall discuss programs and techniques for appraising and improving the performance of individual salespeople. Our study of evaluation begins with an overview of industry evaluation practices. Next, we consider the reasons for evaluation and the obstacles to evaluation of salespeople. Beginning with the general requirements for a good evaluation program, the remainder of the chapter is devoted to evaluation programs and procedures.

## INDUSTRY PRACTICES

A review of industry practices involves a look at three basic questions.

1. *Do all companies evaluate their salespeople?* The answer is "yes." Whether they are large or small, in consumer, industrial, government, or export sales, sell goods or services, employ one or several thousand sales representatives, all companies evaluate their salespeople. Whether consciously recognized, simple or complex, formal or informal, based on objective measures or executive opinion, evaluation takes place in all companies because without it effective supervision of salespeople is impossible.

2. *Do all companies have formal evaluation programs?* The answer is "no." This fact is shown by a survey of 157 sales managers made by the Scott Paper Company.[1] All of the companies in the study reported that they evaluated their sales reps in some way. The percentage of respondents who had a *formal system* of evaluating performance was as follows:

| | |
|---|---|
| Services and Intangibles | 52% |
| Manufacturers of Industrial Goods | 45 |
| Manufacturers of Consumer Durable Goods | 42 |
| Industrial Distributors | 35 |
| Manufacturers of Consumer Nondurables | 32 |
| Wholesalers of Consumer Goods | 23 |
| House to House | 21 |

We see that *formal* evaluation of sale performance is prevalent, but not universal in American business.

3. *Is formal evaluation expensive?* The answer is "yes." Formal evaluation is expensive in money, time, and effort. A good rule is that the more complex and precise the evaluation plan, the more expensive it is. The reasons for this will become apparent in this chapter.

### Why Evaluate Performance?

To this point we see that: (1) sales evaluation is universal, (2) formal evaluation programs are prevalent, but not universal, and (3)

---

[1]Scott Paper Company survey (unpublished).

formal evaluation programs represent an important cost to a company. Why then do we evaluate? Why does your company evaluate sales reps' performance? There are several important management objectives for the evaluation of people who sell. These are:

- To discover where each person needs improvement to make possible individualized personal development.
- To check and evaluate performance standards for salespeople, since poor performance may indicate poor performance standards.
- To spot people who are ready for promotion, salary raises, or assignment to new territories and responsibilities.
- To keep job descriptions current and on target with changing market conditions.
- To supply evidence on salespeople who should be disciplined or fired.
- To cross check the sales compensation plan, training, supervision, recruitment, territory assignments, and operating procedures.

Too often evaluation is considered as a *negative* activity to find out which salespeople are not doing their jobs. To be sure, this is one aspect of evaluation, but the more realistic view of performance evaluation is as a *positive* activity for personal development—to develop winning sales representatives.

### Obstacles to Evaluation

There are important problems in evaluating an individual's sales performance. So common and difficult are these problems that often they are the reasons why some companies do not employ formal evaluation programs and why others use only very simple plans. When we create and operate an evaluation plan, we must recognize that these obstacles will make any plan less than perfect.

### Isolation of the Sales Representative

Most salespeople work without the direct personal observation of their supervisors, who can only rarely observe and evaluate their work as it is being done. For instance, in mass-distributed consumer goods industries such as food, drug, hardware, liquor, and cosmetics, sales supervisors consider themselves fortunate if they can spend one selling day a month in the field with each of their sales reps. How often can your company's sales supervisors travel with their reps? Probably quite infrequently.

The isolation of salespeople creates two problems in evaluating their work. First, evaluation is by inference. Since they can only occasionally observe their reps' performances, sales supervisors must *infer* conclusions from indirect evidence. For example: records for the last quarter show that Joe Green's calls-per-day, new accounts opened, dollar volume sold, and gross margin earned are well below his quota. The supervisor must infer that Green is neglecting his job, and this may be true. But conditions might also have existed where these same facts would lead to a quite different conclusion. For instance, during this period unions struck Green's three biggest customers. Evaluation by inference is often misleading. The evaluator should never forget this. A sales manager, like the law courts when they deal with circumstantial evidence (inferential conclusions), should handle inferential evaluations with great care. Whenever possible, inference should be checked by personal information and observation.

Second, there is a bias with direct observation. When the supervisor evaluates sales representatives by traveling with them, two potential forces of bias are present. First, the sales rep may try to look good by calling on only easy, friendly customers. Anne Larson, field sales supervisor of a toy manufacturer, became curious about the kinds of customers she was visiting when she traveled with her field sales reps. Analysis showed that 80 percent of her calls with sales reps were made on a class of customers who represented 75 percent of the sales reps' volume. Another bias in field observation is that the presence of the sales rep's superior almost inevitably changes the customer's normal behavior in some way. Customers do not react as they normally do when the sales rep calls alone.

Observing salespeople at work is a useful and important evaluation tool, but it should be used by the supervisor with full knowledge of its limitations.

## Isolating and Relating
## Sales Performance Criteria

We cannot evaluate sales reps' performance until we know the functions they should be performing. In even the simplest selling job, it is difficult to identify the specific performance factors that are critical to sales success and then to rate these factors relatively to each other. The problem is determining what creates sales for a specific company, territory, or customer. Service? Advertising and promotion help for customers? Technical assistance? Advice on inventory control or market conditions?

## Lack of Control Over Performance

Another difficulty in evaluation is that the sales rep's performance is always colored, for better or worse, by external conditions over which the individual and/or the company have little or no control. Competition cuts the price. There is a local business recession. A government agency issues a report that is critical of the product. A strike disrupts business. It is impossible to design an evaluation program that takes all such external forces into account in advance of the event.

## Evaluation Facts and Judgments

A recurring problem in evaluation is that we use two kinds of information—fact and judgment. Fact is quantifiable; judgment is not. That is, fact can be stated and used in the form of figures or other fairly exact measures; judgment cannot. An example of quantifiable fact is the number of calls-per-day; of nonquantifiable judgment, the extent of the sales rep's product knowledge. It is difficult to use both facts and judgment in evaluation. It may seem that we are trying to add apples and oranges. But the difficulty diminishes when we remember that we are evaluating sales performance primarily for personal development. We know all we need to know when we find out that on a particular performance standard, fact or judgment, salesman Sam Cohen did poorly. *We know; now we must find out why and develop means to help Sam Cohen improve.*

## DEVELOPING THE EVALUATION PROGRAM

We turn now to designing an evaluation program and managing it effectively. Each sales manager must decide which of the procedures described here are applicable to the company's situation and how complex and sophisticated the evaluation program should be.

## Requirements for a Good Evaluation Program

Before reading further, list below that what you think are the criteria for, or characteristics of, a good sales evaluation program for your company or any company you know. _____

_____

_____

_____

Now compare your list to what management experts generally agree are the critical requirements for an effective evaluation program.

- Realistic: reflects things as they are, the rep's territory, competition, experience, sales potential.
- Continuous, known, expected: rep knows when and how work is evaluated.
- Constructive, not destructive: shows the rep what needs improvement and how to better performance.
- Motivates the rep to improve.
- Provides useful information about the individual and the territory for management.
- Involves the rep in the evaluation.
- Objective, not subjective: based on standards, not on opinions or prejudices.
- Living, changing, adaptive: reflects changing market and environmental conditions.
- Fits the company and the sales group involved.
- Economical of money and time.

These criteria for a good evaluation program are *general* or *ideal* characteristics, applying to *all* companies with salespeople, regardless of size, industry, or nature of the business. *But they are guidelines only.* They are not a formula for the design of an evaluation system that will fit any and all companies. There is no such thing. Each evaluation plan must be tailored to the individual company in which it is used. For one company calls-per-day may be an important criterion of sales reps' performance, while for another company this measure may be meaningless, and new accounts opened may be a more critical standard. One company may evaluate its people annually, another quarterly. Each sales group must design its own evaluation program based on the criteria listed above.

### Steps in the Development of an Evaluation Program

An effective evaluation program involves the five separate, but related steps shown in Figure 7-1.

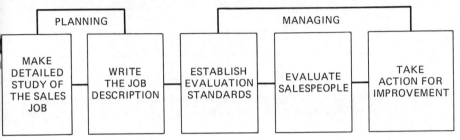

FIGURE 7-1

The first two steps were discussed in Chapter 2; the last three are considered in this chapter.

### Case Study

Before we discuss the steps in developing a sales evaluation program, study the problem below and answer the questions that follow it.

Medical File, Inc. (A)

Ed Larson recently became national sales manager of Medical File, Inc. The company designs and manufactures record-keeping systems for hospitals and other health care institutions. Total sales are $6.5 million, having increased from less than $2 million five years ago.

The company has 15 sales representatives who are paid a base salary plus a commission on all sales. Because most of Medical File's record-keeping systems are custom designed, sales reps are expected to spend considerable time with hospital administrators and their staffs in the development of special institutional record-keeping systems.

When Larson became national sales manager, Medical File did not have a formal sales evaluation program. The former sales manager evaluated the sales reps informally, primarily through field visits. Larson is considering whether Medical File should have a formal sales evaluation program.

*Do you think Medical File should have a formal evaluation program for sales reps? Why or why not?* _____

_____

_____

_____

*What problems might Ed Larson encounter if he continues to evaluate his sales reps informally by means of field visits?* _____

_____

_____

_____

*What difficulties or obstacles do you foresee in setting up and operating a formal evaluation program?* _____

_____

_____

_____

## ESTABLISHING EVALUATION STANDARDS

The third stage in the design and management of a good evaluation program is the selection of the standards that will best indicate how salespeople are doing against the criteria established by the job description. How are we going to measure their work?

### Danger in the Single Standard

The use of a single standard for the evaluation of sales performance has the tempting advantages of being easy for salespeople and their supervisors to understand, and it is usually economical to plan and administer. It is likely, however, to cause problems and create more undesirable conditions than it solves.

To see the kinds of undesirable side effects that can develop from the use of any single standard of evaluation, imagine yourself as a sales representative whose performance is evaluated solely on a gross dollar sales volume quota. You are expected to bring in X number of dollars in sales in the next quarter to meet or exceed your quota. It would be only natural for you to react to this standard by ignoring other important aspects of your work: to control your expenses, to open new accounts, to resist spending the time to introduce and promote new products, to minimize customer service (unless it was to result directly in a sale), and to skip small or less active accounts. It is conceivable that this is just what your company wants you to do. But if it were, it would be a rare exception in today's changing, sophisticated buying and selling environment for a company to want you to overlook any of these important functions. Several standards must be applied for sensible evaluation and supervision of salespeople and to avoid undesirable work habits by them.

### Selected Standards in Use

A great many indices and combinations of performance standards are available to sales management to evaluate the performance of salespeople. The emerging information sciences, the explosion of knowledge around us, and computers have made it possible for us to know, and at great speed and detail, virtually anything we might wish to know about sales performance. The limiting factors are the time and expense of generating, collecting, analyzing, and appraising evaluation information. Time is required for management to design an evaluation reporting and analysis system; time that salespeople must spend in filling out reports on their activities, that salespeople lose from selling while doing this, for collation and analysis of evaluation information; time for management to appraise the results. And the more measurements that are used in the evaluation of sales performance, the more time and money are required to process them.

Consequently, your company must study carefully what is needed to evaluate sales performance and to employ *only the best* of those indices and standards that will give the necessary information.

If your company has a formal evaluation plan, how many standards of performance are used? Should there be more or less? Why? __

## Standards an Individual Choice

No two selling jobs are the same, so performance in each different kind of selling job must be measured by its own standards. The two basic criteria for the selection of performance standards are:

1. *What do we need?* Every manager, because all managers are evaluated on how well they make decisions under conditions of constant uncertainty, wants *all* the information before making *any* evaluation or decision. But information costs money, and the more information and the greater the detail, the greater the cost. Consequently, the critical questions in deciding on the performance standards to be used for a particular sales group are: What can we do without? What information can we afford to buy? What information can we *not* afford to buy? Has your company asked itself these questions?

2. *How efficient is the information source?* Having decided what measures to use in an individual company, critical questions arise concerning the efficiency of the information source. Does it provide the information we want, and only that, or does the cost include unwanted data along with what we want? Is the information accurate to the degree we need? Are we getting more accuracy than we need or can use? Are the data up-to-date? Will the source provide information on time?

## Frequently Used Performance Standards

There are two forms of standards used to measure sales performance: outputs and inputs. Output standards, or the measures of results, tell us *how* a sales representative did. Input standards tell us *what* a sales rep did. The notion is that the results sales reps produce are significantly affected by the kind, amount, and quality of the activities they put into doing their jobs.

An example of the effective use of both types of evaluation standards is provided by a large car dealer on the eastern seaboard. The firm employs 60 full-time sales reps. The dealer's sales manager, Jim McGrath, regularly evaluates sales output by measuring gross dollar sales, net dollar sales after trade-in, number of sales made, gross margin contributed after sales rep's commission, and ratio of new cars sold to used cars sold. But in order to appraise the output results and understand what might have caused them so that remedial action can be taken where indicated, McGrath also measures each sales rep's input in terms of number of days worked, number of phone, letter, direct mail, and personal contacts with potential customers, knowledge of products, company price and service policies, and number of customer complaints. Using output and input measures together, McGrath believes that he has an effective method of evaluating the performance of his sales reps.

The more frequently used standards of performance, along with an indication of what results or activities each standard can be used to measure, are listed below. In evaluating sales performance some of the standards can be quantitatively measured; others are determined by the sales manager's judgment and experience.

---

### OUTPUT MEASURES

---

| STANDARD | RESULTS MEASURED |
|---|---|
| Dollar or unit sales volume | Dollar or unit "score." |
| Customer service calls or assignments | Service provided, amount of customer service work done. |
| Share of market attained | Competitive standing in the territory. |
| Number of orders written | Volume of business, frequency of orders taken. |
| Number of reorders | Frequency of repeat business, customer loyalty, selling skill. |
| Expenses | Selling cost one represents, one's interest in expense control. |
| Gross margin on orders | Contribution to overhead, price lines sold |
| Number of active accounts | Territory coverage, potential. |
| Calls made | Activity rate, aggressiveness. |
| Promotion work done | Amount of nonselling, sales supporting activities. |
| Sales against quota or sales budget | Relative sales results against bogey, standing relative to other salespeople |
| Sales versus territory potential | Territory coverage, sales record |
| Average order size | Nature of business written, size of customer, territory conditions, sales skills. |

**OUTPUT MEASURES (continued)**

| STANDARD | RESULTS MEASURED |
|---|---|
| Ratio of orders to calls made | Time allocation, sales success, territory coverage, sales skill, planning ability. |
| Average of cancelled orders | Sales skill, nature of business written. |
| Number of new accounts opened | Aggressiveness, kind of customers called on, planning ability. |

**INPUT MEASURES**

| STANDARD | ACTIVITY MEASURED |
|---|---|
| Calls per day | Time utilization, application to job, kinds of customers called on, activities on calls, planning ability. |
| Nonselling activities (public relations, etc.) | Attitude toward job, kinds of customers called on. |
| Hours worked per day | Application to job, planning ability. |
| Correspondence, phone calls made | Attitude toward job, selling ability. |
| Problem-solving ideas generated | Creativity in managing oneself and the territory. |
| Management of time | Business ability, efficiency, attitude toward job. |
| Product, policy, and procedure knowledge | Attitude toward company and job, selling ability. |
| Ability as market "intelligence agent" | Value as information source, assistance to company. |
| Personal appearance | Value as company representative, selling ability. |
| Personality traits: judgment, honesty, emotional stability, self-discipline, responsibility | Selling skills, value to company. |

## Sales Quotas

Many sales organizations use quotas as performance standards. A sales quota is a specific performance goal assigned to a sales rep, territory, product line, or other relevant marketing unit. For example, salesman John Dubrowsky's quota may be 2,000 units of product X, 15,000 units of product Y, and 8,000 units of product Z during the first quarter of the next fiscal year.

Quotas are based on company and sales objectives that are established during the planning process. Quotas can be established for virtually any result and time period that are relevant to the particular selling job. Some examples are pounds sold, new accounts opened, sales expenses, displays placed in stores, calls made per day, and number of product demonstrations made. However, virtually all companies that use sales quotas include some measure of sales volume in their performance evaluation programs.

Of all the methods for setting sales quotas, many sales managers believe that the best and fairest one is to base quotas on sales forecasts for particular products, customers, or sales territories. This method reduces the bias that may be introduced by using past sales records or arbitrary goals set by management.

Return on investment (ROI) is one useful measure of sales performance. The formula for determining return on investment is:

$$\text{ROI} = \frac{\text{Net Profit}}{\text{Sales}} \times \frac{\text{Sales}}{\text{Investment (or assets managed)}}$$

Thus, a sales territory with sales of $350,000, net profits of $20,000, and with an investment, or assets managed, of $80,000 would have a ROI of 25 percent. This tells us that this sales territory has earned the company 25 percent on the dollars invested. Whether 25 percent is an acceptable return on investment would depend upon the ROI in other sales territories and upon alternative uses of the company's resources.

## Information Sources for Evaluation

Where do we find the information needed to develop the indices and standards we have decided to use? Following are the major sources of information and a summary of their advantages and disadvantages.

### Company Records

The company's own history is often a useful source of data on which performance standards are built. Invoices, volume experience by territory or customer class, complaints, bills of sale, volume-cost-profit experience with various kinds of promotions and lines, the past performance of individual sales reps, and other aspects of company experience are useful in establishing performance standards for salespeople.

An example illustrates the value of company records. A tire manufacturer expanding from regional distribution in the middle west into the

New England market wanted to establish preliminary dollar sales volume quotas as performance standards for new sales reps in that area. Having never sold in New England, what volume quotas should be established? Investigation showed that the social, economic, and competitive characteristics of the proposed New England sales territories were similar to those of selected midwestern territories in which the company had sold for years. So the company's historical sales volume in these comparable midwestern territories was used to establish the initial sales quotas for the new territories.

The potential advantages:

- Information is not generalized to a whole industry, as some other kinds of evaluation data are, but is particular to the company using the information.
- Data source is known, and in most cases the information is easy to obtain and does not require much time to recover.
- Some kinds of in-company evaluation information are very economical to obtain and use compared to other sorts of information.
- The degree of accuracy and relevance of the data are known.

The potential weaknesses and risks:

- The necessary evaluation information may not be available in past company records.
- In some important respects, company history as represented by company records may not accurately reflect present market conditions.

## Customer Contacts

Customers have close and frequent contact with sales reps. They are, therefore, a valuable source of evaluative information about their performance.

The potential advantages:

- Can provide fresh, vital, up-to-the-minute evaluation information.

– Information is firsthand and not subject to distortion by being transmitted through several senders before reaching the supplier's management.
– Customers are reminded that the supplier company is concerned with them, their operations, and their problems.
– Can provide new ideas on how to improve service to customers.
– Can provide useful comparison of sales reps with competitor's reps.

The potential weaknesses and risks:

– Information is random and unweighted. Customers may give inaccurate or garbled accounts of events.
– Difficulty in appraising the information occurs because all the sales manager receives is an overall judgment that a customer has taken away from a series of events.
– Collecting evaluation evidence from customers may appear to sales reps as an intrusion into their relationships with customers. If so, morale and effectiveness will suffer.

### Sales Reps' Reports

Perhaps the most widely used source of evaluation evidence is the information about their activities that sales reps furnish managers through their reports, both written and oral.

The potential advantages:

– Sales reps have intimate, current knowledge of their territories and of their own operations.
– If the reporting system is designed carefully, salespeople can furnish territory coverage information for supervision purposes along with evaluation data in the same report, thus saving the expense of double reporting for the two purposes.

The potential weaknesses and risks:

– Like most people, sales reps will do what they can to protect

themselves from criticism, to make themselves "look good," to make the job as easy as possible, and to maximize their incomes.
 – Completion of sales reports takes time away from selling. As a result, most salespeople do not like to fill out reports.

These weaknesses do *not* imply that salespeople in general will be dishonest or will deliberately distort reports of their activities. To be sure, there are bad apples in every barrel, cheaters in any human group, and when the manager discovers a sales rep cheating on reports, strong disciplinary action or dismissal should follow quickly.

But more important and prevalent than outright cheating on reports of sales activities is the subtle tendency for a sales rep to report favorably in all instances where there is a legitimate choice on what to report. For instance, if customer calls-per-day is an important performance evaluation factor, how many calls did salesman Joe Ricci make today? He made 10 bona fide calls on customers and happened to run into another customer in a restaurant. They had lunch together and discussed baseball the whole time. How many calls does he report for the day? He is likely to report 11 calls.

This quite human tendency for a sales rep to "look out for number one" in activity reports is a strong reason why so many companies try to collect evaluative evidence on all important job performance factors from more than one source. When a particular evaluation measure is very important and one important source of information on it is what salespeople report about themselves, other collaborating sources should be used.

Earlier we discussed the reluctance that most salespeople and sales managers exhibit when they must take time to do paperwork. Too often sales reporting forms ask for detailed, relatively unimportant information that is difficult and time-consuming for sales people to compile. Salespeople should be asked to provide *only* the information that is required for sales planning, management control, and performance evaluation. Also, sales activity reports should be designed specifically to minimize sales force resistance and reduce the time required to complete the reports.

## Manager's Field Visits

Although most managers cannot find enough time to travel with and observe their people frequently, visits to the field provide important information about the performance of sales reps.

The potential advantages:

- The ability to cross-check other evaluation information with field observation.
- If properly done, demonstrates to sales reps and customers management's interest and concern with their operations.
- Reinforces the importance of evaluation to the sales rep on a personal level.

The potential weaknesses and risks:

- Salespeople may bias field observations by calling only on easy accounts.
- Customers may change their normal behavior patterns, to become tougher or easier, or bring up matters they normally do not discuss with sales reps when they call alone.

### Manager's "Sixth Sense"

Although a manager usually cannot state it in figures or symbols, charts or graphs, the good sales manager has a "sixth sense" in evaluating the performance of the sales group. The manager has usually been a sales rep and is experienced in the industry and the company. Further, the manager knows the members of the sales group as professionals and as individuals. From this knowledge comes a valuable instinct to be used in the evaluation of their work.

Some sales management experts disagree with this contention, arguing that the evaluation of performance can and should be completely objective and scientific, with no room for instinct or the personal judgment of the manager. Interestingly, the majority of those who hold this view are professors and researchers, not salespeople or sales managers. Most salespeople and sales managers support the view that instinct is as useful in evaluation as any of the other more scientific measures; that instead of instinct taking precedence over science in evaluation, or science over instinct, the two complement each other.

The potential advantages:

- Brings the priceless ingredient of experience and insight to the evaluation process.

– Humanizes evaluation, making it more understandable and acceptable to salespeople.
– Serves as an important cross-check with other objective evaluation data.

The potential weaknesses and risks:

– Manager's instinct and judgment may be biased.
– Manager may come to rely too heavily on his or her own judgment against other objective evaluation standards.

## External Sources

External forces influence a representative's sales performance. Shifts in buying power in a territory, population trends, economic activities, number of potential customers—many external forces influence a rep's performance and thereby influence evaluation. To take these forces into account, the good evaluation program includes performance measures that often must be based on information coming from outside the company.

Some examples are:

– Sales of our product are directly related to the total population in each territory. We want to evaluate our reps on this performance factor. What is the population in each of our sales territories?
– We think our sales reps' expense ratio is high. How do we compare with industry experience?
– We want to evaluate how our reps are doing in regard to each person's active, versus potential, accounts. How many potential customers are there in each sales territory?

There are many available sources of this information. These sources are of two general types: government and private. The government sources consist of federal and state agencies and bureaus. The private sources are trade, industry, and professional publications and associations. A detailed discussion of these sources of information is beyond the scope of this book. For more information on external data sources, consult the list of government and private source guides that follows the references at the end of this chapter.

The potential advantages:

- Much outside information is free or inexpensive.
- In some cases, outside information sources provide useful data that the company could not afford to gather for itself.
- Outside sources provide information in some instances that a company itself could not get even if it could afford to.

The potential weaknesses and risks:

- Data may not be applicable to the company's operations, although they may at first seem to be.
- Information available outside may not provide the needed facts, or in the required arrangement or detail.
- Information may be outdated because of the delay between collection and publication.

## Case Study

Before turning to the operation of an evaluation program, let's return to the Medical File case. Read this portion of the case and answer the questions that follow.

Medical File, Inc. (B)

After much thought, Ed Larson decided to develop a formal evaluation program for Medical File's sales reps. He reviewed the job description and selected three performance standards.

1. Sales quota. Each sales rep's quota would be a sales forecast prepared by the national sales manager in consultation with the company's controller. The sales forecast for each rep's territory would be based on past sales records and information on the number of hospital beds in the territory.
2. Calls per day. Although territory size varied, Larson felt that each sales rep should average 2.5 sales calls per day.
3. Selling expenses. Using past experience and industry information, Larson estimated that a rep's direct selling expenses should be approximately 2 percent of his or her total sales.

The evaluation program and these performance standards were presented to the sales reps at a national sales meeting. Although there was some grumbling that the sales forecasts were too high, Larson felt that his evaluation program was received well by Medical File's reps.

*Do you think Ed Larson chose the right performance standards? Why or why not?* _____

_____

_____

_____

*Would you use any other evaluation criteria in appraising Medical File's reps? Why would you use them rather than the ones chosen?*

_____

_____

_____

*Does your company use any of the performance standards identified in this case? If so, what is your opinion of their usefulness in evaluating sales performance?* _____

_____

_____

_____

*Should Larson have involved his sales reps in the development of the sales evaluation program? Why or why not?* _____

_____

_____

_____

## OPERATION OF THE EVALUATION PROGRAM

We have considered the key problems in the design of a formal program to evaluate sales performance. Now we must consider the important questions relating to its successful *operation*. This will involve consideration of who should evaluate salespeople, how frequently evaluation should take place, the follow-up, the sales rep's involvement in evaluation, and training the evaluators to evaluate.

## Who Should Evaluate Performance?

There is an important distinction between who should *design* the evaluation program and who should *operate* it. The evaluation plan should be designed by those in the company with the widest sales experience, managers who know the company, its products, and markets in the greatest detail, and who are experienced in evaluation programs. In most companies, this means that the evaluation program is originally designed, and periodically reviewed, by top sales management and their staff. But who should actually make evaluations and work with them once the plan has been designed? Should it be headquarters sales executives and their staff? Regional sales managers? Field sales managers? Corporate staff evaluation specialists? In the effective operation of an evaluation program, where evaluation should take place is a critical question.

The level in the company where sales evaluation takes place varies in industry. But when you consider the question from an operational point of view, you see that evaluation of a sales rep's performance should be made at the lowest possible level of supervision, preferably by the immediate supervisor. There are a number of reasons to support this conclusion.

### Strengthens the Subordinate-Supervisor Relationship

Evaluation of performance by the sales rep's immediate supervisor places them in a closer working relationship. They must work together on the rep's problems, and they share the satisfaction of improving the individual and his or her work. If well managed by the supervisor, participative evaluation brings the supervisor closer to the salespeople, thereby making other supervisory responsibilities easier and more effective. Morale is improved because salespeople see the interest the supervisor has in their work. They have a chance during evaluation to "work with the boss" on their sales problems.

### Mutual Commitment

When the sales rep and the immediate supervisor participate in the evaluation together, they are both personally and publicly committed to improving the rep's performance and to solving their mutual problems. This commitment is extremely important to both the manager and the rep.

What develops is a mutual understanding or "contract" in which they identify and agree on specific areas where the rep can improve; decide exactly how improvements can be accomplished; how the manager can help; what the rep will do to improve sales performance; how long these actions will take; and how they will know when a problem has been resolved.

## Supervisory Responsibility

The supervisor is responsible for the performance results of the sales group and is judged by how well or poorly they perform. Through their work the manager stands or falls. Consequently, it is only sensible and fair that the manager play a major role in evaluating performance and in working out remedial action based on the evaluations. When the supervisor does not have an important part in evaluation of the sales group's performance, we are likely to see the classic administrative blunder: assigning the supervisor responsibility for subordinates' performance without the necessary authority to remedy their mistakes.

## Communication of Goals and Remedies

Perhaps the most important reason why the sales rep's immediate supervisor should play a major role in evaluating performance is so that the rep and the supervisor both can have a clear understanding of what is right and wrong with performance and what remedial actions must be taken, when, why, how, and by whom. If someone other than the sales rep's immediate supervisor evaluates sales performance, a third party is introduced, communication is immediately made more difficult, and resentments can quickly appear. They both begin to ask of third party evaluation: What standards are being used? What is meant? Why was that decided? What information is being used? Why was it recommended that I solve my problems that way? What right does someone else have to judge my work? But when the evaluation of a third party is not imposed upon the sales rep and the manager, when they are forced to interpret the meaning of the evaluation, they each know precisely what the situation is. Evaluation communication is clear.

### Frequency of Evaluation

How frequently should salespeople be evaluated? The question posed here relates to the frequency of *formal* evaluation, not to routine evaluations and remedial changes that are made almost daily in normal sales operations. Clearly, when a sales rep is judged to have made a mistake of some significance (evaluation), it should be brought to the rep's attention as soon as possible, not stored up against some future formal evaluation date.

But apart from individual, routine corrections, how often should salespeople be evaluated under a formal evaluation program? Industry practice varies, as indicated by the Scott survey cited earlier in this chapter. All companies in the study reported that they used some form of sales evaluation. Of the 36 percent who reported they had a *formal* system of evaluation, the frequency with which they evaluated their salespeople was:[2]

| | |
|---|---|
| At least every 3 months | 30% |
| 3 to 6 months | 27 |
| 6 to 12 months | 21 |
| 1 to 2 years | 15 |
| 2 to 5 years | 7 |

We see that 57 percent evaluated their people at least twice a year and 78 percent at least annually.

Why does industry practice vary? How can we decide what is the best frequency for evaluation of a particular sales group? To answer these questions, think of the two extremes of frequency that are theoretically possible. At one extreme, we could formally evaluate salespeople after every call; at the other, we could evaluate a person's work only on retirement. Immediately you reject these extremes as impractical and useless. Of the first you might say, "No company could afford a formal evaluation plan with such frequency." Of the latter, your reaction is, "But it wouldn't do anybody any good, not the sales rep, the company, or the sales manager."

Refinement of this analysis leads to the critical questions that must be answered to decide what frequency of evaluation is optimal for your company or any other individual sales group.

## Time Required to Evaluate

Each formal evaluation plan operates on its own evaluation time cycle. The time cycle is the sum of the amount of time necessary to complete all steps in the evaluation program. With simple plans, the

[2]Ibid.

evaluation time cycle is short, perhaps only a week or so. With more elaborate plans, the time cycle may run to months. Consider the example of a time cycle analysis made by an office equipment manufacturer:

| ACTIVITIES IN THE EVALUATION CYCLE | TIME REQUIRED |
|---|---|
| Data collection | 90 days |
| Information processing | 10 days |
| Supervisor's work with salespeople on performance evaluation and improvement plans | 5 days |
| Total Evaluation Time Cycle | 105 days |

This, of course, is not to say that this company spends 105 full-time days on each evaluation cycle. Rather it means that 105 days are needed to complete an evaluation cycle. Another company might require a month or two weeks.

One of the answers to the question about how frequently we should evaluate emerges from this example: we cannot formally evaluate more frequently than our evaluation time cycle will allow. If the cycle requires 105 days, we cannot formally evaluate more frequently than that. The evaluation time cycle sets a bottom limit on the frequency of formal evaluation that is possible under any given evaluation program.

## Intrusion of Evaluation

The sales rep's and supervisor's jobs are made up of *current* and *future* activities. Current activities are those performed in the present to achieve immediate results. Future activities are those performed in the present to achieve future results. For salespeople, selling, calling on customers, opening new accounts, providing service, and filling out reports are current activities, functions that must be performed now, today, to achieve immediate results. For the supervisor, traveling with salespeople and calling on customers are current activities, today's responsibilities for immediate payoffs.

Evaluation, however, is for both salespeople and their managers, a *future* activity. It is performed not to gain immediate benefits, but to achieve desired future gains. All future activities are based on the concept of *investment:* giving up something of value in the present in the expectation of receiving something of greater value in the future. The college student gives up present income in the expectation that a college education will produce greater personal, social, and economic returns in the future. You, by reading this book, are giving up your present time in the expectation of receiving greater benefits in the future.

In short, future activities *intrude* on current activites; they are a cost in time, money, energy, and attention on current activities.

Evaluation, as a future activity, intrudes by taking time, energy, and attention away from current activities and by costing money. When we are evaluating past performance to improve future performance, we cannot be selling, calling on customers, or performing any other current activity.

Therefore, another criterion for how frequently to evaluate is how much intrusion on current activities can be tolerated. How much time can salespeople and managers in your company spend away from their present activities in order to evaluate? There is no all-inclusive answer. This is a judgmental decision to be made by each company in light of its own needs and conditions. One company may decide that for the sake of future performance their salespeople and supervisors must forego a considerable amount of present activity in the expectation of more substantial future gain. Others may severely limit evaluation, preferring to emphasize present gains over potential future benefits.

## Time Required for Remedial Action

The last criterion that should be applied in answering the question how frequently should we evaluate is: how long does it take salespeople to solve problems that are indicated by the evaluation and how long does it take them to perform the functions on which they are evaluated?

This is only common sense. It is pointless to evaluate salespeople more frequently than they are able to react to the evaluation. If, for example, an important performance criterion is the number of new accounts opened and it takes an average of six months to open a new account, it makes little sense to evaluate this activity more often than semiannually.

In summary, we see that the best frequency of formal evaluation for a particular sales group is the frequency that is established in relation to the evaluation time cycle; is no more intrusive on present selling and management activities than is acceptable; and takes into account the time required to remedy mistakes, solve problems, and perform the activities being evaluated.

## Evaluation Follow-up

*Rating* or score keeping simply tells us what a sales representative did. But if the formal *evaluation* plan is a good one, it will show what specific selling activities each individual did well or poorly and, either directly or by deduction, it will give us the reasons and causes behind these results. Essentially, a good evaluation program indicates *where changes are and are not required to improve each individual's selling performance*. Therefore, unless something is done about evaluation, unless it results in worthwhile change, it is a waste of money, time, effort, and attention. Evaluation must continue through follow-up, the identification of remedial actions to be taken, and the check by the supervisor that the remedial plan is being followed.

However, should it be necessary for the sales manager to follow up to see that salespeople make the necessary changes that are indicated by their evaluations? Should the manager's supervisor have to follow up to be sure that required changes have been made? After all, isn't that their job? The answer to all of these questions is "yes." Follow-up is necessary because the indicated remedial activities frequently involve changing work habits or making the job more difficult. All of us, when left to our own devices, tend to resist change by returning to our old habits, the old ways of doing business, to the easiest, most pleasant way of working. Without follow-up, like water flowing downhill, salespeople will revert to their old ways, to repeating the same mistakes.

Some procedures used to ensure performance evaluation follow-up by salespeople and supervisors are: regular post-evaluation reports from sales supervisors to their superiors summarizing the steps their people will take to improve specific aspects of their performance; subsequent progress reports; special entry on a sales rep's regular activity report where the manager states the problem(s) the last evaluation showed, the plan for correction, steps taken to solve it and results to date; when traveling with a rep, the supervisor is careful to review progress and status on particular problems shown by the evaluation; special reports from salespeople to the supervisor concerning specific problems uncovered by evaluation; reports by individual salespeople at sales meetings on their plans and progress toward solutions.

*Does your company employ some follow-up system on evaluation? If not, should there be? How?* _____

_____

## Degree of Sales Force Involvement
## in Their Own Evaluations

The degree of the sales group's involvement is the extent to which they are allowed or required to participate in the evaluation of their own performances; how much they are consulted in the process and how much detail they are given about results. Industry has adopted one of three policies, two extremes and a middle position. These can be characterized as: no participation, complete participation, and selected participation.

We must avoid considering these three policies, especially the two extremes, on any other basis than the business considerations of a particular company and market. The best policy is the one that best serves the particular company. These policies cannot be judged, nor choices made between them, on ideal, social, or ethical grounds. One policy is not better or worse than the others because it is more "democratic," or "humane," or "considerate." The real question is: Given our market, products, competition, customers, and sales force, what is the best policy for *us?* For instance, in some companies a restricted budget for evaluation, or the need for constant, speedy evaluation, or the pressure for the performance of current activities, or other important considerations not only justify a no-participation policy, but make it the only policy possible. Each policy is applicable to particular conditions and is a "good" or "bad" policy in relation only to how well it fits the conditions.

To study which policy would be best for your company, we will analyze the advantages and disadvantages of the two extreme policies. The middle ground policy of selective participation, of course, shares the advantages and disadvantages of the two extremes.

### No Participation

This policy is based on the premise that management is best qualified to set standards and evaluate results and that the results of sales evaluation are the property of management to be used in any way they see fit.

The potential advantages are:

– Salespeople are not taken from selling activities by participation in evaluation.

221

- Salespeople cannot dispute evaluation because they know nothing about it.
- This policy is less expensive because there is no data from salespeople to process and evaluate.
- Less time is needed for evaluation because less data are compiled.

The potential disadvantages are:

- Evaluation is less complete because no data from salespeople are included.
- Because evaluative data are less complete, they are usually less accurate.
- The lack of participation by salespeople may make the evaluation less useful for personal development purposes.
- This policy may have a negative impact on the morale of salespeople, who see a no-participation policy as selective, unilateral, and high-handed.

### Complete Participation

This policy is based on the proposition that the sales rep and the company share a common interest in evaluation of performance, that salespeople have useful information to contribute and that evaluation is for the guidance of all those concerned.

The potential advantages are:

- This policy adds the sales rep's intimate knowledge of the territory, customers, personal operations, and habits to the evaluation, thereby making the evaluation more complete and usually more accurate.
- Communication of job requirements between salespeople and their supervisors is improved.
- A genuine interest by supervision in what the sales rep is doing is communicated.
- Salespeople are able to see specifically how they may improve their performance because they know precisely how and why they are evaluated.

– This policy may have a positive impact on the morale of sales-people, who see a complete-participation policy as open and supportive of their self-development.

The potential disadvantages are:

– Salespeople must divert time from selling to participate in the evaluation program.
– Salespeople may challenge and debate performance standards and results.
– Costs of collecting, processing, and analyzing data from sales-people may be high.
– Because more data are compiled, the time required to complete the evaluation cycle will be longer.

## Selected Participation

This policy seeks a middle ground between the two extremes. It is viewed as a method of achieving some of the benefits of both of the other procedures.

## Case Study

Before we consider methods for involving salespeople in their evaluation, let's return again to the Medical File case. Read this portion of the case and respond to the questions that follow.

Medical File, Inc. (C)

At the end of the first year of the evaluation plan's operation, Ed Larson compiled the following information on Medical File's 15 sales reps.

While reviewing the information, Larson made the following observations.

1. Six sales reps met or exceeded their quotas and nine did not.
2. Sales of three reps (Cross, Reynolds, Todd) were more than 30 percent below their forecasts.
3. Selling expenses of four reps (Baker, Cross, Goodman, Watson) were 3 percent or more of their sales.

## MEDICAL FILE'S REPS' PERFORMANCE

| SALES REP | SALES FORECAST | ACTUAL SALES | PERCENT OF FORECAST | SELLING EXPENSES | PERCENT OF SALES | CALLS PER DAY |
|---|---|---|---|---|---|---|
| Linda Baker | $ 506,500 | $ 531,600 | 105.0% | $ 15,758 | 3.0% | 2.0 |
| Michael Cross | 472,100 | 328,700 | 69.6 | 11,965 | 3.6 | 1.3 |
| John Gates | 465,900 | 396,900 | 85.2 | 11,220 | 2.8 | 3.1 |
| Calvin Goodman | 427,000 | 368,000 | 86.2 | 12,180 | 3.3 | 3.3 |
| Robert McAndrews | 450,000 | 580,200 | 128.9 | 6,696 | 1.2 | 2.5 |
| David Murphy | 544,200 | 664,800 | 122.2 | 10,684 | 1.6 | 3.0 |
| Diane Reynolds | 583,000 | 406,400 | 69.7 | 10,716 | 2.6 | 3.9 |
| Lester Richards | 614,700 | 513,400 | 86.4 | 5,028 | 1.0 | 2.1 |
| Gerald Simmons | 522,600 | 462,700 | 88.5 | 6,756 | 1.5 | 2.7 |
| Thomas Smith | 479,600 | 510,400 | 106.4 | 9,492 | 1.9 | 2.9 |
| Lawrence Todd | 638,100 | 383,800 | 60.1 | 8,288 | 2.2 | 1.8 |
| Susan Tyson | 470,600 | 590,500 | 125.5 | 11,872 | 2.0 | 3.0 |
| Ruben Vargas | 432,300 | 582,000 | 134.6 | 9,936 | 1.7 | 3.5 |
| Thomas Watson | 432,100 | 412,800 | 95.5 | 12,972 | 3.1 | 2.1 |
| Joseph Whelan | 485,700 | 452,500 | 93.2 | 7,776 | 1.7 | 2.3 |
| Company Total or Average | $7,524,400 | $7,202,700 | 95.7% | $140,570 | 2.0% | 2.6 |

4. Six reps (Baker, Cross, Richards, Todd, Watson, Whelan) were below the expected 2.5 sales calls per day.

*What should Larson do with the information he has compiled?* __

_____

_____

_____

*How would you recommend that the evaluation be followed up?*

_____

_____

_____

*Which specific sales reps do you feel should receive special attention? Why?* _____

_____

_____

_____

## Methods of Involving Salespeople in Their Evaluations

Companies that involve their salespeople to some degree in their own evaluations use a variety of techniques or combinations of them to accomplish this.

### Evaluation Interviews

Many companies require that sales supervisors review the evaluation with each person in a personal interview after each evaluation cycle. Sometimes called a performance appraisal or periodic development interview, the evaluation interview involves an open and free discussion between the sales rep and the manager. This interview is intended to permit the sales manager to transmit evaluation results to the sales rep; clarify any necessary points; object or raise questions; and to allow the supervisor and the sales rep to agree upon the action that must be taken.

Companies using the evaluation interview report that it is a very important management activity. They point out that in addition to translating evaluation into meaningful action by the sales rep and reemphasizing the company's performance standards, the evaluation interview is a strong motivator; a source of detailed market information for the supervisor; an additional chance for the supervisor to evaluate the sales rep; and an opportunity for the supervisor to train the sales rep further.

Despite the importance and proven benefits of evaluation interviews, many sales managers are reluctant to conduct them. The major reason is that they are afraid the interview will be an unpleasant, embarrassing experience. Although this is possible, careful preparation and the proper frame of mind can increase the chances that these interviews will be a strong positive element in the evaluation and development program.

The following guidelines are suggested for the sales manager who conducts evaluation interviews with subordinates:

1. Do your homework! Prepare for the interview by thoroughly reviewing the sales rep's records and performance history.
2. Select the right place, where you will be alone, and the right time, when you are relaxed and feel helpful toward the subordinate.
3. Open the interview by establishing a relaxed atmosphere. Reassure the rep that the interview is to help him or her do a better job and that you are ready to help in any way you can.
4. Encourage the rep to talk. Listen carefully to what the rep has to say. Show your interest and check your own understanding by asking questions.
5. Present a balanced review of the person's work performance, citing positive factors as well as those needing improvement. It is usually best to begin with a positive factor. Some interviewers use the "sandwich technique" where strong and weak points are alternated.
6. Establish and maintain throughout the interview a logical, helping orientation. To the greatest extent possible, deal with facts, not hunches or opinions. Remind the rep that the purpose is to help him or her do a better job. A "shape up or ship out" interview is *not* an evaluation development interview. It is a disciplinary interview. Remind the rep that you are there to help solve problems.
7. Don't end the interview until you and the rep have agreed to a remedial action plan, including what both of you will do to help improve specific weaknesses brought out in the evaluation.

8. Be careful not to make, or even imply, promises, such as a salary raise or promotion, that you are not sure you can keep.

## Management by Objectives

Although management by objectives (MBO) is a planning and motivation process (see Chapter 5), many companies use its basic concepts in their sales evaluation programs. Using MBO in performance evaluation allows salespeople and managers to concentrate on specific performance goals and results. In this way, much of the bias of individual personalities is removed from the evaluation.

When applied to sales evaluation, MBO is a process by which salespeople and their managers agree upon relevant activities, target dates, and goals that will be used at a later date as standards to evaluate sales performance. Many companies also include individual self-development goals, such as improvement of interpersonal skills, improvement of technical skills, and preparation for advancement, as part of the goal-setting process. Since MBO requires that performance goals be set by the sales manager and the sales rep together, the evaluation focuses on goals the rep helped to develop. Thus, the rep is more committed to their achievement than might otherwise be the case.

As an evaluation procedure, MBO has all of the advantages and disadvantages of a complete-participation policy. In particular, proponents of MBO contend that this procedure will lead to increased sales force motivation. Further, MBO requires that performance appraisal be an ongoing process. "This is what we should have done last quarter. How did we do?" By giving constant feedback, the sales manager is able to pinpoint opportunities for improvement in each rep's performance and personal growth.

## Self-Evaluation by Salespeople

Another device that is used to increase the sales rep's participation in formal evaluation programs is for the rep to evaluate performance at the same time and on the same standards as the superior. The two evaluations are compared and form the basis for the performance interview. It is interesting that when this technique is employed, salespeople are usually harder on themselves than their supervisors are. Such a technique has the advantages of drawing salespeople's attention to specific aspects of performance and highlights clearly for them what changes must be made. In addition, this technique, when properly managed, makes it easier for the supervisor to work with salespeople on their evaluations and to attain their enthusiastic, constructive cooperation for improving their performance.

### Formal and Informal Evaluation of the Program by Salespeople

Involvement is also achieved by the supervisor soliciting the salespeople's appraisal of the evaluation system itself, either informally or formally. Informally, when traveling with sales reps, the manager seeks their reactions to, and comments about, the evaluation program. Is it measuring the right activities? In the right terms? Over the proper time period? Is there something the sales rep wants to report about this performance that the plan does not allow? Comments to evaluative questions about the plan can be gathered in field visits, increasing sales reps' participation in the plan.

The same kind of participation is achieved more formally by making the evaluation plan a topic for constructive analysis at formal sales meetings, where individual sales reps or a panel present their ideas and suggestions about the plan.

### Case Study

As discussed in the previous section, it is important to follow up the evaluation and to involve salespeople in their evaluations. Many sales managers use evaluation interviews to involve the sales rep and to probe for remedial actions. Read the following portion of the Medical File case and respond to the questions that follow.

Medical File, Inc. (D)

After reviewing sales reps' performance data, Ed Larson decided to conduct an evaluation interview with each rep. Two reps he wanted to see as soon as possible were Diane Reynolds and Lawrence Todd.

Diane Reynolds is a young woman who joined Medical File three years ago. Her previous job was assistant accounting manager in a medium-sized suburban hospital. During her first two years on the job, Reynolds impressed the former sales manager with her enthusiasm and dynamic personality. As a result, just before Ed Larson became sales manager, she was transferred to a new territory with excellent potential.

Like his predecessor, Larson was impressed by this sales rep's positive attitude and personality. However, he was disappointed that she had not come close to achieving her sales quota. He had also heard several disturbing reports from her customers. The general impression Ed Larson receives from customers is that she has difficulty adapting Medical File's record-keeping systems to specific needs of customers. They acknowledge that Reynolds makes an excellent impression and knows the health care field well, but they are not impressed with her product knowledge. One hospital administrator said, "Diane makes a great PR gal, but I don't have any confidence in her ability to solve our problems."

Lawrence Todd, in terms of service, is Medical File's oldest sales rep. He has always been among the top producers and respected by his peers. In fact, most of the other sales reps expected Todd to be promoted to national sales manager when the former manager left.

Ed Larson's relations with Todd have been pleasant, but distant. He realized that Todd was disappointed, but he felt that the rep's pride would help him overcome this and enable him to continue his record as a top sales producer. Unfortunately, although Todd has the sales territory with the greatest potential, his actual sales have been much below the forecast.

When Larson called to arrange a field visit, he was immediately confronted with an angry response from Todd. "I told you the sales forecast was too damn high! How do you expect anyone to meet an unrealistic goal like that?"

*Refer to the guidelines for conducting an evaluation interview. Briefly outline how Larson should conduct the interview with Diane Reynolds.* _____

_____

_____

_____

*Should Larson conduct the evaluation interview with Larry Todd differently? If so, briefly outline the approach he should take.* __

_____

_____

*Should Larson have involved Medical File's sales reps more in the evaluation program? Why?* _____

_____

_____

_____

## Training the Evaluators

When we accept the proposition that the basic purpose of all sales evaluation is the development of selling skills, we are committed to a difficult and complex management process, even though the particular evaluation system involved may be quite simple.

Because evaluation is such a complex process, supervisors and other executives who do it must be trained in its use. It is not true that because a person is skilled in a field, he or she is thereby well qualified to appraise the performance of others. A top sales executive is not necessarily a great evaluator of others' sales performance. Managers must be trained, counselled, and guided on how to evaluate. Good evaluators have the skills, experience, and insights to know:

- The significance of each performance standard being used; for example, that the number of promotions secured with customers is in part a measure of the rep's aggressiveness.
- How to spot meaningful patterns of results; for example, a rep's calls/day have been trending steadily up or down.
- The significance of the interrelationship between several performance indices; for example, the relationship between number of new accounts opened and sales expenses.
- How to use performance measures to imply conclusions about individual selling skills; for example, that most accounts and orders are small may imply that a rep is not skillful in handling large accounts.
- How to cross-check evaluation evidence by placing one set of observations against another; for example, sales rep's activity reports against field visits with the rep.
- How to explain problems and deficiencies to salespeople and work out remedial action with them.
- How to be as objective and unbiased as possible; not to evaluate

people against the evaluator and his or her experience, or whether the evaluator likes them, but against the established performance standards.

These skills and insights of the evaluator do not "come naturally," nor are they necessarily the result of normal field selling or supervisory experience. They must be deliberatly transmitted to evaluators by some form of indoctrination or training. Some methods of training evaluators follow.

## Evaluation Manual

Collective company experience is assembled in a how-to-do-it instruction manual which new evaluators are expected to master and experienced evaluators to review periodically.

## Seminars

Supervisors who are assuming evaluation as a new responsibility are gathered in a group for a training seminar. Under the direction of skilled evaluators, they study cases, problems, and exercises in sales evaluation. They hear lectures and instructions and exchange their views and insights with experienced evaluators and their contemporaries.

## Observation and Critique

An experienced evaluator is assigned to a new evaluator and together they work through a number of individual evaluations. The experienced evaluator shows the new evaluator what to look for and how to prepare sales evaluations.

### The Problems and Promise of Evaluation

Performance evaluation is a sales management process that is difficult and inexact. It is an art striving to become a science. But as uncertain as it is, industry experience has proven that if it is used with full recognition of its problems and limitations, it pays real dividends. Information from the evaluation process is especially important to the sales manager who is concerned with the growth and development of individual salespeople. And all sales managers must be!

## Brain teasers

|  | Agree | Disagree |
|---|---|---|
| 1. The basic purpose of sales evaluation is to rate or rank sales performance against objective standards. | ____ | ____ |
| 2. The single, most important problem in designing a good evaluation program is securing top management's support for the concept of performance evaluation. | ____ | ____ |
| 3. In general, the fewer standards of sales performance that are used, the better. | ____ | ____ |
| 4. Performance standards for salespeople within an industry, for example, small electrical appliances, tend to be the same in all companies in the industry. | ____ | ____ |
| 5. The most accurate source of evaluation information for salespeople is information they furnish about themselves through their reports. | ____ | ____ |
| 6. The regular evaluation of performance is a continuing function of top levels of sales management. | ____ | ____ |
| 7. The follow-up of sales evaluation is a continuing and important function of field sales management. | ____ | ____ |
| 8. Sales reps should always participate actively in their own performance evaluations. | ____ | ____ |
| 9. Many sales managers fear evaluation interviews because they are unprepared. | ____ | ____ |
| 10. Generally it is necessary to train and orient evaluators only when an evaluation program is very complex. | ____ | ____ |

## Activities

1. Discuss evaluation with a sales executive of a company with a formal evaluation program. List the reasons and conditions this manager cites as favoring and not favoring the use of any sales evaluation system in this company. Do you agree? Why?____

2. *A friend of yours with 10 years experience as a saleswoman with two companies has just been hired by a third company as national sales manager. In discussing her new job with you, she says, "What a challenge! You know neither of the companies I worked for before had evaluation programs for their salespeople. One of the first things I'm going to do is design and put into operation a good, hard-hitting sales evaluation program. It'll be easy and quick to set one up. I should have it working in a matter of weeks. What do you think?" Outline your reply to her.* _____

_____

_____

_____

3. *What performance standards does the company you studied in question 1 use in evaluating sales performance? Do you think these are the right measures? Why? Would you make any changes in the measures used? Why?* _____

_____

_____

4. *With your wife, husband, or a friend, thoroughly discuss the question: Should college students take an active part in evaluating their own class and course performance and setting their grades? Take notes on this discussion, organizing them in yes or no columns. Now study your lists. How, if at all, do they apply to the question of salespeople participating in their own evaluations?* _____

_____

_____

5. *Make a list of the specific skills and knowledge people in your company would have to possess to be good evaluators of sales performance. Identify which of these would have to be "trained into" an evaluator and which the evaluator should know from experience or common sense. What does this analysis indicate about training evaluators in your company? Why?* _____

_____

_____

# SELECTED REFERENCES

## Overview of Evaluation

FOURNIER, FERDINAND F., "No Praise for Salesman's Appraisal," *Sales Management,* March 3, 1975, pp. 40–42 ff.

KEARNEY, WILLIAM J., "Performance Appraisal: Which Way to Go? *MSU Business Topics* (Winter 1977), pp. 58–64.

*Measuring Salesmen's Performance.* New York: National Industrial Conference Board, 1965.

RIEDER, GEORGE A., "Performance Review—A Mixed Bag." *Harvard Business Review* (July-August 1973), pp. 61–67.

## Developing the Sales Evaluation Program

STANTON, WILLIAM J., and RICHARD H. BUSKIRK. "Evaluating Sales Force Performance," in *Management of the Sales Force* (5th ed.). Homewood, Ill.: Richard D. Irwin, 1977.

STILL, RICHARD R., and EDWARD W. CUNDIFF, "Controlling and Evaluating Salesmen's Performance," in *Sales Management: Decisions, Policies and Cases* (2nd ed.). Englewood Cliffs, N.J.: Prentice-Hall, 1969.

STROH, THOMAS F., "Quotes and Performance Appraisals," in *Managing the Sales Function.* New York: McGraw-Hall, 1978.

WOTRUBA, THOMAS R., and MICHAEL L. THURLOW, "Sales Force Participation in Quota Setting and Sales Forecasting," *Journal of Marketing* (April 1976), pp. 11–16.

## Operation of the Evaluation Program

BROWN, RONALD, "The Appraisal Process," in *From Selling to Managing.* New York: American Management Association, 1968.

EVERED, JAMES F., "Keeping the Sales Force on Target," *Sales and Marketing Management* (December 1978), pp. 77–79.

HANAN, MACK, and others, "How to Evaluate Salesforce Performance," in *Take-Charge Sales Management.* New York: Amacom, 1976.

HENRY, J. PORTER, and staff, "Failing at the Controls," *Sales Management,* July 9, 1973, pp. 28–29.

JACKSON, DONALD W., JR., and RAMON J. ALDAG, "Managing The Sales Force by Objectives," *MSU Business Topics* (Spring 1974), pp. 53–59.

"Portfolio of Sales Control Forms, Special Report," *Sales Management*
August 18, 1975.


## SOURCE GUIDES FOR EXTERNAL DATA

ANDRIOT, JOHN L., *Guide to U.S. Government Serials and Periodicals*.
McLean, Va.: Documents Index, 1970.

COMAN, EDWIN T., JR., *Sources of Business Information*, (rev. ed.).
Berkeley: University of California Press, 1964.

FRANK, NATHALIE D., *Market Analysis: A Handbook of Current Data
Sources* (2nd ed.). Metuchen, N.J.: Scarecrow Press, 1969.

JOHNSON, H. WEBSTER, *How to Use the Business Library*, (4th ed.).
Cincinnati: South-Western Publishing, 1972.

WASSERMAN, PAUL, and others. *Encyclopedia of Business Information
Sources*. Detroit: Gale Research, 1970.

WECKESSER, TIMOTHY C., JOSEPH R. WHALEY, and MIRIAM WHALEY, *Business Services and Information: The Guide to the Federal Government*. New York: Management Information Exchange, 1978.

# 8

# YOUR FUTURE AS
# A SALES MANAGER

*After reading this chapter, you should be able to demonstrate your learning as follows:*
- *Identify the major future trends that will affect your job as a sales manager.*
- *Improve the management of your time by better planning, discipline, and organization.*
- *Develop a personal plan for career advancement.*

We have completed the full cycle of activities that are required in managing people who sell—sales personnel planning, recruiting, selection, training, leadership, compensation, and evaluation. In this chapter, we change our focus from your sales people to *you,* the sales manager.

The preceding chapters should help you to develop and manage a professional sales organization. Now we consider what you ought to know about managing *yourself* and *your* continued professional growth and development. To do this we begin by previewing the future of selling and sales management. What will your business world be like? Then we turn to one of the sales manager's most pressing problems, now and in the future—managing time effectively. We conclude with specific suggestions for your professional development.

## THE FUTURE OF SALES MANAGEMENT

What will your business world be like in 5 or 10 years? Predicting the future is risky in any circumstances, and prediction is even more difficult in the rapidly changing environment of sales management. However, some trends can be identified. The most important factors that will affect your future as a sales manager are international sales, changes in the people who sell, selling in service and nonprofit organizations, the energy crisis, and the increased professionalism of sales.

## International Sales

As increasing numbers of American firms become involved in international markets, more and more sales managers find themselves dealing with salespeople and customers in foreign countries. Important, and sometimes baffling differences in culture, social customs, business practices, political policies, and legal restrictions make the international sales manager's job quite different from that of his or her domestic counterpart. Several of the problems you will encounter if you are involved in international sales are:

1. Selling is viewed as a low status occupation in many foreign countries. Consequently, it is more difficult to attract and retain qualified sales recruits.
2. Studies show that the costs of maintaining a foreign sales force are three times higher than the costs of a domestic sales force. Included in these higher costs are travel, living expenses, use of interpreters, and less efficient use of time.
3. Training and motivation of individual sales reps are more difficult than they are in the United States. Language and cultural differences slow down training, and cultural and economic conditions can reduce the effectiveness of many forms of sales incentives.
4. Turnover is higher for foreign salespeople. Higher turnover increases costs and decreases selling effectiveness.
5. In some foreign countries what we consider to be bribes to secure business are considered to be standard business practice and not at all unethical.
6. The countries abroad vary widely in the degree of marketing sophistication they have achieved. Some seem only a step advanced from our era of the Yankee Peddler, others are as advanced as we are.

As a sales manager dealing with international salespeople and customers, you must be keenly aware of these and other problems and conditions. In the American market top sales supervisors and salespeople sell by creatively adapting their product to the specific needs and conditions of customers. It is the same in managing an overseas sales force. Sales management techniques and procedures must be adapted to the specific needs and procedures of foreign markets.

### Changes in the People Who Sell

We have discussed the impact of affirmative action on sales management, and we noted the changes in the attitudes of people who sell. The sales manager of today and for the future supervises salespeople who are different from those of 10, or even 5, years ago. To cite just a few of these differences:

- More women, blacks, Hispanics, and other minority persons in selling.
- More salespeople with college educations, many have master's degrees.
- Changed attitudes toward work in relation to recreation and other uses of time.
- Different concepts of marriage and the family.

These and many other new conditions mean that your role as a manager of people who sell will be different from your predecessors. You will spend more time getting to know your people—their likes and dislikes, attitudes, personal goals, strengths, and weaknesses. You will be challenged to work with many types of people. This will at times be frustrating, but it is also exciting and personally rewarding.

### Selling in Service and Nonprofit Organizations

Personal selling has come to be recognized as an important business getting technique by many service and nonprofit organizations. For example, banks and other financial institutions have developed training programs in personal selling for branch managers and other officers. And the military recruiter has one of the most difficult jobs of all in selling young men and women on careers in the armed forces.

Because personal selling is so new to most service and nonprofit organizations, sales management in these fields is in an early stage of development. These organizations are drawing heavily on managers and

on sales management practices and techniques that have been successful
in other industries. What is emerging in personal selling for service and
nonprofit organizations are adaptations of successful sales management
procedures taken from the long selling experience of tangible goods manufacturers and retailers. This continues to be a very exciting development
in the history of personal selling.

### Energy Crisis

Much has been said and written about the energy problems of the
United States. There will be no easy solutions, but it is clear that energy
will be in short supply and very expensive.

Although everyone has and will be affected by the energy crisis,
sales reps and their managers face special problems because of the particular nature of personal selling in the company's total marketing program. To do their jobs salespeople must *get to* customers and it is here
that the energy shortage introduces important handicaps. Sales reps will
not be able to travel as extensively or call on customers as frequently as
they did in the past. You and your reps will have to rely more heavily on
public transportation. Telephone selling will become more and more prevalent and important. Sales reps will have to plan and schedule their trips
very carefully considering *both* customer coverage and fuel conservation.
Prescheduled appointments with buyers will become a requirement for
good territory coverage.

It will all add up to *new* ways of selling and managing the people
who sell.

### Increased Sales Professionalism

We are all familiar with the professions of law, medicine, and
teaching. The concept of professionalism includes these conditions: special training, personal dedication, and established standards of conduct.
In the years to come there will be increasing concern for making sales
management more professional. Already public opinion and government
regulations have imposed many controls and restrictions on sales practices and operations. In part, these have forced salespeople and managers
to become more professional. But there has also been substantial pressure
from within selling for increased professionalism. This trend will continue in the future.

The professionalism of selling is a major goal of Sales and Marketing Executives International and other organizations in selling. Proponents of increased professionalism call for the adoption of a code of ethics, increased training, and even certification. In fact, one author has proposed the creation of a Certified Sales Manager for those who meet high professional standards. This designation would be similar to the certified public accountant and other professional certifications.

### Learning Exercise

*Five important trends that will affect the future of sales management have been projected. Do you agree with them? Why or why not?* _____

_____

_____

_____

*What other factors do you feel will affect your job as a sales manager in the future? Why?* _____

_____

_____

_____

## TIME MANAGEMENT

Many sales managers report that managing their time is one of their most difficult problems. Time management will be an even more important skill in the future. Three keys to managing your time well are planning, discipline, and organization.

### Planning

As a manager you plan for the optimal use of the resources at your disposal. Often the most limited resource is time—yours and your subordinates'. Some suggestions for better time planning:

1. Establish priorities for your activities. One author suggests a "to do list" on which the manager ranks activities according to A, B,

or C priority. The manager concentrates on completing the A priorities before turning his or her attention to the B and C activities.

2. Anticipate major tasks that will come up in the future. By thinking ahead you will spend less time on "fire fighting" and more on "fire prevention."
3. Establish deadlines for yourself and your salespeople and adhere to them.
4. Let your plans and your schedule be flexible. Develop contingency plans so you are ready for changing conditions and emergencies when they arise.

### Discipline

Good time management is based on self-discipline and the development of good work habits. There must be a sincere desire to avoid bad work habits and to manage time effectively. Some suggestions:

1. Don't procrastinate. The person who is going to do something tomorrow never seems to get it done.
2. Be alert to unnecessary interruptions such as casual visitors and unimportant telephone calls. You must have blocks of uninterrupted time if you want to accomplish a major task such as writing a report or preparing a sales forecast.
3. Train yourself to be brief. Too frequently managers waste time on unnecessary details when writing or speaking.
4. Avoid requests for special favors. Quite often special requests have no relation to the manager's or the company's goals.

### Organization

The third characteristic of effective time management is organization. Carefully study the tasks you must perform. Get yourself organized to accomplish them. One trick is to prepare a daily or weekly work schedule to organize your work. Other suggestions for organization:

1. Consolidate activities whenever possible. For example, it may be better to take one long trip to visit your sales reps in the field rather than several short ones.
2. Delegate tasks to your subordinates. Don't try to do everything

yourself or you will discover that there is never enough time remaining for important management responsibilities.
3. Concentrate your efforts on major tasks whenever possible. In particular, don't try to do several things at once.
4. Identify the key, most important problems so you do not waste time on less important matters.

## Case Study: Titan Enterprises

Bob Rockwell became sales manager for Titan Enterprises, a large distributor of electrical appliances, eight months ago after 10 years as a successful salesman. Lately, he has felt under pressure to accomplish everything he has to do.

Rockwell usually arrives at his office at 8:30 a.m. He begins the day by reading his mail, and he tries to take care of all paperwork and office duties before lunch. After lunch he calls on accounts with his sales reps. He also has several major accounts of his own.

On Friday, Rockwell's day was more pressured than usual. At 9 o'clock, before he had even read all his mail, a sales rep called to discuss a price quote for a large customer. Since Rockwell's secretary was on vacation, he had to spend several minutes going through the files to find the needed information to respond to the sales rep. Then, when the rep hung up, Jeff Marcus, a lawyer who has an office in the building next door, stopped by to arrange a tennis match for Sunday. Rockwell decided he needed a break and went with his friend for coffee at a drugstore down the street.

When he returned, the phone rang again. It was his boss, the general manager, asking for the quarterly sales report, which had been due the previous Monday. Rockwell explained that he still needed reports from two sales reps, but that they were promised by next Monday. As soon as the reports came in, Rockwell would compile the results and get the quarterly report out the next day. Why, he thought, were there always so many reports?

After lunch, as Rockwell was leaving to call on an account, his wife called. Since they were having guests for dinner, would he pick up a bottle of wine? Also, would he make a special effort to get home early so he could take the kids to McDonald's for dinner while his wife got ready. Rockwell said he would try.

When he finished his call on the customer at 3:30 p.m., Rockwell phoned his office to check before going home. The receptionist told him that he was to call another major customer immediately. He did and was informed of a shipping error that must be corrected at once. He returned to the office and spent the next two hours correcting the error. Then he left for home and arrived at 7 p.m.

When he arrived, without the wine he had forgotten, Rockwell was met by an angry wife. The guests were coming at 7:30, the kids were hungry, and they both needed to get dressed.

1.   *Review the events of Bob Rockwell's day. How could he have reduced the pressure on himself?* _____

_____

_____

_____

2.   *What appear to be Rockwell's priorities? What should they be?*

_____

_____

_____

3.   *Have you had a day like this recently? Did you handle it differently?* _____

_____

_____

_____

4.   *Prepare a list of the 10 biggest wasters of your time. What can you do to eliminate or minimize these time-wasters?* _____

_____

_____

_____

## YOUR PROFESSIONAL DEVELOPMENT

As a sales manager, or someone who aspires to work in sales management, you are on your way to a rewarding career. Studies of corporate promotions have shown that effective sales reps and managers have an excellent promotion track record. In addition to further advancement in sales management, you can also move into executive positions in product management, market research, sales and market planning, customer relations, sales training, and other staff positions. Further, sales management has often been a rewarding career path to top management positions.

This section offers some suggestions as to what you can do to enhance your chances for career advancement. The first step is to understand yourself.

### Understand Yourself

You cannot begin to plan your career and develop yourself toward your goals until you understand yourself. Take a few minutes to complete the following list of your strengths and weaknesses.

My Strengths                                    My Weaknesses

_____             _____

_____             _____

_____             _____

What did you discover? Do these lists give you some ideas of how you can improve your management skills? Are you receptive to new ideas? Do you relate well to superiors, subordinates, and peers? Do you spend too much time on details and not enough on major problems? Are you a better planner or implementer? How well do you give and take direction? Honest answers to these and similar questions will give you insight into what you need to do to become a better sales manager.

### Manage Yourself

In the discussion of time management, the importance of controlling your time on the job was emphasized. Now we are going one step further to suggest that you use the same planning and management techniques to help you control your life. You will have to make careful decisions about your personal and professional priorities. A leading executive career counsellor suggests that career planning and corporate planning are similar.

Career planning follows the same general logic as corporate planning. The corporate planner asks, "What business are we in?" The career planner must ask, "What do I really want to do?" The corporate planner asks, "Where is our market?" The career planner must ask, "Where are my best opportunities?" The corporate planner asks, "What resources do we have?" The career planner must ask, "What are my personal assets and liabilities.?"[1]

This expert goes on to suggest three major steps in career planning.

1. Set a realistic long-term goal.
2. Set intermediate goals and make intermediate plans that will help you reach your long-term goal.
3. Relate your intermediate plans to your long-term goal and schedule.[2]

*What is your long-term career goal?* _____

_____

_____

_____

*What are your immediate goals and how do you expect to achieve them?* _____

_____

_____

_____

*How are your intermediate goals and plans related to your long-term career goals?* _____

_____

_____

_____

Two important considerations must be added to the self-analysis you have just completed. First, what sort of balance do you want between your career and your personal life? Of course, personal commitments will vary between individuals, family status, and age, but they are always

---

[1]Alan N. Schoonmaker, *Executive Career Strategy* (New York: American Management Association, 1971), p. 3.
[2]Ibid., pp. 129–30.

important for us personally. You will not have a satisfying, productive career as a sales manager if you always have the feeling that your career is in conflict with your personal or family life. This requires that you make a careful review of your career goals to strike a balance between your career and personal objectives, a balance that is appropriate *for you, your family, and your company.*

The second important consideration is to make self-development a major career activity. Make time for your own development as a manager. The same benefits realized by your salespeople from continuous training will be yours if you make a concerted effort to improve your management skills. Suggested techniques for self-improvement are: read and observe, exchange experiences with other managers, and practice.

### Read and Observe

An effective sales manager is always looking for ways to improve. One way is to keep up-to-date by reading business, industry, and professional books and journals. As noted in the introduction to this book, the suggested references at the end of each chapter are to help you to obtain more information on a particular topic.

To assist you further in self-development, a short list of general business and marketing publications with which you should be familiar includes:

| | |
|---|---|
| *Advertising Age* | *Industry Week* |
| *Business Week* | *Journal of Marketing* |
| *Dun's Review* | *Management Review* |
| *Fortune* | *Marketing Times* |
| *Industrial Distribution* | *Sales and Marketing Management* |
| *Industrial Marketing* | *Wall Street Journal* |

Observation can also help you become a better manager. Who was the best boss you ever had? What made this person a good boss? How about your peers? What can you learn from them? We all can learn a great deal from others if we observe them carefully and make a deliberate effort to learn from our observations.

### Exchange Experiences

Take advantage of every opportunity to exchange ideas and experiences with other sales managers, both in and outside your company. Two ways to do this are by attending continuing education programs at colleges, universities, and professional associations and by joining trade and professional organizations.

Continuing education programs have important benefits for the sales managers who attend them. A recent study identified these benefits as the learning of new techniques and exposure to new ideas, the reinforcement of basic knowledge, and the exchange of ideas with other sales managers. The latter is perhaps the most beneficial, especially to the inexperienced sales manager. Most management seminar leaders stimulate the interaction of participants by using cases, role playing, group discussion, and similar participative techniques. Also, evening bull sessions, coffee and meal breaks provide seminar participants with the chance to learn from each other.

Another means of learning about sales management practices is to join a professional or trade organization. Sales and Marketing Executives International and the American Marketing Association offer programs that are targeted on sales management. Also, many industries have trade associations that promote the interests of their members. One sales manager summarized the benefits of associations in the following way:

> . . . They save your sanity (or even your job) by giving you immediate information—important facts and figures from studies and reports important in your work.
>
> Associations provide opportunities to make valuable contacts, to meet big guns in your field.
>
> Perhaps most important: they give you a showcase for your talents, a platform for your ideas and opinions, a chance to grow in new directions meaningful in your career.[3]

## Practice Your Management Skills

A good strategy for professional advancement is to take every opportunity to practice and challenge your management skills. There are many ways to do this. To suggest a few: take on a leadership position in a community, religious, or professional organization; volunteer for special projects for your company (for example, to evaluate a new product idea); speak to a marketing or sales management class at a local college; write

---

[3]Jo Foxworth, "Join Professional Group and Work: It Pays Off Big," *Marketing Times* (January-February 1979), p. 7.

an article for a trade publication. Such activities give you a chance to practice management skills—to learn by doing.

In this regard, if you are now a sales rep aspiring to management, ask your boss to involve you in some management activities. Ask to interview a few sales applicants, help plan a sales meeting, contribute to the training of new sales reps. Most sales managers will appreciate your offer to help, and this is another way to evaluate your own potential for management.

### Learning Exercise

*Prepare a professional self-development plan for the coming year. Be specific as to what you will do to improve the weaknesses you identified on page 244.* _____

_____

_____

_____

## CONCLUSION

When we finish a book, we like to think, "Well, that's it. I've read it carefully and I understand it. I know all about that subject now!" But, of course, this is never true. Perhaps we can say this about some books of fiction, but *never* about books in sales management.

This book is a beginning, not a conclusion. In it we have presented many concepts and ideas from the collective experience of a large number of salespeople and their managers and from research. But this experience and knowledge are not "laws." In sales management there are no laws that can be memorized to achieve instant success. Good sales management is an *individual, personal* process. It can't be *taught,* it must be *learned* by continuous individual self-development. Self-development begins with knowing the experience and knowledge of others and continues, day in and day out, to build on this base through the individual experiences, observations, and personal insights of the sales manager.

Sales management is exciting and rewarding. It takes place in an environment that changes almost daily. Nothing is certain. The rewards and satisfactions for success under these conditions are substantial.

So sales managers can never stand still. They must constantly change and grow or they soon become obsolete. We hope the concepts in this book have caught your interest in continuing growth and self-development and that they will help you achieve a satisfying and prosperous career in sales management.

## SELECTED REFERENCES

### Future of Sales Management

JOHNSON, WALTER H., Jr., "Ageless Global Strategy Guides Today's Marketers," *Marketing Times* (May-June 1978), pp. 10–15.
KURTZ, DAVID L., H. ROBERT DODGE, and JAY E. KLOMPMAKER, "The Future of the Personal Selling Function," in *Professional Selling* (rev. ed.). Dallas: Business Publications, 1979.
MAZZE, EDWARD M., "Personal Selling in the Future," in *Personal Selling: Choice Against Chance*. St. Paul, Minn.: West Publishing, 1976.
STROH, THOMAS F., "Sales Management in the Future," in *Managing the Sales Function*. New York: McGraw-Hill, 1978.

### Time Management

ANDRAS, P.F., "Self-Management: The Key to Success," *American Salesman* (May 1970), pp. 42–43.
HENRY, J. PORTER, and staff. "Spending Time, Buying Nothing," *Sales Management,* May 28, 1973, pp. 27–29.
HENRY, J. PORTER, and staff. "Wasting Time," *Sales Management,* September 23, 1974, pp. 55–56.
RILEY, ROBERT T., "Time Management: Effectiveness 1st, Efficiency 2nd," *Marketing Times* (September-October, 1978), pp. 10–12.

### Your Professional Development

FOXWORTH, JO, "Join Professional Group and Work: It Pays Off Big," *Marketing Times* (January-February, 1979), pp. 7–9.
JACKSON, DONALD W., JR., and JOHN L. SCHLACTER, "The Continuing Education Needs of Sales Managers," *Training and Development Journal* (November 1978), pp. 8–10.

KERSHAW, ANDREW, "How to Get Yourself Promoted," *Marketing Times* (March-April 1979), pp. 22–23.

KUTCHER, FRANK E., JR., "Needed: A Personal Marketing Plan," *Sales and Marketing Management* (February 6, 1978), pp. 42–43.

SCHOONMAKER, ALAN N., *Executive Career Strategy*. New York: American Management Association, 1971.

STANTON, WILLIAM J., and RICHARD H. BUSKIRK, "Careers in Sales Management," in *Management of the Sales Force* (5th ed.). Homewood, Ill.: Richard D. Irwin, 1978.

# INDEX

**Advertising**
definition of, 10
for sales recruits, 50–51, 54
Affirmative action, 51, *See also* Equal employment opportunity
Age Discrimination in Employment Act, 51
American Management Association, 183
American Marketing Association, 247
Anastasi, Anne, 74
Application forms, 64–65
Aptitude tests, 75. *See also* Psychological tests
Attitude and training, 97
Awareness of self, 155–56

**Bartels, Robert, 3n**
Behavior
complexity of, 120
elements of, 120–21
Berelson, Bernard, 120n
Bern, Ronald L., 53n
Black, James M., 70
Bonus, 187
Business games, 104

**Call reports.** *See* **Reports of sales reps**
Career planning, 244–46
Change, responses to, 5–6
Character references, 65–66

Chesapeake Life Insurance Company case, 63–64
Civil Rights Act, 51
Combination compensation plans, 176–77, 187–88
Commission, 185–87
drawing account, 186
regressive, 186
sliding, 186
varied, 187
Communication
in evaluation program, 216
in leadership, 155
as motivator, 174–75
Compensation
level of, 181–82
methods of, 182–88
bonus, 187
combination plans, 176–77
commission, 185–87
salary, 185
objectives of, 181
trends in, 176–77
combination plans, 176–77
emphasis on profitability, 177
fringe benefits, 177
Compensation plans
criteria for, 178–80
development of, 180–89
implementation of, 189